The Undersea Discoveries
of Jacques-Yves Cousteau

LIFE AND DEATH
IN A CORAL SEA

The Undersea Discoveries
of Jacques-Yves Cousteau

LIFE AND DEATH
IN A CORAL SEA

Jacques-Yves Cousteau
with Philippe Diolé

Translated from the French by J. F. Bernard

A & W Visual Library
New York

This paperback edition published by A & W Publishers,
Inc., 95 Madison Ave., New York, N.Y. 10016,
by arrangement with Doubleday and Company, Inc.,
245 Park Avenue, New York, New York.

Library of Congress Catalog Card Number: 69-13003
ISBN 0-89104-089-7
Printed in the United States of America

The Cousteau Society is dedicated to the protection and
improvement of all life. We invite your membership and
participation in support of this effort.
The Cousteau Society — 777 Third Avenue
New York, N.Y. 10017

Contents

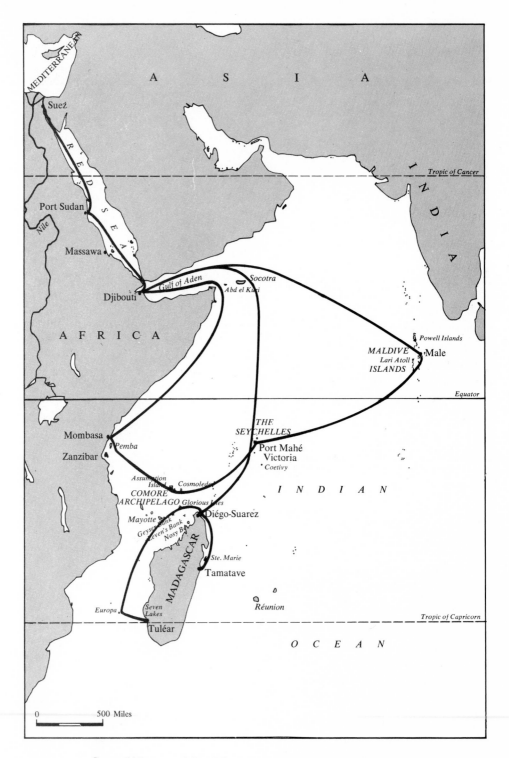

General itinerary of the *Calypso* from March 1967 to February 1968.

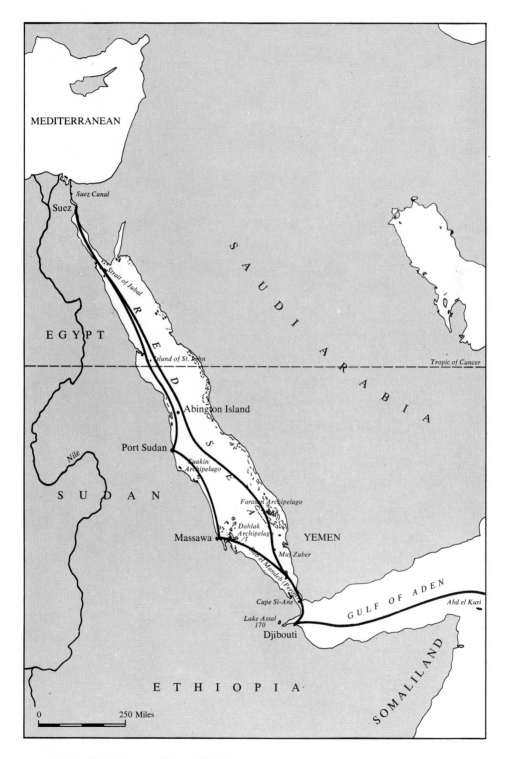

Detailed itinerary of the *Calypso* in the Red Sea from May to September 1967.

Aboard the *Calypso*, in the Red Sea.

ONE

The Unending Quest in the *Calypso*

Coral and the friends of coral.
Coral as it kills, eats, lives, and dies.
The Red Sea, with triggerfish and shark, whale and dolphin.
Funding the expedition.
Musée Océanographique.

Through the window of my mask I see a wall of coral, its surface a living kaleidoscope of lilac flecks, splashes of gold, reddish streaks and yellows, all tinged by the familiar transparent blue of the sea. I am suspended at the rim of a coral reef, supported and surrounded by the still water. Above, red-speckled fish, as blue as the sea itself, swim in lazy circles; and below, I see the limey parasols of the *Acropora* like trees in a petrified forest.

Butterfly fish and angelfish watch indifferently as I continue my descent along a cliff wholly covered by marine life forms. The shells of giant clams are ajar to display the emerald flesh bordered with a curious zigzag pattern of midnight blue. Sponges, like human hands, clutch the wall; and miniature thickets of black coral shelter colonies of minuscule crustaceans.

It is all strange, unearthly, and yet familiar. Strange, because the sea, once it casts its spell, holds one in its net of wonder forever. And familiar, because this is by no means my first experience with the teeming coral life of the Red Sea. But each new expedition, and every new dive, revives in me the same excitement and astonishment that I felt when I was first here, in 1951, with my old friend Frédéric Dumas and with Professor Pierre Drach. Drach was the first scientist aboard the *Calypso*. And Dumas had been my companion during my first dives;

(Left) J.-Y. Cousteau examining corals in the Red Sea.

(Right) A group of Chromis (damselfish) and Abudefdufs (sergeant-majors) swimming among coral, alcyonarians, and sea fans.

together, we had explored the sea, and it was Dumas who had done the initial testing of the Aqua-Lung, which Émile Gagnan and I invented in 1943.

That was seventeen years ago. And now, the water is still warm and silken. There are the same grottoes to investigate; and the same species of fish fleeing in fright before the unaccustomed being that is man. I see the same ascidians, looking for all the world like tiny, swollen wine-skins. And I am wary of the same dragonfish — the *Pterois* — the beauty of whose gauze-like "wings" belies the deadly poison that tips them.

I sink slowly to the base of the coral wall as a rainbow of color circles slowly in the water around me. There are triggerfish, with vivid blue lines and streaks, their Fernandel eyes eternally curious, staring at butterfly fish and imperial angelfish striped as though by the brush of some color-mad genius. I see surgeonfish, handsomely attired in profes-sional blue, with golden spots on either side of their tails, accompanied by their scalpels — the Moorish idols, whose pennantlike dorsal fins re-semble nothing so much as the instrument of a primeval surgeon. And, of course, there are sharks. There are always sharks, like sentinels, cir-

cling slowly, cruising over the sandy bottom. They watch.

Such, in brief, is the world of coral. I suspect that such a description may appear strange, and even flippant, to a reader; or at least to the reader who has never seen for himself the submarine life of the tropical seas. One who lives on dry land might well be astonished (not to say alarmed) at one's first sight of the new "human environment" — the world of the sea.

In this book, which is, after all, devoted to the world of coral, I should begin by describing what we might call the scenery, or the countryside. I should say first that it is a world of breath-taking splendor; next, that it lies in the Red Sea and in the Indian Ocean, and finally that it is much more a world of animal life than a world of plants, despite the fact that I refer to such fanciful things as coral "thickets" and "branches." The analogy between coral and plant life is an obvious one because of the resemblance in form between the two. Let us keep in mind, however, that these "plants" actually are closely knit colonies of animals, of complex cellular organisms with digestive systems that they manage to keep occupied by virtue of tiny but effective weapons. And let us remember, too, that there is a great deal about coral that we do not know.

We do know, however, that coral kills, eats, lives, and (as we shall see) dies. Its collective life is often cruel, but it is always fascinating to the observer. And it is that life, in its complexity — at least to the extent that we are aware of the facets of that complexity — which is the subject of this book. The living organisms that are coral constitute, as it were, countries in the sea. I propose that we visit them together, for, as in all strange lands, the traveler is much better off with an experienced guide. It takes a long time to understand the world of coral, and no two parts of that world are quite the same.

The first of those countries, the Red Sea, holds many memories for me; memories of events, but also of animals of all kinds (sharks, particularly) and, above all, of old friends. Among the latter is Pierre Drach, who, since our experiences together in the Red Sea, has made a name for himself by his work in marine archaeology in the Mediterranean, and who is with us again on this expedition.

When Drach, Dumas, and I were first here in 1951, I recall, there was a particularly large busybody of a shark in the area where we were diving. That day, this monster decided, without any provocation other than Drach's presence, to make a meal of the good professor. I was in the water near Drach, and I saw the shark making for him with murder in every motion of its body. I shouted with all my strength. But Drach is a scientist to his fingertips. When he concentrates, he concentrates; nothing can distract him. And he was then in the middle of a series of observations in what he regarded as his underwater laboratory. I reached him with two frantic strokes and struck him on the shoulder, pointing to the shark, which was now nearly upon him. Drach gave me, and then the shark, a withering look, shrugged his shoulders in a Gallic what-the-hell gesture, and returned to his examination of a patch of polyzoans. The shark, in the face of such scorn, cautiously circled around Drach for a few moments, and then swam off and was never seen again.

It was on this same expedition — in fact, during this same dive — that we went deep enough to feel the first symptoms of that state of semi-consciousness known to divers as "rapture of the depths," a state attained at a depth of between two hundred and two hundred fifty feet, in which euphoria takes over and illusion and reality combine in dangerous, and sometimes fatal, proportions.[1] On this occasion, we saw masses of white branches — sea pens — like the canes of hundreds of blind men, protruding from the wall of coral. Strange life forms, half real and half nightmare, surrounded us as we sank down into the world of dreams, and a multitude of sea fans like ostrich plumes caressed my face as I passed. By then, we were about two hundred fifty feet beneath the surface, and I could see, stretching temptingly below me, as far as my eyes could reach, what seemed the infinite sweetness and quiet of a blackness that would yield up the secrets of the universe if only I were to go a bit deeper ...

On that occasion, fortunately, intelligence and the instinct for survival asserted themselves before it was too late. Yet, this tour along the edge of mortality accomplished something. On that day, I came to know that the purpose of my life lay down there, in what people call "the depths." The trouble was, at that time there was hardly any equipment with which one could penetrate those depths and survive. And so, on that same day, I swore to myself that I would do all I could to build

[1]See Appendix I, pp. 259.

(Left) Damselfish swimming among acro-
porarian umbrellas.

(Upper right) A handsome specimen of
black coral.

(Lower right) A diver under an acroporar-
ian formation. In the foreground, a coral
wall on which are found many of the life
forms associated with coral.

equipment to cross this second frontier of the "silent world," even to its
depths. Thanks to the Aqua-Lung, we had already been able to penetrate beneath the surface of the sea. On that day, however, I realized
that we had still a second frontier to cross, a frontier beyond which the
Aqua-Lung would be inadequate. For that reason, I conceived and
caused to be built the diving saucers (or minisubs), which we have with
us on the present expedition. The testing and use of the saucers has been
one of our main activities, and it will be one of the subjects of this book.

Since 1951, I have often returned to the coral world. In 1963, we
chose the Red Sea as the site for the construction of our undersea houses
in Project Precontinent II — an unprecedented scientific experiment by
means of which men were enabled to spend the entire week at a depth
beyond eighty feet; and, in another experiment, an entire month beyond
forty feet.

Now, several years later, I am here again. But this time I came to

the Red Sea to keep a rendezvous that I arranged years ago. I came with better means than ever before, with much greater experience, and with such equipment for diving and exploration as I hardly dared dream of on that day in 1951. I came, moreover, armed with the determination (of course) to realize, in maturity, all the ambitions of my youth.

On February 17, 1967, the *Calypso* sailed from Monaco for the longest expedition that I had ever conceived. It became, in fact, an expedition without limits in time and space — a permanent expedition. The proof is that at this moment, three years later, as I write these lines, it is still going on. Our mission, like the sea itself, is boundless and unending.

It is true that, in the past, the purpose of the *Calypso's* voyages have been specific and definite. On one of them, for instance, we had the intention of photographing the submarine mountains of the Atlantic Ocean. On this occasion, however, the voyage's purpose is no more limited than its duration. We will be gone for years, and, in that time, we will explore the secrets of the sea, no matter what those secrets are or where they are contained. That is not to say, of course, that we have no operational plan; on the contrary, that plan is the most comprehensive that we have ever prepared, since we have the scientific support of the *Musée Océanographique de Monaco*. The plan is, essentially, to become residents of the sea — or wanderers, if you will — so that we may seek out new knowledge wherever it is to be found and for as long as the *Calypso* will carry us.

I do not think there has ever been a similar oceanographic expedition or one undertaken in the same spirit. For my friends and I have concluded, on the basis of the years we have spent exploring the sea, that an enterprise such as ours requires a total dedication and a willingness to forgo the amenities of life. Such was the spirit that animated, I think, the explorers who first circumnavigated the globe in their sailing ships.

An expedition, as one may suspect, involves a great deal of preparation. This was particularly true in the present instance, since it was to be a voyage of indefinite duration. Even after the feverish activity that always accompanies a departure, there is still much work to do. All our supplies and equipment must be checked, stowed, and trimmed — and that was more than enough to keep all hands busy until we reached the Suez Canal, which, in early 1967, was still open. We passed through the canal without incident and shortly afterward cast anchor at the spot we had chosen for our work.

It was not until my first dive of the expedition, however, that I could really believe I was there, once again, in the tepid waters of the Red Sea, swimming about under the watchful globular eyes of the trig-gerfish and the hard gaze of the sharks. It was a moment of absolute bliss; and all the more so, since at the very last moment before sailing from Monaco, it had seemed that the expedition might have to be post-poned indefinitely. Only a short time before our departure, I had been involved in an automobile accident and had suffered two fractured ver-tebrae. Everyone was upset, and nearly everyone insisted that our depar-ture be put off until I was better. I and my vertebrae, however, both sensed that the best possible treatment would be to bathe in the waters of the Red Sea. We were very possibly right. Nonetheless, there were times, even in the water, when movement itself was pure agony. To this day, I am like a child who does not quite know what he is strong enough to do and what he is too weak to attempt. I can dive; that I know. But to what depth? That remains to be seen. In the meantime, I handle myself like a piece of Meissen china. The alternative would have been to post-pone departure; that is, to postpone the realization of the dream of my life, to disappoint my friends aboard the *Calypso* — and to miss the opportunity for a voyage around the world with new engines, new tech-niques, and new diving equipment such as had never been used before for oceanographic observation and research. Seen in that perspective, I doubt that I had any trouble in making up my mind what to do.

The first dive of this expedition was at Shaker Isle, a coral island off which we cast anchor at eight o'clock one morning. I told everyone aboard, "This is going to be a hard one. First of all, we'll have to see what we can do, and then we'll have to get with it right away. And we'll have to do more than one thing at a time."

We began by dispatching two teams on barges. Each team consti-tuted what we call "a subject"; that is, a particularly photogenic diver, a cameraman, and a lighting man. They were to reconnoiter the bottom to find an appropriate theme for our first film of the voyage.

While they were at work, we raised the SP-300 (the diving saucer)

Two Arabian fishermen come to the *Calypso* to ask for fresh water.

from the hold and set it on deck, and André Laban, an engineer, and Georges Barsky, a cameraman, got ready to go down in it. By ten o'clock, the saucer was in the water. From the bridge, I could see its round yellow top fading into the blue of the sea; and at that moment I felt that the expedition had really begun. Everyone on board, I think, shared my feeling.

Most of my companions aboard the *Calypso* had just come from a winter in France and from the hostile waters of the Mediterranean. Now, they were able to experience once more the sweetness of blue water sparkling with the rays of the tropical sun, and the silken warmth of that water against the body. For me, however, this was a more important occasion. It marked the beginning of the greatest adventure of my life, one that I had anticipated for years. For on that day was to take place the first dive in a new kind of life under water.

To be sure, this was to be nothing more than a dress rehearsal. Still, our job was so complex and comprehensive that it was necessary to put our diving teams into action as soon as possible, so that we might be in a position to draw conclusions from this first dive. We therefore spent the whole day at work in the sun and in the water. The only interruption was for lunch in the wardroom, which was the occasion for an impas-

(Right) a diver wearing one of our new diving suits, which includes a helmet with built-in telephone.

(Below) An eel hiding among coral.

sioned discussion of the merits and defects of our equipment. There was much marshaling of interesting facts and conjecture. Albert Falco, for one, was enthusiastic about the equipment he had been testing, and he was categorical in his conclusion that the new tanks of the self-contained diving suits allowed for dives of much longer duration than the old ones, and that the suits themselves were entirely satisfactory. On the other hand, it came out that the underwater lights, which were handled by our lighting men, were difficult to focus directly on what the camera was filming. After a bit of discussion, I concluded that the solution was to mount the lights on the camera itself, and to mount the batteries on the cameraman's oxygen tank. We've followed that practice for almost three years now, and it works beautifully.

There was one failure, however, that I am still forced to live with. I had conceived a rather presumptuous plan, by which the cameraman, after having filmed a sequence, would use the underwater telephone to describe what he had filmed. His description would be recorded on a minicassette on deck. The purpose of this extra step was to help us in adding commentary and explanation to the film, since we would then have on hand the cameraman's on-the-spot observations. The problem was (and is) that the tape recordings were unintelligible when the cameraman was at a depth of one hundred feet or more. The density of the air that a man must breathe at that depth deforms the human voice into an imitation of Donald Duck. And there the situation remains today.

Another fiasco — and this one more complicated, because the equipment is more complex — was a scheme I had devised for making an electronic montage of films. On the bridge of the *Calypso,* I had installed an electronic device (really the first stage of a computer) to which was attached a typewriter. The theory (illusory, as it turned out) was that we would be able to break down filmed scenes into numerical symbols. B17, for instance, would indicate a lone shark swimming from left to right on the film; and Z64 would mean that a shark was swimming from right to left with a diver. Then, if the film editor needed, say, a scene of a lone shark swimming from left to right, all he would have to do would be to press a button ... Very good. Except that nothing worked. First, we had problems in programming the computer stage; then we had problems in using what we had programmed; and then — then the problems began to pile up into an insurmountable mountain of diffi-

Navigating among coral formations — an activity that requires constant attention to one's depth finder.

culties and we threw up our hands and decided, for the time being at least, to forget the whole thing.

By the end of our first day at anchor, and despite a few reverses, I was once more struck by the efficiency that everyone demonstrated in bringing a whole complex of activities to a happy conclusion. I am constantly amazed and delighted by the *Calypso's* ability to do three things at once. Perhaps tomorrow, I think, we will be able to do *four*. Today, we did some very useful work with our two diving teams and with the SP-300. Not bad at all, especially considering that we were really only testing our equipment.

André Laban, who went down in the diving saucer to a depth of more than three hundred feet, was reticent about the beauty of the bottom. But then, he is not a great talker under any circumstances, and he makes a point of keeping his opinions to himself. Moreover, there was not much point in his talking, since the saucer is equipped with cameras and Laban is an expert cameraman. He rubbed the water off his shaved skull and said, "There was some nice black coral. You'll see some more on the film."

It was an intriguing statement. I know from experience that the bottom of the Red Sea is full of surprises. I can say, in fact, that the happiest hours in my diving experience have been spent there. The Red Sea is a corridor of marvels, undreamed of by those who have never seen it, and we are familiar with almost every coral reef in it. There my friends and I have been able gradually to explore the world of coral, a world that offers a profusion of life unmatched by any other area in the

world. When we first began to dive in the Sea, we were almost over-
whelmed by the wealth, the diversity, and the complexity of what we
saw. There was so much that it seemed we would never be able to make
any sense out of it. Then, bit by bit, we began to unravel the meaning of
that universe which is so alien to man. It is a world in which animals,
both mobile and sedentary, still hold the first place, while man is rele-
gated to a level of subordinate importance.

From year to year, we have learned to live in that world, side by
side with sharks, which are the last great predatory beasts over which
man has no control. They are less understood, less vulnerable even to
modern weapons, and more ferocious, than the predators of the jungle.
And, by way of apprenticeship, we had to learn to live with them. The
Red Sea, then, has been the scene of our most moving experiences and
our greatest joys. We return to it again and again, and each time it is
brought home to us that we are doing the work of pioneers, that so far as
the sea is concerned, we are the advance guard of humanity.

Now that our equipment had been tested and had proved satisfac-

Diver from the *Calypso* approaching a grouper to feed him.

tory, the *Calypso* weighed anchor to sail through the labyrinth of the
Farasan Archipelago, which stretches more than three hundred nautical
miles in length and thirty nautical miles in width along the coasts of
Hedjaz and Yemen. Except for the Australian Great Barrier Reef, this
archipelago is the greatest coral complex in the world. Several years ago,
in an attempt to arrive at some understanding of its development and
biological equilibrium, we left a team of scientists on the island of Abulat for a month. Even so, we just began to scratch the surface. Now,
however, in March 1967, we were merely passing through on our way to
the south. We would be back later. Our primary concern for the moment
was to test our new equipment and to establish a practical working rou-
tine for our personnel. We had to measure the *a priori* methods, which
we had conceived on dry land, against the inflexible rule of reality. And
as always on such expeditions as ours, we had to give our team a chance
to "ripen" before we got down to serious work. This entire process is an
integral part of our mission, for that mission, as we conceive it, entails
the application of the most modern technology to the exploration of the

A shipboard conference to work out the program for a dive. From left to right: André Laban,
Frédéric Dumas, J.-Y. Cousteau.

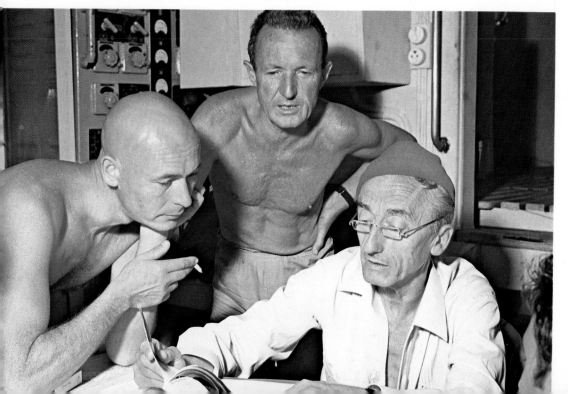

depths. And we aim to do this, moreover, within the framework of maritime tradition — a tradition that implies total dedication and a spirit of self-sacrifice.

The basic rule aboard the *Calypso* also reflects that tradition: one must never take unnecessary risks. In order to follow that rule, every man must know exactly what he is supposed to do and must have achieved a mastery of how to do it. This requires a rigorous and continuous program of training in a variety of fields, for diving involves dangers to which, obviously, the scientist in his laboratory and the cameraman in his studio are not exposed.

In addition to the classic dangers of underwater exploration and of deep-sea diving, there are those of the sea itself. The *Calypso* is not an ordinary ship, and its expeditions are not pleasure cruises. When we are in search of a particular specimen of marine life or when we have a particular stretch of bottom to explore, we often must cast anchor and send down divers in the worst possible conditions. There is much more on the sea, and under the sea, than is dreamed of in the lounges of ocean liners. And that, essentially, is the reason why, aboard the *Calypso,* everyone in the crew of thirty is constantly "on watch," no matter what kind of work he is doing, and is always ready for action.

One of the principle dangers of our trade is implicit in the necessity for studying, at close range, animals whose reactions are unpredictable. The most obvious such beast, of course, is the shark, whom by now we look upon as an old acquaintance. But there are also the members of the order of cetaceans: dolphins, porpoises, and the largest of the mammals — whales. On this trip, we intend especially to study the sperm whale and the grampus, both of which enjoy a well-deserved reputation for ferocity. Neither of those great mammals has been subjected to systematic observation before.

Other risks are those implicit in being required to take to the sea in small boats in any kind of weather, and in launching the diving saucer. Not the least of the dangers is met among the beauties of the coral reef, where light boats are sometimes smashed to pieces and divers injured. Then there is the additional menace, in a tropical sea, of all the things that nature has equipped with stings, spines, and poison: sea anemones, stinging coral, jellyfish, Siphonophores, to name a few.

I confess that I feel more than a hint of pride when I think of the degree of training, experience, and physical stamina that our teams have attained in order to be capable of so many activities under such conditions. Indeed, the variety and quality of our equipment is matched by the personnel aboard. The history of the *Calypso* is important to me for its scientific importance and its technological value, but above all it is a story of human adventure. I can more easily recall the person with whom I did something than remember what I did. Our discoveries have been, in effect, the result of a common life and of shared risks, day by day and over a period of time.

My first rather dangerous experiences with sharks, in fact, were shared with Frédéric Dumas, my son Philippe, and Albert ("Bébert") Falco, a *Marseillais* who joined our crew at the age of sixteen. On the present cruise, we are all together again; and we are going to have, we hope, bigger and better adventures. As I write, I can see, in my mind's eye, Albert's glistening silhouette in the water, and Philippe's, with its long, swimmer's lines. And I can see circling sharks, attracted by a chunk of meat that Canoë Kientzy, one of our most audacious divers, is holding out at arm's length.

I would like to tell the day-by-day story of our common life aboard the *Calypso*; but that would be beyond the scope of this book. It would be the story of a series of often exhausting activities, of dives at all hours of the day and night regardless of the condition of the sea or of the divers themselves. For our work requires men who regard marine life with single-minded devotion and who are wholly dedicated to our adventure. Our work would be impossible to accomplish unless there were an exceptional *esprit de corps* aboard the *Calypso*. And our work goes far beyond the professional duties and personal preferences of each member of the team. Everyone, at least initially, is responsible for everything; everyone is expected to pitch in and do any work that is called for, on deck or in the water.

That we are able to achieve such awareness of ourselves as a team is astonishing when one considers what a mixed bag we are. There are divers, cameramen, writers, engineers, and, above all, scientific researchers: biologists, zoologists, geologists. The scientists, regardless of nationality, who have lived aboard the *Calypso* have always been willing to perform even the most menial tasks when they felt it would be helpful to do so. (Perhaps it helped a little that, at Frédéric Dumas's suggestion, such chores were called "practical field work.") We have had our decks swabbed, our lines hauled — and our radar repaired — by such men as Professor Richard Edgerton of MIT and Professor Pierre Drach of the Sorbonne, among others.

We have very few rules aboard the *Calypso*; and none of them has anything to do with the way one dresses, or does not dress, or with the way one looks. Everyone has complete freedom to do whatever he wishes to his appearance. There are many beards, of course, and some long hair; and one skull, belonging to my friend André Laban, that is religiously shaved every single day. On the whole, all regulations boil down to one principle: we must never stop learning. Our work is to try to understand the sea, its problems, and its exploration. Within that context, we are forever attempting new variations on old themes, experimenting with new equipment and new uses for equipment. Each research theme that forms the subject of a film is, as it were, a separate chapter, a particular riddle that must be solved; and the solution requires certain knowledge and skills, physical exertion, and often, the design and manufacture of equipment. This holds true whether one is studying sharks or sea urchins, whales or starfish. There is, therefore, an endless variety of experiences, and a different kind of work every day. And that is the "adventure" of the *Calypso*.

People are curious about how we finance our research and exploration. Usually, they think that we receive large subsidies from public or private institutions; this is not so.

The *Calypso* belongs to, and is managed by, a foundation that I organized in 1950 and of which I am still president, the *Campagnes Océanographiques Françaises*. This organization gets its funds from various sources: author's royalties, television fees, industrial royalties, and research grants.

The *Musée Océanographique de Monaco*, founded by Prince Albert I, of which I am the Director, provides logistical support for the scientific aspect of our expeditions, but it is not in a position to finance the expeditions themselves. The *Calypso* depends, however, in matters of research, on the scientists available through the Musée. Our biological studies, for instance, are planned by Professor Raymond Vaissière, who is Associate Director of the Musée and a professor at the University of Nice. He was one of the "oceanauts" of Precontinent II, and he was the first scientist to spend a month doing underwater research in the Red Sea. So he has had more than a little experience in the use of diving as a means of marine research and in oceanographic biology. My own connection with the Musée, as well as the first funds that were made available for the *Calypso* and its equipment — indeed the whole direction that my life and work have taken — all are due to the efforts and guidance of my late friend Professor Louis Fage.

For geology and geophysics, we are fortunate enough to have the guidance of Dr. Gunther Giermann, a member of UNESCO's Intergovernmental Oceanic Conference, who has been our own geological consultant for many years. In geophysics we also have the support of Dr. Oliver Leenhardt, who, with Commandant Jean Alinat, took the seismic soundings that have given us an idea of the sedimentary structure of the various basins of the oceans, and also of the nature of the great deeps and their rock formations.

The *Musée Océanographique* is run by two groups: an Administrative Council and an Executive Committee. The members of the committee are all scientists, half of them French and half of other nationalities, and include the most eminent oceanographers of France, America, Italy, Germany, Norway, and Sweden. Even the USSR is represented, in the person of Lev Zienkevitch, professor of marine biology at the Oceanological Institute of the Moscow Academy of Sciences. Marine research requires so many skills and so much expertness that we cannot afford to dispense with close international co-operation among scientists. (Besides, the voyages of the *Calypso,* and our work, go far beyond the limits of Europe.) This international committee is in full charge of scientific matters, while the Administrative Council is concerned with budgetary matters and generally with means and methods.

As I have said, the *Musée Océanographique* is in no position to provide funds. Prince Albert I of Monaco, its founder, left a considerable amount of capital to the institution, but, over the years, the successive devaluation of French money has caused that sum practically to vanish. The Musée now depends for its survival on income from admission fees (which, happily, are sufficient for its basic needs). In order to do serious research, therefore, we are obliged to fall back upon contracts with the French Government, and particularly with CNEXO — the National Institute for Oceanic Exploration.

TWO

Twentieth-Century Noah's Ark
Equipping the Calypso.
The Red Sea and its coral.
Death by pollution.
To the Maldives.
Encounter with a Japanese trawler.

Shortly before our departure, Prince Ranier of Monaco and Princess Grace had visited the *Calypso*. As a gift, they had brought us a mascot, a dog named Zoom, whose size and unparalleled energy seemed rather excessive for a ship as cramped for space as was the *Calypso*. Eventually, however, his face, with its built-in plea for affection, his dangling ears, and his loose, wrinkled skin all worked their magic on us, and we learned to forgive Zoom his exuberance. He was, after all, a Saint-Hubert — a hunting breed that is highly prized in France. Zoom became everyone's pet. (Even a pair of sealions that we had on board for a while took to Zoom without reservation, and this despite the fact that Zoom had been madly jealous of them at first.)

I have mentioned that our ship was cramped for space. The reason is that she is not a large vessel, particularly when one considers the amount of material and the number of people (about thirty) that we normally carry on an expedition. And then we must count the assortment of animals that we usually have on board at one time or another — seals, otters, albatrosses, pelicans. And Zoom, of course. Visitors often are astonished that we all dare to sail around the world in what seems to them to be hardly more than a modest-sized "boat."

The *Calypso,* though small (some 350 tons), is admirably suited to our needs. When Philippe Tailliez, Frédéric Dumas, and I were discuss-

Raymond Coll (left) and Michel Deloire climbing aboard the *Calypso* after a dive.

ing, back in 1947 and 1948, what sort of vessel would be best for marine research, we could not have imagined anything that would be more suitable than the *Calypso*.

The *Calypso* is a former mine sweeper, built in the United States for the British in 1942. After the war, I was able to buy her in Malta as war surplus. I did not even have to change her name. The British had thought of her as Calypso, nymph-daughter of Father Ocean himself. It was, if one believes in such things, a "sign." And so, *Calypso* she remains — thanks mainly to the generosity of Loel Guinness, by virtue of which I was able to buy and to modify the *Calypso*.

Mine sweepers are expected, in the course of their duties, to be sub-

On the after deck of the *Calypso,* from left to right: Jacques-Yves Cousteau, his son Philippe, Michel Deloire (the cameraman), and Canoë Kientzy (our chief diver).

jected occasionally to underwater explosions. For that reason, the *Calypso* is an exceptionally sturdy ship, with a double hull of wood, double planking, and very narrowly spaced timbers. Her two engines and propellers give her a speed of ten to ten and one half knots. She is superbly easy to handle, and her shallow draft enables her to maneuver in and out of treacherous coral reefs with a minimum of trouble.

It was necessary, of course, to make extensive alterations before the mine sweeper could become an oceanographic laboratory. We added a false stem, among other things, and a well which goes down about eight feet below the water line and in which there are eight portholes. From there, we can see — and film — what is going on in the water, even when the ship is in motion. In addition, a double mast of light metal was built as far forward as possible on deck. It serves as a radar antenna, as a sort of upper bridge from which to observe and direct a difficult passage, and as a crow's nest from which we can observe the larger marine animals — whales, for instance.

In addition to such structural modifications, the *Calypso* is equipped with the most advanced means of marine exploration. I am

Ludwig Sillner, our German photographer, questions Cousteau about an unusual fish.

Albert Falco on an underwater scooter. The vehicle is equipped with a camera.

not referring to the more or less classic material of oceanography; we are divers, and our purpose is to know what lies beneath the surface of the sea. (I say "beneath the surface" because the sea is not a surface, as most people feel instinctively. It is a volume, a quantity, into which we descend and in which we work and observe. That is the basis of the modern concept of oceanographic research.) For centuries, scientists were forced to rely upon dead fish for observation. Now, for the first time in the history of science, man is able to study fish alive and in their natural habitat. This equipment is perhaps the chief cause of the crowding that I've spoken of. Our first few days aboard ship, it was almost impossible to move about the deck without climbing over crates and boxes. We had been collecting all sorts of tools and instruments for months before sailing, and material was being delivered to the ship up until the moment that we pulled away from the dock at Monaco. We had not even had time to check and test some of this material.

The heaviest and most cumbersome pieces of equipment were the Galeazzi tower (the "Tourelle Galeazzi"), which was capable of going down to depths of almost a thousand feet, and the SP-300, or diving saucer, which we had already made use of in the Red Sea.

It is not really because of the duration of the expedition that the *Calypso* was so crowded. It was because we had so many separate projects to undertake — each of which required its own special equipment. Here, it might be helpful to outline the equipment we carry, because we consider it all indispensable to a study of the sea, such as we conceive it.

1. First, of course, there is our diving equipment, which is considerable. It comprises the most modern equipment available, all of it perfected by CEMA — the Center for Advanced Marine Studies, which I founded at Marseilles in 1953 and of which I am still president. CEMA designs and builds the prototypes of all our instruments. On this trip, we were taking along a new, self-contained, and streamlined type of diving suit, the headpiece of which has a built-in movie camera and a telephone. (We had just tested this equipment during our dive of the previous day.) The suits are black, with a single yellow stripe down the side — so elegant, in fact, that we could hardly wait to try them out. We also carry a decompression chamber, and underwater scooters of a new design. Moreover, there is a special kind of air compressor that could fill all our tanks — simultaneously, if need be. There are tanks containing a helium mixture, to be used for deep-sea diving so as to avoid nitrogen narcosis and decompression accidents. (The Galeazzi tower could also be used as an emergency decompression chamber.)

2. There are numerous small craft aboard, all of which are needed for reconnaissance and exploration, and for the observation and protection of our divers. These boats must be always available, easily handled, and capable of use in the open sea. They must also be sufficiently light and fast for us to get close enough to the large marine animals to film them (whales, dolphins, seals, etc.). Therefore we have runabouts, inflatable rafts, and inflatable skiffs — and an excellent collection of outboard motors. More than once we've used our runabouts — which are unsinkable, and of metal — for a purpose unforeseen by the manufacturer. Filled with water and placed on the rear deck, they make splendid pools for fish, seals, and otters.

3. The diving saucer requires special equipment, particularly a powerful crane aft to raise and lower it. Moreover, we have to have a qualified electrical engineer aboard to service and maintain the saucer.

4. To be able to film properly both on the surface and in the water,

On the after deck of the *Calypso,* Maurice Léandri makes a last-minute inspection of the antishark cages. The cages, which are equipped with floodlights, are about to be lowered over the side for filming.

(Below) One of the *Pomacentridae* — in this case, the blue-banded angelfish, which has blue and yellow stripes. Its scientific name is *Pygoplithes diacanthus,* but the natives call it simply the pavilion fish. It is seen here with Amphiprions (clown anemonefish) and, in the background, a Chromis.

as well as from the diving saucer, we must carry fifteen underwater cameras, six commercial dry-land cameras, and a variety of special automatic cameras for filming in the deep. Then, since underwater filming requires an enormous amount of artificial light, we must have an untold amount of waterproof lighting fixtures and miles of special wiring. To use and care for all this cinematographic equipment, we have with us five cameramen and their assistants.

5.   There is a closed-circuit television system, by means of which we can see everything that happens either on the ship or in the water.

6.   We have an ultrasonic telephone, the ERUS, for communicating with the diving saucer and with the divers, and for the divers to be able to talk to one another.

7.   There are tape recorders to record sounds and voices on board and in the water, particularly the sounds of dolphins and whales, and indeed the whole chorus of noises that pervade the "silent world" of the sea — the peculiar groaning sounds made by some fish, the clicking of the crustaceans, and so forth.

8.   And finally, the *Calypso* is equipped with all the most up-to-date navigational aids: automatic pilot, radar, navigational sonar, and also a special sonar device for use in very deep water.

This collection of unusual equipment was assembled on the basis of years of experience, and with much care and effort. So far as I am concerned, it also entailed considerable technical research and a heavy financial burden. And now, it was time to put it all to work; or rather to see if and how it would all work.

On March 4, we neared the island of Seil Makawa. The approach was difficult. The water, though a marvelous blue flecked with sunlight, was rough and shallow. I did not think a dive would be worth while, and so I sent Barsky and Bernard Delemotte (who is one of our best divers) ashore to see if there was anything worth filming on the island.

While they were gone, we had time to test a new piece of equipment, the "toboggan slide," delivered just as we were about to sail from Monaco. It is similar to that found on any children's playground. It hooks onto the fantail of the *Calypso*, and its purpose is to allow a team of divers to get into the water as expeditiously as possible, one after the other. The apparatus took an extraordinarily long time to hook up, but it worked very well — although it was funny to see grown men throwing themselves down a slide as though their lives depended on it. (Zoom was not amused. He howled and bayed constantly as he saw his friends disappearing one by one into the sea.) The only difficulty was that the divers, who were wearing the new diving suit, lost their headpieces during the slide. But Falco was certain he could work out something to correct that defect.

Next, we tested our new underwater vehicle, an improved model of scooter. The rider of the scooter wears a self-contained diving suit, and he is shielded in front by a convex plexiglass bubble. The scooter is propelled by an electric engine. We found a few "bugs," which would have to be worked out. For one thing, the vehicle was too light. For another, the handgrips were too fragile; one came off in the hand of my friend Canoë (who often does not know his own strength). Our mechanics set to work immediately to correct the defects.

Finally, we put our sail-surfers into the water for the first time. They worked beautifully, and they are proving to be a delight and a pastime throughout the voyage.

Barsky and Delemotte came aboard to announce that, on the island, they had found a group of young Arabs, from thirteen to twenty-five years old, who were spending a month in the area, fishing from their boat. This was the customary Arab small boat, or *boutre*, with maroon sails. They used the island to salt and dry their catch and to sleep; and, naturally, the sky over the island was dark with circling sea gulls watching for a chance to steal the fish. As scarecrows, the Arabs used live birds, nailed to posts, whose flapping wings and cries were supposed to frighten, and perhaps to warn, their brothers overhead.

These young fishermen, living in solitude and privation, depend for their lives on the sea and the sun. They have no homes other than the sand on which they sleep, and their only personal possessions are their tiny prayer rugs. From the sea, they take not only their fish, but also the salt for their primitive salting process.

The parched island, the constant hot wind, and the macabre scarecrows gave a nightmarish cast to the whole scene.

On March 5, we passed through Bab el Mandeb strait—in bad weather, as usual. On the sixth, we docked at Djibouti, where we took aboard Dr. Leenhardt (our geophysicist from the *Musée Océano-*

One of the lobsters of Abd el Kuri, standing at the entrance of its hole gazing at the divers.

graphique) and our photographer, Ludwig Sillner, a German. We left the same morning and, a few hours later, we arrived at the Shab Arab shoal, where we set up two buoys.

We were now more crowded than ever aboard the *Calypso*; so much so that no one could be alone even for a moment. Ludwig Sillner solved the problem for himself by making a shelter on the spar deck out of green tarpaulin, which he held together with bits of string. His furnishings were simple: an air mattress. At night, when it rained, he was drenched, of course; but the rain was warm, and he did not mind. Better alone and wet, he said, than in a crowd and dry. "Sillner's hut" we called it. There he spent his free time, surrounded by boxes and cans (we use the spar deck to store everything that we have no other space for), doing those mysterious things that all photographers seem to do when

A lobster feast aboard the *Calypso* — under the watchful eye of General Cambronne, who presides over all our meals.

left to themselves.

The odd thing is that Ludwig Sillner, who is a photographer par excellence, is not a commercial photographer at all. By profession, he is a ball-point pen manufacturer's representative in the Arab countries. During his travels about the Red Sea, he took up diving, and then, as a hobby, turned to underwater photograph. I had first met him at Port Sudan three years earlier, and when I was looking for a photographer for the present expedition I thought of him. I've never regretted it for a moment. In addition to his skill as a photographer, he is extremely useful for his knowledge of all the Middle Eastern languages and dialects. Moreover, he is an engaging and rather colorful sailing companion.

The water at Shab Arab was so rough and the air so foggy that it was impossible to use our cameras. Since there seemed to be little hope that conditions would improve for the next few days, we decided to visit the Goubet, a famous gulf of the Red Sea. Before leaving Djibouti that morning, one of our crew had by chance asked a local Arab diver about the Goubet. "Ah, sir," the man had replied, "it is a most extraordinary place. It is bottomless, and it is inhabited by monsters so large that they can drag down lines attached to 200-liter cans. Moreover, in 1963, Commandant Cousteau went there with Frédéric Dumas and his best divers, and they were so terrified by what they saw that they ran away."

Naturally, we were eager to see the place in which, according to local gossip, we had earned so ignominious a reputation. I must report, however, that the Goubet was a disappointment. It is an inland sea or gulf that connects with the Red Sea by a narrow pass in which there is a very strong current, running up to seven knots. The surrounding area is very beautiful, and very wild, being dominated by volcanic mountains bare of foliage and marked in shades of red, yellow, and black.

Once in the Goubet itself, we lowered the diving saucer to a depth of over six hundred feet without catching sight of even a small monster. The divers then suited up and went down also, but they saw nothing more remarkable than some very large sea urchins. There seemed to be very few fish of any kind. It is my guess that the "Goubet monster" of Arab legend was originally a manta ray, seen by some shepherd from a hill top. Manta rays are plentiful in this area, and it must happen occasionally that they wander into the Goubet and — because the inlet is so narrow and because mantas are not the most intelligent of beasts — have trouble finding their way out again.

Sunday, March 12, we anchored at a point west of the island of Abd el Kuri. Here, again, the landscape was wild, even alien. A mountain range of reds and blacks rose out of the sea like molten lead, the whole flecked with pink by the setting sun. Along the length of the island, there was a white ridge that seemed about seventy-five feet high — probably salt, or guano, or both. We saw a small creek winding through the mountains. For a moment, I considered sending a boat ashore, but then the wind changed to the southeast and we quickly had to change anchorage. We sailed to the north of the point, prudently bypassing the shallows.

We had been at anchor no more than thirty minutes, all told; during that time, we thought we had seen two human heads peeking at us from behind a small hill. and now that we were moving away, we saw two men running down to the beach. They were no doubt chagrined at having been too shy to show themselves before, for visitors are rare at Abd el Kuri, and the natives number only about a hundred and fifty.

We reached our new anchorage about nine o'clock, and then I dispatched two parties to the shore, a photographic team and a moving-picture crew. While waiting for their return, Falco and another young diver, Christian Bonnici, decided to do a little reconnaissance on their own, and a series of short dives produced a treasure of sorts: about seventy-five pounds of lobster.

Abd el Kuri is astonishingly beautiful, and surprisingly rich, but it has very little fresh water. So we were informed by four natives who arrived shortly in two small boats. They were more eager to see our ship, however, than to tell us about their island, and, after offering them tea, I took them on a tour of the *Calypso*. Sillner, our interpreter, was under water with his cameras, and my explanations consisted mostly of gestures. They gave every sign, however, of understanding what I was trying to tell them. They were particularly amused when Marcelin Naguy, our sound engineer, turned the television camera on them and showed them their images on the screen. At that happy moment, Sillner appeared and immediately began an animated conversation with them in Arabic, a language he speaks to perfection. The five men — four of them black as coal, and one a Nordic type — presented a striking contrast as they shouted Semitic gutturals at one another, and the *Calypso* sounded for all the world like a marketplace of old Araby. Finally, our guests departed, happy as children, with gifts of water, sugar, bread, preserves, and rope.

Shortly afterward, our reconnaissance teams returned, and their film and photographs wholly confirmed the natives' boasts of the beauty of their island.

By March 13 we were at Socotra, off the coast of southern Arabia. It is an island of respectable size, about one hundred miles long, with fifteen thousand inhabitants. The main occupation is pearl fishing, from which the natives themselves apparently derive little profit. They live in clusters of primitive huts scattered over the island in a veritable Stone Age society over which presides, we were told, a sultan.

Socotra is memorable for its lobsters. We found them everywhere, in heaps, in six to eight feet of water. Without even trying, we picked up about a hundred and fifty pounds of them. It was the moulting season — which is also the time at which they reproduce — and their shells were still soft. For the next few days, we were to have lobster for every lunch and every dinner as our chef plumbed the depths of his genius to produce a line of delicacies that ranged from conventional broiled lobster to a succulent soup, or *bisque* of lobster heads.

By now, our psychological ties to land had been perceptibly loosened. We were even beginning to lose interest in the surface of the sea itself, and we were looking forward with increasing enthusiasm to the opportunity to exchange the stark horizon of Socotra for the fluid images of underwater scenery. To us, whose lives center in the sea, the "real world" is beneath the surface of the oceans, in waters that have become second nature to us. The entrance to that world is just off the rear deck of the *Calypso,* and it is a world characterized by colors, forms, and a way of life that are alien to what we have become accustomed to from centuries of human activity on dry land, and especially from several centuries of indifference to that submarine world. And it was now time to return to the very source of life, human and otherwise: to the sea.

We sailed from Socotra the same night about eleven o'clock. It was a marvelously still and clear evening, and the stars shone with a brilliance unsuspected by inhabitants of our smog-ridden cities. I went to bed almost immediately, but I was awakened at two o'clock by Laban, who excitedly told me to go up on deck. The *Calypso,* I found, was sailing through a stretch of water made luminescent by tens of thousands of floating globes. I immediately ordered the lights on the stem to be turned on, and then I ran below to get Barsky, our cameraman. By the time we returned to the deck, however, there was not a sign of the globes. We circled back, but still there was nothing. We will never know, I suppose, what they were. Perhaps they were jellyfish, but perhaps not. The incident is interesting because it illustrates what we are up against in our work of observing and recording life in the sea. Time and again

(Above) The entry to the *Calypso's* "false nose." It is a well, made of metal, which leads to the observation chamber (below) situated ten feet below the surface of the water.

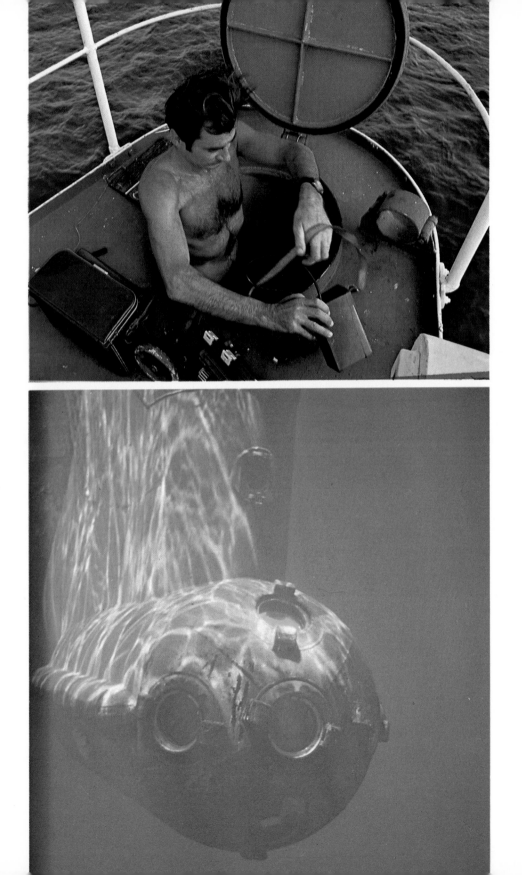

we have come across phenomena eminently worthy of being investigated — only to have them disappear before we could make even a visual record. And this despite the fact that we have trained ourselves to set up our equipment as expeditiously as humanly possible. Without being unduly pessimistic, I would say that, for every success we have had in filming or recording a matter of scientific interest, we have had ten failures.

The present voyage is not altogether an oceanographic expedition in the same sense as previous ones. We have an unusual mission, a mission that, in all modesty, we believe we are best qualified to accomplish. It is to determine what the future has in store for the world of coral.

I have said that coral is a living organism. Like all life forms, coral may sicken and it may die. Better than anyone else, divers know the dangers that human civilization holds for marine life. Pollution destroys sea life as well as human life; and oil tankers, particularly, on their runs across the coral areas of the Red Sea and the Indian Ocean, represent a serious threat to marine fauna. It is possible — indeed, it is likely — that, unless there is a great change in the near future, disaster will follow. And it will be a disaster of which man himself will be not only the perpetrator, but also one of the victims.

Our intention on this expedition is to find out what harm has been done so far to marine life, and what has caused it. I have thirty years of diving experience, and sixteen years of experience in the Red Sea and the Indian Ocean. I think I am in a position to judge whether the damage that human technology has worked on life in the tropical seas — particularly with respect to coral — is irreparable, or merely superficial, or somewhere in between those two extremes. The reason for my concern is obvious. I have devoted my life to the sea. Certainly, I will not allow it to be dirtied, degraded, and polluted, without protest.

At the time of this writing, it has been three years since we sailed from Monaco to find out the truth, no matter how unpleasant that truth might be. At the time of our departure, "pollution" was a word, and a fact, that few people found disturbing; and even fewer people were concerned about pollution of the seas. Since that time, however, public opinion — especially in the United States — has been stirred up by man's crimes against nature, crimes that have been multiplied and aggravated with the passing years. A program of correction is being undertaken, and I hope a reversal may be accomplished. But public opinion is still concerned chiefly with pollution of the cities, of the air, and of fresh water. That is understandable, since it seems at first glance that man is more seriously affected by those things than by the sea. There are a few people, nonetheless, who are aware of the fact that the sea is also in danger, and that pollution of the seas will have a catastrophic effect upon life on land; for the seas are the great regulators of life on the whole planet.

In January 1967, while we were planning this expedition, it was my intention to compile a record of pollution of the seas; and my ultimate purpose was to use that record to awaken as many people as I could to the enormity of the stakes for which man plays when he disturbs the delicate balance of life in the sea. This book is, among other things, that record, insofar as coral life is concerned. And the conclusion drawn from the observations I have set down is inescapable. The world of coral, which spreads like some great fairyland of beauty and color over a great portion of the earth, is dying.

Why? It is difficult to answer that question honestly. There are several causes, and certainly, one of them is oil spillage from tankers and underwater wells. Another is probably a biological imbalance provoked by human interference in a variety of forms. Biologists everywhere are at work, trying to understand what is happening to the sea. But it is already a great deal to know that something is happening, and that man can still remedy the situation if only he has the necessary knowledge of the causes and, above all, the will to act upon it.

At the present time, we were to begin our observations of coral with a visit to the atolls of the Indian Ocean, in the vicinity of Ceylon and India. This was the first phase of our plan.

En route toward the Maldive Islands, on March 14 and 15, we encountered a large number of sperm whales, or cachalots, and everyone aboard was suddenly fired with enthusiasm for these enormous creatures. Some climbed up to the observation deck, and others went below into the *Calypso's* "false nose" to begin filming them. We could see the mammals spouting all around us, their great bodies shining in the filtered sunlight of the sea. Even so, they were too far away from the cameras to be captured on film.

Almost at the same time, we had another surprising encounter, this one with a Japanese trawler — which is a rare enough occurrence in the Indian Ocean. In the late-afternoon light, it seemed hardly bigger than, and very similar to, the *Espadon,* except that its metal hull was covered with rust from one end to the other. At Djibouti, someone had told us that a Russian oceanographic vessel was in the vicinity, and we first thought that we had, by some coincidence, followed the same course as our Soviet colleagues. We slowed and drew closer to the ship. We now saw that it was a fishing boat, and we could see men waving and making signs to us from the deck. Between gestures, they seemed occupied in

[1] The *Espadon* (swordfish) is a vessel belonging to the Center for Advanced Marine Studies of Marseilles. It is a modified trawler, and it is normally used for carrying supplies to a "buoy-laboratory" anchored off the coast near Toulon.

We encounter a Japanese trawler in the middle of the Indian Ocean and discover the difficult lives led by these modern "gypsies of the sea."

taking aboard buoys similar to some we had seen in the water a half hour earlier. We caught sight of a gigantic tuna flopping about on their deck.

I had a boat lowered, and Falco and Maurice Léandri (who is the embodiment of curiosity) crossed the narrow stretch of water that separated the *Calypso* from the Japanese trawler and were invited aboard. They were no sooner on deck than a trio of the fishermen threw a swordfish and a tuna into the boat and made directly for the *Calypso*. Once aboard our ship, they darted about exploring every foot of it, from the engines to the radar antennae, pausing only to examine the diving saucer, and chattering away among themselves. Since no one aboard spoke a word of Japanese, we contented ourselves with accepting the swordfish and tuna with polite little bows; and then we stood helplessly aside while the fishermen satisfied their curiosity about the ways of the inscrutable Occidentals.

Aboard the trawler, however, the Japanese captain was becoming impatient and began shouting, in tones that were intelligible even to us, that it was time to get back to work. We presented the three Japanesee aboard the *Calypso* with bread, sugar, and wine, and they left, hissing happily like a flock of geese. The Japanese captain invited Barsky and Léandri, politely but firmly, to return to the *Calypso*. Visiting hours were over.

The Japanese fishermen, young and old, were impressive specimens, muscular and strong. Their faces were open and, like those of children, candidly reflected every emotion. Over all, they had the look of determined, but wholly engaging, pirates.

We were astonished at their endurance, particularly in view of the primitive lives they led aboard the rust-rotten trawler. They subsisted on a steady diet of fish and rice, and slept all together in a dormitory-like cabin below deck. Their only clothing consisted of rubber pants and gloves. We could not help admiring the courage and enterprise of such men. If the sea belongs to them, it is because they have learned to deserve it. I imagine that the fishermen of Brittany or of New England in the nineteenth century must have been such men as these. If Melville's heroes are alive today, they live in Japan.

The only one aboard who did not share the general admiration for our visitors was our dog, Zoom, who had been seized with an instant

The shaft of our starboard propeller has broken, and the propeller is jammed against the rudder. The *Calypso* is going around in circles.

dislike for the diminutive Japanese and had had to be forcibly restrained from devouring them on the spot.

On March 16 and 17, we sailed through a monsoon. And on the eighteenth, at about two o'clock in the morning, the starboard propeller shaft broke with a snap that reverberated throughout the ship. (My guess is that there was no connection between the weather and the accident, only that, by an inflexible law of nature, if anything can go wrong, it will.) with the shaft broken, the rudder was blocked, and the *Calypso* was turning helplessly in a circle. We were about eighteen hundred miles from the nearest port.

By the time I got up on deck, almost everyone else was there — Falco was already wearing his diving mask, along with his pajamas — and there was much excited discussion. I had the engines shut off right away, and as soon as we were motionless, Falco, as chief diver, dived from the stern to survey the damage. He surfaced almost immediately to report that the shaft indeed was broken and was jammed against the rudder. The propeller and the shaft would have to be removed before we

Our divers succeed in freeing the rudder and securing the propeller, which weighs about four hundred fifty pounds.

could budge. Bonnici and Raymond Coll suited up and joined Falco. We lowered the anti-shark cage, not only to protect the divers while they were working but also to give them the benefit of the cage's two powerful lights. Nonetheless, I was uneasy. It is difficult to be sanguine about the situation of three friends who are the only lighted objects in a black ocean full of perpetually ravenous sharks.

After forty minutes of hard work by the divers and worry by everyone aboard, a hoist was hooked up to the propeller and to the forward bracket, and they were made to slide forward until the shaft was disengaged. Then the divers fastened the prop to the rear bracket by lines, and the shaft was hoisted up on deck. At three forty-five, the engines were started and the *Calypso* continued on its course.

Our situation was not good. I realized it, and so did everyone else on board. We were in the middle of the Indian Ocean, halfway to the Maldives, and there seemed little point in turning back. We were limping along at a speed of five knots, on a single engine — which, to us, represented an intolerable waste of time — a tiny speck on the vastness of a hostile sea. But then we remembered. What did time matter when one was on an endless voyage? What counted was what we would be able to observe in the sea once we reached the Maldives. And so we resigned ourselves and cultivated the virtue of patience. Only then did I notice that my back had begun hurting again.

On March 20, shortly before reaching the Maldives, we had the opportunity of filming a group of sharks fighting over the carcass of a dolphin that we found. We used two small boats for the filming, with Michel Deloire in the water and Delemotte acting as his bodyguard.

Our technique was to attach the carcass to the *Calypso* and let it trail from the stempost. Since we dive off the quarterdeck, we estimated that this arrangement would give our divers time to climb aboard if the sharks became too aggressive. There were, nonethless, a few close calls. The sharks seemed to take a special interest interest in Coll, and the largest of them — a real monster — finally became openly hostile.

I was kept informed of what was going on by means of our underwater telephone system, and I immediately ordered everyone back on board. The last to climb the ladder was Delemotte. When he was halfway up, the monster jumped out of the water with such force — and such good aim — that Delemotte would undoubtedly have lost at least a leg if he had not had the presence of mind, and the good reflex action, to pull his legs away from the shark's gaping maw barely in the nick of time.

After that, the diving and camera teams stayed down for only short periods, and there were no more incidents, although we continued filming throughout the morning. We obtained what I consider to be some really extraordinary footage — even though the cameras jammed more than once. Those who see these films will never know, probably, just what was involved in making them.

THREE

The Indian Ocean:
Exploring in the Maldives

Socialist sultanate.
Coral building blocks.
The doctorfish and other friends of coral.
The great coral parasols—and cemeteries.
An infinity of atolls.
How to eat coral.
The great eels and how they disappear.

On Tuesday, March 21, 1967, shortly after five o'clock in the afternoon, we sighted the first atoll of the Maldive Islands, the Lari Atoll. It was our first sight of land in several days, and we could see coconut trees waving in the breeze and a beach glistening invitingly. And then, night began to fall.

I was hesitant to take the *Calypso* through the reefs in the growing darkness. During the day, it is possible to tell the depth of the water by its color. But at twilight it is the easiest thing in the world to misjudge the bottom and to smash into a bit of jutting coral. I dispatched a small boat, equipped with strong lights, to inspect the reef, and, with the information sent back from it, we managed to anchor safely almost alongside the reef.

As soon as we had stopped the engine, we set to work. The diving saucer was launched for an initial reconnaissance of the area, and went down the slope for a distance of more than five hundred feet, but visibility was poor. The tides were running strong, and the water was troubled and cloudy. Nothing more could be done that night.

The next day was hardly better, and since we were in need of a supply of fresh water, I decided to take advantage of the opportunity to visit the islands. The Maldives, lying in the Indian Ocean to the southwest of Ceylon, were once famous as a port of call on the historic spice route. Today, however, they are merely one among many coral atolls characterized by remoteness and poverty. Their chief — and only — industry is the raising of coconuts. First colonized by the Portuguese, the Maldives were a British possession from 1802 until 1965, at which time they became an independent nation.

We sailed around the atoll near which we were anchored, and entered the port of Male, the capital of the archipelago. We were immediately greeted with the news that the good people of the Maldives were celebrating the second anniversary of their independence and that during the celebrations — which were to last for three days — the port would be closed. Indeed, we were told, the entire country would be shut down.

It was an unexpected setback. We visited everyone we thought might be able to help us: health inspectors, the police, customs, government officials. Everyone was extremely polite and hospitable; but there was nothing they could do for us. Wait, they said. And so we waited. And nothing happened.

On Thursday, the twenty-third, the Maldivans were still celebrating, and our water shortage was growing serious enough to make us uneasy. At this point, our enterprising Barsky went ashore to see what he could do. He returned a short time later with a companion named Farouk Ibrahim who, it turned out, was the Chief of Customs of the National Airport. Ibrahim was an intelligent and very likable man, and blessed with a sense of humor.

After the standard tour of the *Calypso,* we invited our guest to remain for lunch, an invitation which he accepted with alacrity. During the meal, he told us the astonishing story of his uncle.

This uncle was called "Didi" — as was Ibrahim himself and, it seems, everyone who lives in the Maldives. During World War II, the uncle happened to be a member of the native government at the moment when the British asked the Maldivans to grant them a ninety-nine-year lease for a naval base. The government, at the instigation of Uncle Didi, peremptorily refused. Shortly thereafter, Didi was hustled aboard a British vessel and disappeared. The British then notified the Maldi-

(Right) A Maldivan returning with a block of coral to be used in construction.

(Below) One of the graceful sailboats of the Maldivans.

Jean-Paul Bassaget
having a chat with
Zoom.

vans that the vessel had been sunk and that Uncle Didi had been lost.

The story, told with great emotion, illustrated (we gathered) how happy the Maldivans were to be free at last.

After lunch, Farouk Ibrahim took us ashore for a jeep ride and a tour of the island. We visited the airport, where a new landing strip, constructed entirely of coral, had just been completed, to accommodate the one plane that visited the Maldives each month. The houses of the island, like the landing strip, are also made of coral. For centuries, we discovered, the Maldivans had been using their coral reefs as their exclusive source of supply for building materials. An ideal subject for our cameramen, I thought: the Maldivans chipping away blocks of coral and loading them into their elegant little sailboats.

Despite the relative poverty of the Maldives, the islanders are far better off than the inhabitants of those arid little spots of land in the Red Sea that we had visited so briefly. There is an abundance of coconut trees and of fresh water. The islands lie low in the sea, but have adequate vegetation. The beaches are made not of sand, but of pulverized coral. There is no lagoon, but there is a barrier reef, and whenever the tide is low, we were told, a team of "masons" sails out to quarry the coral "stone." This is made possible by exceptionally low tides — so low that clusters of madreporarian corals and half-open giant clams can be found practically at the surface.

The archipelago itself extends over a huge area, but the individual islands are not far apart and the inhabitants communicate from island to island by walkie-talkie. Many of the islands are inhabited, and wherever there is a fresh-water well, it seems that at least a fishing village has been built around it.

Everywhere we saw tiny cemeteries under palm clusters. The tombs themselves, crosses and all, were made of coral. Everything here is bound up with the sea, even life and death.

There are approximately ninety-three thousand Maldivans, inhabiting an area of some 115 square miles. They are a handsome people, more Indian than Arab in appearance. About half of them are Moslems and half are Protestants (thanks to the efforts of English missionaries), and mosques and churches stand side by side in all villages.

The standard of living is not so low as one might imagine, since the sea provides more than an ample supply of food. The economy, however, is still at the stage of bartering, and the islands' sole resource — copra, or coconut meat — is exported to their nearest large neighbor, Ceylon. For that reason, Ceylonese influence is perceptible in all areas of Maldivan life. I was particularly struck by the fact that the Maldives offer an example of advanced socialism, particularly with respect to what the natives gain from the sea.

In honor of our visit — and since he was not in a position to stamp our passports or provide other official courtesies — Farouk Ibrahim offered us, in parting, a delicious drink of coconut milk.

Back aboard the *Calypso,* we decided to make use of the delay in obtaining our authorization for water to explore the sea bottom around the island. Accordingly, Falco took one of the small boats to the north side of the atoll and, after spending the day in exploration, had to report that the water was still too turbulent to be of much use to us. Sillner was unable to obtain a single underwater shot.

Other members of the expedition occupied themselves in other ways. Delemotte and Bonnici went in search of groupers and eels. Georges Barsky, Raymond Deloire, and Marcelin Naguy returned to film scenes of the Maldivans quarrying their coral blocks, and they did so well that all we needed besides those scenes were a few continuity sequences. By now, we had reached the point where all tasks were almost perfectly co-ordinated. Everyone aboard had had so much experience in all phases of our techniques that we could carry on several jobs at once — as I had always wished we could do. The immediate future looked bright.

That night, however, Falco, Delemotte, and Deloire had bad news. All they had seen during the day had been cloudy and therefore

(Above) One of the
beautiful fishes of the
reefs: A *Holocanthus,* or
queen angelfish.

A school of small fish
(Chromis) around a
stylaster.

(Above) Two *Chaeto-dontidae*, or butterfly fish, probably a male and a female, feeding on coral.

The *Calypso* at anchor off a *platier* (level reef).

unfilmable water; a bottom like a desert; and dead or dying coral. We listened in disappointed silence. All except Jacques Roux (whom everyone calls "Gaston," for no known reason), the electrical engineer in charge of the diving saucer. He sat there with a smile on his face; and I knew him well enough to know that he must have something up his sleeve. Because he was an engineer, Roux's job on the *Calypso* was a strictly technical one, and those who use the saucer have come to depend on his meticulous care and attention to the slightest detail in everything that concerns the saucer. But this engineer had conceived, at some point in his career, a passion for the sea and its beauties, and he dived at every opportunity purely for the pleasure of it. Once his work was done, no power on earth could have kept him aboard the *Calypso*. Often, we would hear a splash at night, and there would be Roux, with a small light in his hand, going for a swim among the coral. His friend Marcelin Naguy, our sound engineer, often went along, and we could see their lights moving about underwater four or five hundred yards from the ship.

I had often tried to convince Roux and Marcelin of the dangers of these nocturnal dives, but they would simply nod, say "Yes, yes. You're right, of course," and go right on diving whenever they felt like it. I couldn't find it in me to forbid them to go. I liked them both too much to deprive them of their sport — and, moreover, I shared their passion for the sea and marine life.

On this occasion, Roux sat there on the desk with his enigmatic smile until we were all looking at him. Then he walked over to the railing and, leaning over, pointed to something in the water that we could not see. He laughed, and offered no further explanation. "You'll have to see for yourselves," he said, and he plunged into the water. There was nothing to do but follow him. We did, and with Roux in the lead, we discovered under the *Calypso* what we had been looking for all day around the island: an underwater paradise of crystal-clear water, an abundance of fish, and very few sharks. It was as marvelous as it was unexpected. For the rest of our stay, the spot was known as "Gaston's Isle." And, of course, I have never had the heart since then to try to stop his nighttime diving.

It is impossible even to guess why, surrounded by comparatively uninteresting areas of bottom, there was this delightful oasis of life.

Maldivan natives examining our minisub aboard the *Calypso*.

Gaston's Isle must be regarded simply as one of those mysterious surprises offered by a coral sea. There we found great pink sea fans rising from the bottom, to which bronze-colored feather stars had attached themselves. There were mauve limestone algae that, with sponges of red, yellow, violet, and green, and an occasional feather-duster worm, combined with the yellows and blues of the *Acropora* into an extraordinary specimen of nature's nonrepresentational art. Across this background moved a rainbow of tropical fishes, ready, at the least provocation, to disappear into the coral recesses. They appeared undisturbed, however, by our approach, and after watching us for a while, they returned to their individual interests. Among them was a species with elongated and pointed noses — the astonishing long-nosed butterfly fish (*Forcipiger longirostris*) — searching for food among the coral; and there was the *Chelmon rostratus,* with a false eye on its back.

It was there, at Gaston's Isle, that we shot the first sequences of our film on the world of coral; that is, the views of the great *Acropora* parasols, so large that a diver could swim around under them as though they were trees. An abundance of sea fauna such as we have never seen anywhere else in the Indian Ocean became actors in our film. There was the trumpet fish, for example — an animal so gregarious that it cannot resist joining schools of fish of other species — swimming among tight banks of yellow snappers and soldierfish.

It was at Gaston's Isle also that we were able to film the doctorfish — so called because of its scalpel-sharp spine — which is able to change color suddenly and without apparent reason. Normally, the doctorfish is green or dark blue. But in a school of doctorfish one sees a fish sud-

(Left) Hassan Didi, our Maldivan friend, has just had a ride in the mini-sub and is delighted with it.

(Facing, above) The red fish in the coral massif is a Myripristis and belongs to the *Holocentridae* family. In the background are some *Pomacentridae*: Chromis (reef fish) and Abudefdufs (sergeant-majors).

(Facing, below) The trumpetfish (*Aulostomus*).

denly turn white. We do not know why. It may be a signal of some sort, or part of a mating ritual. In any case, the color change is sudden and unpredictable, and it was an exercise in patience for our camera crew to have to stay constantly alert to capture it on film.

On Saturday, March 25, Barsky and Dr. Leenhardt — whom I had appointed ministers plenipotentiary to the Maldivan government, because of their superb sense of diplomacy — went ashore clutching copies of letters that I had earlier obtained from the French Embassy in Ceylon. By noon, their diplomacy had borne fruit, as it were, and a boat arrived bearing a supply of mangoes and lemons. During the afternoon, a small motorboat, pulling a barge, arrived with the five tons of water that we needed. Jean Philippe Adrien Plé, one of the party who had gone ashore to buy supplies, reported that the natives were so poor that with a modest amount of cash he could have bought out the marketplace from one end to the other — but then there would have been nothing left for the Maldivans to buy. We all congratulated him on his good judgment in resisting the temptation to make a vulgar display of French economic power.

Later in the evening, we welcomed aboard a representative of the Maldivan Government who had been assigned to accompany us while we were in territorial waters. His name was Hassan — Hassan Didi, of course — and he was an amber-colored aristocrat related to the Maldivan national hero who was the political reformer of the archipelago.

Hassan was a man of great dignity, and of even greater solemnity, who seldom smiled. His gravity, combined with his youth, impressive physique, and intellectual gifts, made of him an engaging companion, and one who, moreover, was to be of considerable service to us.

The next day, Sunday, we sailed northward early in the morning, arriving at Gaha Faro, one of the Maldive atolls, at dawn. We sent out a team to the northeast at 6 A.M.; one to the north at 8:15; one westward at 8:30. And by 9:00, Laban and Barsky were under water in the saucer. Less than four hours after our dropping anchor, all our teams had been deployed and were at work. Despite some difficulties because of strong currents and troubled water, we were able to take some worth-while pictures and film sequences of fish in the area, and particularly of such reef animals as the ascidians and hydrozoans. One team found an interesting wreck that had been described and photographed earlier by Hans Hass, a German biologist and photographer.

Those who have never been to sea, and even surface sailors, can have no idea of how our work changes from one hour to the next, and how a bottom can offer contrasting spectacles of which one has no hint before diving. (There are, of course, certain indications that give a diver a general idea of what to expect — such as the color of the water.) For instance, after swimming among marvelously colored madreporarian corals and tropical fishes, we suddenly came upon a stretch of puny, grayish coral, some of which was covered with that green mucus that, as we know from experience, signals the decline of coral. Its presence indicates that the coral in question is no longer defending itself against the intrusion of other life forms — in this case, against the green algae that cover the now lifeless branches of madreporarians. It was obvious that some biological disaster was in preparation here. Unfortunately, part of our mission was precisely to visit such coral graveyards, so that we might gather information on the death of coral as well as on its life.

If I may draw a conclusion from our experiences and observations at the Maldives, it is that thriving communities of marine life are now relatively rare in this area. We do not see here the profusion of life that is characteristic of the Red Sea — great undersea cliffs, covered by coral thickets, where each individual life form seems to be constantly struggling to defend its place against intruders. In the Maldives, every time

Long-nosed butterfly fish (*Forcipiger longirostris*) and a member of the *Acanthuridae* family, the surgeonfish or doctorfish.

(Below) A specimen of "stinging coral" (*Millepora*) with unusual coloration. The small yellow branches on the gray sponge are Hydrozoa.

we found a spot where life was particularly abundant, we noticed that the area seemed to be dominated by a single species of coral or other fixed fauna. There were fields of elkhorn coral, meadows of sea fans, and rows of brown sponges in the shape of chalices, with each species occupying an area often not more than thirty or forty feet from that of the next life form. And almost everywhere, we saw an abundance of giant clams, their shells ajar to show the flesh, which varies in color from clear blue to dark violet, according to the individual clam.

Monday, March 27, we were within sight of the Powell Islands, which are part of the Maldives. The Powells comprise two islands, Etingili and Alifuri, and we anchored north of the former in a protected spot. The natives welcomed us in a singular manner: We had no sooner cut our engine than fishing boats, powered by sails, pulled alongside. The occupants of the boats bade us welcome with elaborate gestures — and then, when they were certain they had made themselves understood, they changed their tone and signaled quite clearly that they wished us to leave immediately. They made no threats, nor were they rude; but they were quite firm about it. Happily for us, Hassan Didi, the government representative, was aboard, and he quickly explained that we wished them no harm. The atmosphere cleared as he spoke, and we were then welcomed to the Powell Islands and treated as honored guests. Coconuts – the traditional gift of welcome in the islands – were handed aboard, and we returned the courtesy by offering them cigarettes. It was then explained to us that the islanders were wary of strangers because their waters had recently been invaded by commercial fisherman – Japanese, especially – and all their fish taken, which was not something to make them welcome foreign visitors with open arms.

Here, in the Powell Islands, we were able to witness and to film the natives fishing for a species of tuna called bonito. It was a noteworthy sight, and we managed, not without difficulty, to obtain a striking sequence. At this time of the year (in the spring), the natives fish for tuna by an unusual method. They begin at night by going out into shallow water and picking up crabs, which they then crush and attach to their hand nets early the next morning. They go out again into shallow water and, with the crabs as bait, catch small fish which are themselves to serve as bait for larger game. These little fish are kept alive in the water at the bottom of the fishing boats. The boats are rather deep, and they are made in such a way as to take on enough water to keep the fish alive. Since the boats are always on the point of sinking, two men are permanently assigned to bailing duty, to make sure that the water does not reach a dangerous level.

At around seven o'clock in the morning, the boats raise their sails and make for the deep, in groups of six or eight, until they sight a large number of birds circling overhead. On the sea, where there are many birds there is usually a school of tuna. As soon as the presence of a school has been verified, the fishermen begin throwing overboard handfuls of the bait from the bottom of the boat. Then they begin fishing, using bamboo poles — four to each boat — a line about twelve feet long, and an ordinary galvanized hook. No sooner is the hook in the water, it seems, than a tuna is pulled aboard. The fishermen do not even bother to unhook their catch. The tuna (which average about two feet in length) flop around so violently that they usually unhook themselves. In fifteen minutes, a single boat can easily take in twenty fish, and an average day's catch for a boat is about six hundred tuna. Each fish is worth one rupee. The catch is divided up that evening on the beach. A quarter goes to the government, a quarter to the owner of the boat, and half to the fishermen. This traditional division of spoils has served as a model for all other commercial activities in the socialist sultanate: 25 per cent to the state, 25 per cent to the employer, 50 per cent to the employees.

During the morning, we worked at filming this extraordinary fishing expedition. Early in the afternoon, however, it occurred to me how much more unusual it would be if we could have scenes showing not only the islanders pulling in the fish, but showing also the other side of the story — the fury and the folly of the fish as they snapped frantically at the fishermen's lines. I therefore asked Marcellin, our sound engineer, if it would be possible to hook up a self-contained underwater television camera to a small boat. He said it was. So, the television camera was screwed to the underside of a runabout facing the rear. We also hooked up, in the same way, two movie cameras — a 9 mm. and a 25 mm. All night long we worked and improvised to make sure that everything would function. By 3 A.M., we were ready.

Hassan got permission for us to have our runabout towed by one of

Hydrozoa, in a fernlike formation, in the midst of coral.

the fishing boats. And everything seemed to be working perfectly. The fishing boats took on a record catch. The extraordinary spectacle was duplicated on the television monitor, with thirty or forty tunas frantically grabbing for the hooks and being pulled up into the boats. In hot pursuit of the tuna came the sharks, who swallowed the smaller fish in great mouthfuls. It was a scene of almost unbearable cruelty and violence. Then Laban, very upset, told me that only the 25-mm. camera had been working, which meant that we would have only close-ups. We had to start all over again. This time, there were perhaps fewer tuna on the screen at once, but we shot two spools of film with which we are extraordinarily pleased.

While we were filming the tuna catch, Falco was in the diving saucer on the west side of the island, moving through a field of brilliantly colored sea fans and a dense school of Zanclidae, or Moorish idols — a species that, aboard the *Calypso,* we have nicknamed the "radio fish" because of its elongated, antenna-like dorsal fin. At a depth of between a hundred fifty and two hundred feet, Falco found a series of ascending grottoes — some of them ten or twelve feet deep — like a giant staircase

An angelfish (*Pygoplithes diacanthus*), with its blue and yellow stripes, and a Moorish idol (*Zanclus*). Aboard the *Calypso,* the latter is known as a "radio fish" because of its antenna-like dorsal fin.

leading to the surface. Perhaps they had been carved aeons ago by some disturbance on the surface when the water level in this area was a hundred fifty feet lower than it is now. If so, the grottoes would be a fossil bank. This was all conjecture, of course, but it occurred to me that perhaps we would be able to check this out in other regions of the Indian Ocean.

The next step for us was to gather coral samples, which we would send back to Monaco for analysis. I therefore organized a dive on the north side of the island. Two teams, each comprising two divers, went down in relays to depths of between a hundred fifty and two hundred feet and removed fragments from the coral wall. They carefully noted the exact depth at which each specimen was taken, so that carbon testing could determine the ages of the coral at different levels.

Once we had taken all the necessary samples, we had time to show our gratitude to our Maldivan representative, Hassan Didi, for his services. This took the form of a ride in the diving saucer, from which Hassan emerged overcome with enthusiasm. The experience, he told us, had been a revelation to him. If so, it was one of which this aristocrat of the sea was entirely worthy.

During our first weeks in the Maldives, I must confess that we were — not disappointed, but disconcerted, by what we saw. There were no complaints from the divers, of course; we had come so far on one engine precisely so that we might "acclimatize" ourselves to the world beneath the surface of the sea, and our teams were taking full advantage of our stay here for that purpose. Our reaction, I think, had more to do with the vastness of the phenomena we were observing than with those phenomena themselves. It was a matter of scale. Even though we think of ourselves as knowing the sea comparatively well, our experience has been limited to certain fairly well defined areas. In theory, we know that the sea and the bottom are very different from one region to another; but what makes the sea such a marvelous adventure is that it is really impossible to imagine, unless we have actually seen it, to what extent it differs from one place to the next. In the Red Sea, for example, and in the Mediterranean, we had become accustomed to observation on a comparatively limited scale. But here, in the Maldives, nature seemed boundless, and it was necessary for us to adjust our minds to a new order of magnitude. The Maldive region is an immense area in the In-

Heterocongers, or garden eels, dig into the sand at the approach of a diver.

dian Ocean composed of a seeming infinity of atolls — more than two thousand — which rise from a plateau lying at a depth of about a hundred thirty feet. Once we go beyond the immediate vicinity of the reefs, we no longer see any coral, and very few of the brightly colored fish that one might expect to find in a tropical sea. But we do see other things: sharks, naturally; but also manta rays, and even a grampus — a member of the whale family with a particularly fearsome reputation. (Falco assured us, however, that the beasts are easily trained, and that, in California, he had been able to strike up a real friendship with one.) The sea bottom around the Maldives, therefore, is composed of sandy expanses and is inhabited by the great beasts of the sea.

Each atoll of the region is a veritable mill in which coral is ground, a factory for making sand. Coral grows by absorbing calcium from the water. But as the coral reefs grow, they are demolished by fish — the parrot fish, principally — who eat the coral. The Maldivans also, as we have seen, use coral as a building material. Little by little, therefore, the natural protection from the sea afforded by the coral reefs has been compromised. The underwater walls of the atolls are losing their cohesiveness, and the islands are in danger. The history of the Maldivans may be summed up in the tale of the man who worked busily at sawing off the branch on which he was sitting. A number of the islands of the Maldives have already been dismantled to the point where they have recently sunk into the sea.

To one who knows the story of sand, this comes as no surprise. I have mentioned the fact that parrot fish eat coral. The truth is that they graze on coral like sheep in a meadow. Then, they spew out what they have eaten in the form of a cloud of sand. It is estimated that a single parrot fish produces five tons of sand every year. This sand, which is pulverized limestone, dissolves once more in the water until a point of saturation is reached, at which time it recrystallizes in the form of "beach rock," or sandstone — which is the indurated form of parrot-fish detritus. Below this mass of beach rock there is sand, broken only by an occasional sloping cliff that has been worn smooth by the incessant action of falling sand.

The whole is constantly being swept by tidal currents that move first in one direction and then in another, at a speed of two knots. High tide brings clear water from the open sea into the vast lagoons of the

A triggerfish watches over the eggs that it has deposited in an opening of coral. Above is a *gomphos,* or wrasse, belonging to the *Labridae* family.

islands, while ebb tide carries out water that has been clouded by the intense fermentation of life in the reefs and in the microatolls of the interior.

The north and southwest sides of these atolls usually offer the greatest abundance of fish. The islands and reefs lying slightly to the interior of the great atolls, and opposite the channels through which the tide flows, are usually (but not always) oases in which marine life congregates in a profusion unequaled anywhere in the world. In this case, however, we had explored the north side of the island in vain.

Before leaving the Maldives we returned to that underwater paradise we had baptized Gaston's Isle. But now the currents were so strong, and the water so turbulent, that we could work for only two 1-hour periods each day, while the tide was slack.

We were working near the island of Funidu. The bottom was mostly flat, relieved only by a succession of shallow basins, which we visited, one after another, as one would a series of antechambers at Versailles. Sunlight penetrated the water to heighten the colors of the fish

(Above) There are several species of *Tetraodontidae,* of which some exhibit surprising colors. The one shown here is probably a *Mappa.* All species puff up their bodies when frightened.

One of the most extraordinary sights to be found in tropical seas is a colony of fixed animals (or sessiles, as they are called). This biotope comprises alcyonarians, antipatharians, annelids, and madreporarians. The whole is cemented together by calcareous algae.

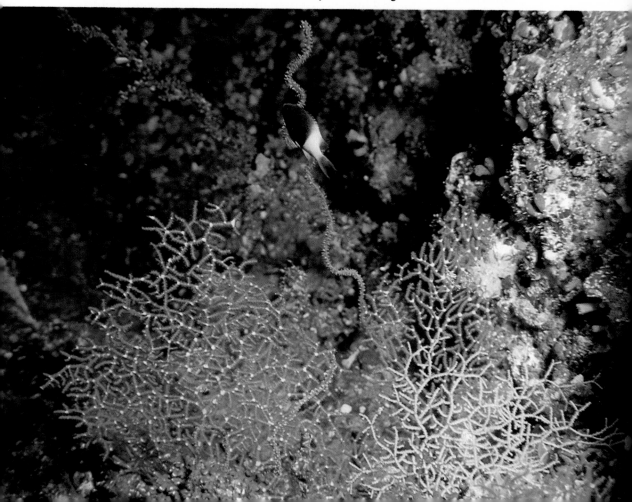

and to brighten the hues of the coral: there were thickets flecked with lilac, pink, and blue, and massifs from which grew branches of gold. At one point, a curious eel emerged halfway from its lair to inspect us, but lost its courage and — despite Frédéric Dumas's friendly overtures — fled.

I was amazed at the lines of fish who swam around us in perfect formation, fin to fin, following some mysterious instinct and bound on some unfathomable journey. When seen through human eyes, these formations of fish, all of the same species, looked like nothing so much as a river within the sea. Occasionally, a shadow on the surface of the water or a movement by a diver would cause the line to accelerate its pace, and then the river would become a cascade or a torrent. If we moved toward them suddenly, the group would scatter in all directions, their bright colors looking like a display of fireworks against the sky blue of the sea.

Off the island of Oulele — on which the Maldivans had built their coral airstrip — we had occasion also to observe once more the garden eel (*Heteroconger longissimus*) which has the disturbing habit of burying itself in the sand. We had seen garden eels earlier at Madeira, and Laban had seen some in Mexican waters. And here we saw them again, balancing their rope-like bodies on the sandy bottom.[1]

To film these garden eels of Oulele, we used, as in filming the tuna catch, two cameras: a 9 mm. and a 25 mm. These were coupled with a television camera, which served as a monitor, and the whole complex was connected to a boat on the surface. Since garden eels live at a depth of about a hundred to a hundred and twenty-five feet, this arrangement made it possible for the men in the boat to see what was happening in the water.

The only trouble was that as soon as a diver came anywhere near an eel, the animal immediately disappeared into the sand. I therefore ordered the three cameras to be placed on the bottom and focused for horizontal shots. When this had been done, everyone returned to the surface.

A considerable time elapsed between the departure of the divers and the emergence of the eels. But emerge they did, cautiously, inch by inch, until they were certain that the intruders were indeed gone. Then

[1]Another species of this peculiar animal was discovered by Hans Hass, which zoologists have christened *Xariphania Hassi* in his honor.

they went about their business, which consists in searching for food in the current by balancing themselves on their tails, like question marks, and facing the current. As soon as we saw them on the television screen, I pressed the starter button and the two cameras below began to record the scene. Obviously, this was the only way to film the garden eel.

To give a little variety to the scene, I sent a diver down. As he approached the cameras, the eels fled into the sand again as soon as he had come to within five or six yards of them. Seen from a distance, it looked as though a beautiful carpet had disappeared by magic into the earth.

When we had all the film we wanted, we decided to try capturing a garden eel. We wanted to put it in a special aquarium so that we might study the habits of its species. A team went down, armed with a ball-point airlift (a suction device) and a syringe containing a concentrated solution of MS-222 (a soporific for fish), while we watched on the monitor screen. As soon as the divers approached, the eels plunged into the sand on schedule. The suction was applied to the spot where one of the animals had disappeared. It was in perfect working order — but it caught nothing. Delemotte, who was one of the divers, felt the spot with his hand and discovered that the hole had been plugged — or rather, cemented shut — by a mucous substance that the animal had discharged through its skin. And there was no sign of the eel itself.

With the help of our doctor, we prepared a more potent solution of MS-222. Our plan was to inject it into several holes before attempting to draw out the eels with the suction device. But Frédéric Dumas had a better idea. He suggested that we cover two or three holes with plexiglass domes and then inject a strong dose of MS-222 into the enclosures. The eels would then either fall asleep in their holes or emerge from them and fall asleep under the domes. In either case, we would be able to capture specimens.

Dumas's method proved to be a spectacular success. After the domes had been in place for a while, the animals decided that it was safe to emerge from their holes; whereupon they went to sleep almost immediately. All we had to do was gather up as many as we wanted. We then placed the specimens within a shallow, enclosed aquarium to observe how these creatures dig their holes. The aquarium itself was placed on the sea bottom, so that the eels might be in their natural environment.

We were in for a surprise. The natural enemies of the eels, which we had not yet seen, showed up, and the aquarium was suddenly surrounded by small wrasses and triggerfish, which tried desperately to attack the eels through the glass of the aquarium.

Finally, we released our prisoners, and Deloire filmed their flight. One swam away immediately and disappeared into the distance. Another began burying himself in the sand as fast as he could. But he was not fast enough. A wrasse seized the protruding end and pulled him out, and another wrasse grabbed the other end. It seemed that the wrasses were the victors. But, in the sea, no victory is ever final. Out of nowhere, a grouper came upon the scene and, in one gulp, swallowed both the wrasses and their prey.

Our stay in the Indies was exciting and rewarding in every respect. Yet, I could not forget that the *Calypso* was operating on drastically reduced power. Alone in my cabin, I worried and fretted until a decision was made. We would have to abandon our observations here and make for the east coast of Africa, which was the only place where we could hope to have our propeller shaft repaired. I was not looking forward to the long trek across the Indian Ocean on a single engine, but there seemed to be little choice. The monsoon season was almost upon us, and it was within the framework of that phenomenon of nature that I had to analyze our situation.

At the same time, it occured to me that it had been a month since we had received any mail (at Djibouti), and, during that time, no one aboard had had any news of their families in Europe. The next mail call would not take place until we had reached Diégo-Suarez, on the coast of Madagascar, in three weeks. So, I authorized everyone aboard to send telegrams home, and to have answers wired collect to the *Calypso*. And then on April 7, we weighed anchor and began our slow journey back across the vastness of the Indian Ocean

FOUR

The Indian Ocean:
Exploring Around the
Seychelles and Cosmoledo

What coral is really like.
How a reef captures its food and eats it.
Tentacles waving in the night.
Sea fans, tree shapes, walls,
and discs of coral.
Photographing under floodlights.
The monsoon approaches.

As our first stop en route to Djibouti I had selected the archipelago of the Seychelles. To reach these islands, we had to travel southwest across a considerable expanse of the Indian Ocean, over which few ships pass, and I was anticipating some interesting meetings with the larger forms of marine life. I knew that, at that time of year and in that region, we would have a chance to observe sperm whales, for these mammals have fixed routes which they follow on their migrations and along which they hunt for food. It was not necessary for me to organize a formal "watch." Such things take care of themselves spontaneously aboard the *Calypso*. There are always one or more of our men on the observation deck, on the alert for the spouting of a whale. I know I can depend, with absolute confidence, on the enthusiasm and curiosity of my friends, particularly with respect to the larger marine animals. We reached the equator, however, without having seen even the smallest specimen. But we did not give up. We sailed westward for a time, hoping to run across a whale "lane," but in vain. It was puzzling. We had been here before at this time of the year, and there had been sperm whales aplenty. We had been able to follow and observe them for days on end as they traveled in small family groups of three or four members.

The sperm whale, or cachalot, while not as large as some of the whalebone, or baleen, whales, is nonetheless a formidable mass of muscle and blubber. The species is often found at a depth of almost two thousand feet. Sometimes it goes as low as thirty-five hundred feet, and — though rarely — down to four thousand feet. I can imagine what those fantastic dives into the black world of phosphorescent creatures must be like.

Although we saw no sperm whales, we did see an abundance of grampuses and dolphins. The latter provoked much excitement aboard. We all crowded into our underwater observation room and watched and filmed to our hearts' content. These mammals, it seemed, were playing a game with the *Calypso*. They would swim back and forth just ahead of the prow, in order to take advantage of the increased amount of oxygen in the water caused by the ship's motion. They seemed to find this an amusing pastime. And I could swear they had seen us watching them and were performing as much for our benefit as for their own.

On the eighteenth we arrived at Mahé-Port Victoria, the capital of the Seychelle Islands.

The Seychelles are very different from the Maldives. For one thing, they rise high above the water, and, with their bluffs, are reminiscent of the islands of Polynesia — Bora Bora, for example, or Moorea. Geologically, however, they resemble not at all the coral and volcanic islands of the Pacific. The Seychelles are mountains of red and brown granite, and they are covered with vegetation as varied as it is beautiful.

In earlier times, the Seychelles were an important port of call on the route to the Indies; but now they are off the main shipping lanes, and traffic to and from them is minimal. No civilian aircraft land there. The archipelago was discovered by the Portuguese, and then it passed into the hands of the French, who named the capital Mahé, in honor of Mahé de la Bourdonnais, a French navigator who participated in the founding of the city. The archipelago itself was named after Moreau de Séchelles, a French high commissioner. The Seychelles became a British possession in 1810, during the Napoleonic Wars; but French is still the language of the natives, despite the best efforts of the British, for the past century and a half, to impose their own tongue.

The Seychelles produce and export sugar cane, coffee, tobacco, vanilla, black pepper, and an essence used in the making of perfume. At one time, the goods of three continents — Europe, Africa, and Asia — flowed into the islands, and the superb botanical gardens of Mahé reflect that era of prosperous commerce.

If one is looking for an earthly paradise, however, one can more easily find it on the islands that lie close to Mahé but are more removed from civilization: Fregati and Silhouette — and Praslin, which is an island of sea coconuts and black parrots.

Our sojourn in the Seychelles was good for a single worth-while sequence. Deloire and Barsky were able to film a species of amphibious fish, *Periophthalmus koelreuteri* — more commonly, and much less grandly, known as the mudskipper. It is acknowledged to be the most amphibious of all fishes, for it can stay out of water for longer periods than it spends in the water. When on land, the mudskipper carries a supply of water in the gill cavity, and it also gulps air. It is at home on mudflats and among mangrove roots, where it propels itself by "walking" on its pectoral fins and — in order to move hurriedly — by means of rather spectacular, froglike leaps. In the water, however, the mudskipper swims quite normally. Its diet consists of insects and small crustaceans, in pursuit of which it makes optimum use of its highly functional popeyes to keep watch in every direction.

We were pressed for time, as I have mentioned, because of the approaching monsoon season, and we could not linger here. I know, moreover, that the Seychelles are not particularly well endowed so far as coral reefs are concerned. But on the other hand, it would be the ideal spot to study the mollusks and crustaceans that abound here — a fascinating subject which, perhaps, we may be able to investigate at some time in the future. The Seychelles stand on a gigantic and very old socle, or base, of coral, the top of which is not more than about a hundred and sixty feet beneath the surface of the sea. The plateau thus formed — which is an environment suitable for mollusks — falls off into steep cliffs and slopes that descend precipitously as much as three miles.

Before the monsoon caught up with us, however, I wanted the opportunity to continue our observation of coral life, and Dumas, Falco, and I studied our charts carefully until we concluded that the little island of Cosmoledo seemed to offer the best conditions for diving. Cos-

Chromis among the branches of sea fans.

(Above) A female parrot fish grazing on coral. Following her is a *Siganus*.

(Below) Alcyonarians — the so-called "soft coral." Unlike true coral, they do not secrete calcareous exoskeletons. At night, they swell up to twice their normal size.

moledo is situated to the northwest of Madagascar. It is a British possession, and is attached, for administrative purposes, to the Seychelles. We
decided to take our chances there.

We dropped anchor on April 24, north of a beautiful beach near
the Isle of Menay, which we had chosen as the site of our first exploration. The anchorage was difficult enough. I had to try three times, and
three times the anchor did not touch bottom. Nevertheless, I was unwilling to go in closer to land, for I wanted above all to have swinging room
in case the wind rose. By my fourth try, there were already three teams
of divers in the water — a situation that I do not like, even though I
know that all my divers, except perhaps Sillner, the German photographer, know how to avoid the propellers. This time, however, the anchor
held.

A half hour later, one of our boats returned with five enormous fish
caught off one of the inner islands. The best of these were for our table.
The rest would be chopped into pieces and distributed among the fish in
the water by the divers — to create a friendly atmosphere. This is standard procedure with us, and it is known aboard the *Calypso* as the "feeding detail."

Our diving teams were in action morning and evening. I am always
amazed to see to what extent underwater work depends on the temperaments of the individual divers; the results, happily, are uniformly excellent, but they are obtained by very different methods. Diving, like so
many human occupations, reveals the secret character of men — even of
men whom one thinks one knows very well.

Our long-time diving companion Albert Falco, with an athlete's
build that is distinguishable even under the water, is characterized by
persistence in the face of difficulties. He has had more than sufficient
experience to know instinctively what to do and how to act with marine
life forms; and he is particularly good with sharks, into whose reactions
and behavior he seems to have a special insight. He is one member of a
team, in which Christian Bonnici is the other diver. Bonnici is younger
than Falco, more flexible, more sensitive, and marvelously intuitive.

Falco — or Bébert, as we call him — and Bonnici were working at
capturing specimens by the use of Quinaldine, a soporific. When the
fish were sound asleep, Falco and Bonnici placed them in a plexiglass
container resembling an eelpot. This time, there were angelfish with al-

ternating stripes of yellow and dark blue. And they had been lucky enough to catch a specimen of the spectacular *Forcipiger longirostris,* or long-nosed butterfly fish, which is disc shaped and striped with blue and gold, and has a small mouth set at the end of a snoutlike extension. The snout is useful in seeking out the tiny invertebrates that lie among coral and are the butterfly fish's principal nourishment. Both the angelfish and the butterfly fish are remarkable for their beauty and for their comparative rarity. The purpose in capturing them was to send them (by air) to the *Musée Océanographique* at Monaco.

A second team comprised Michel Deloire, Bernard Delemotte, and Yves Omer. All three are equally expert in handling large marine animals and cameras, at any depths and in whatever circumstances. This team first organized the "feeding detail," of which we now make constant use.

Our third team is composed of Sillner and Dominique Sumian. On this occasion, they were down about 125 feet, taking pictures "in the Sillner style." After a short time, Sillner appeared alongside the *Calypso,* but he did not come aboard. His day, obviously, was not yet complete. I amused myself for a while by watching him. He is short and round, and he swims frog fashion. Or perhaps he reminds me more of a tetraodont, or porcupine fish, when its spines are down and it is floating here and there, apparently dreaming but actually aware of everything that is going on. Sillner was wearing around his neck the cameraman's rosary of gadgets: cameras, filters, light meters, lenses, range finder. He saw me watching him, smiled, waved, and disappeared into the water, oblivious to anything but his work. A shark could snap at Sillner, and he would never notice it unless it were a very effective snap indeed. We have learned that if we disturb him while he is diving, we do so at our own risk. The slightest interruption causes an angry explosion of air bubbles to rise to the surface.

When Sillner has finished his day's shooting and climbs aboard, he immediately deposits his equipment over the whole of the *Calypso,* from stem to stern. No one can move without bumping into one of Sillner's thingamajigs. Then, when it is time for his next dive, there is a cry of rage, and the accusation that we've "hidden all my equipment," that we have "ruined everything," and that he is "not going to put up with this any longer." Then, because we are all so fond of him, we gather up all his equipment, from every corner of the ship, and bring it to him. He blushes, and everyone laughs.

Sillner's teammate, Dominique Sumian, is the perfect companion for him. Dominique is the one man capable of protecting our photographer from sharks and from the results of his intense preoccupation with his work to the exclusion of all else.

Sumian — who is known aboard the *Calypso* as "Doumé," which is the diminutive, on his native Corsica, of Dominique — is a remarkably capable diver. He is also extraordinarily strong, and it is always a pleasure to watch his long, swimmer's body in the water. Like most of our team, however, Sumian is a gentle and patient giant, and we have learned to depend upon his ability to remain calm in the most trying circumstances. In the three years he has been with us, our respect for his ability has grown constantly. And, like many of the young men aboard, Sumian seems to have given meaning to his life by sharing our life.

Dominique began as one of our chief divers, and later he became the pilot of the diving saucer. In the near future, he will take on even greater responsibility as commander of our research submarine, the SP-300.

At Cosmoledo we discovered that conditions for diving were not ideal. But then, they seldom are; so much so that we regard the ideal as the exception. Here, there were strong currents and turbulent water. But it was worth it, for never before had we seen so many fish in one place.

On the plateau along the coast, down to a depth of forty-five to fifty feet, there was an incredible profusion of tropical fish of every shape, form, and color. At less than twenty feet, three big groupers came out of their holes to inspect us. There were pointed-toothed wrasses and enormous parrot fish and such "rivers" of fish as we had seen off Funidu, in the Maldives. It seemed a submarine paradise, untouched by man.

The face of the cliff along which we were descending was not vertical — but almost. And, for once, it held more life than any I had seen in the Red Sea. Everywhere, enormous sea fans were waving. It was like a fairyland — but the current was so strong that I was out of breath by the time I climbed aboard the *Calypso* again. But I did not feel even a twinge in my back.

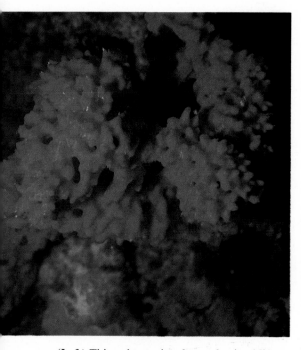

(Left) This red mass is a form of animal life. It is a colony of sponges.

(Right) A coral massif encrusted with red sponges. An eel shows its teeth from the safety of its lair; next to it is an angelfish.

The true wonder of Cosmoledo, however, is that the place has remained unspoiled — filled with fish, turtles, and birds, none of which have yet learned to be wary of man. How long can it last? I wonder. I had the very strong feeling that, on this cruise of the *Calypso,* we were taking a final inventory, and that the end might not be far off; that Cosmoledo would go the way of so many such paradises that the touch of man has destroyed. Something, surely, could be done to protect it. But it is not certain that man will be willing to take the necessary means.

It may be that I use the word "paradise" too liberally. Cosmoledo may indeed be a paradise; but it is a redoubtable one. The danger — or at least the greatest danger — is not from sharks. Many smaller fish are just as dangerous. One such is the *Pterois,* or dragonfish, which is a thing of great beauty as it swims surrounded by veil-like fins tinted in shades of pink and blue. Those fins, however, are as dangerous as they are lovely, for they are, in reality, poisonous stingers. The unlucky diver who is careless with a dragonfish runs the risk of edema, of paralysis, and perhaps even of death. Even worse are the scorpion fish, for most of the 118 species have a sharp, poisonous spine on the tail, and its puncture — particularly on the trunk of the body — is often mortal. Poison is a weapon commonly encountered in the world of coral. It is the offensive and defensive arm not only of the fauna that live among coral, but of the coral itself. The group of invertebrates to which coral belongs is characterized by the use of urticant, or stinging, cells — called nematoblasts — which are tiny weapons of extraordinary effectiveness. These cells are, in fact, minuscule capsules that explode under the effect of excitement or danger and shoot out a tiny line, covered with hooks, which lodges in the target. It is worth noting that almost all the fixed animals of a coral reef possess that weapon, which is used primarily to obtain food but also to ward off enemies. It is very painful and dangerous to the unwary diver. For that reason, in this area our divers never go below without a protective suit. The tropical seas are a country in which poison reigns supreme.

As numerous in tropical waters as fish may be — and they are particularly abundant around Cosmoledo — they are not the most common of the marine animals. That distinction is reserved for coral, and for the fauna that are found with coral — the fixed, or stationary, life forms. I should explain here that I use the word "coral" in a general sense, to designate polyps characterized by an outer skeleton of limey material.[1] In its proper sense, "coral" is applicable solely to the precious red coral *(Corallium rubrum)* of the Mediterranean. Red coral belongs to a distinct genus. It is an octocorallan; while what we usually call coral is a hexacorallan. (In other words, red coral has an axial symmetry of eight parts, while other "coral" has an axial symmetry of six parts, or of a multiple of six.)

The madreporarian corals, which I have mentioned earlier, have polyps similar to sea anemones, but they live within a limestone exoskeleton they create by secretion. Madreporarians are the most abundant reef-forming corals in waters in which the temperature does not go below 70 degrees F.; that is, in seas between 32 degrees north and 27 degrees south of the Equator. They come in a variety of colors: pink, blue, purple, yellow, green, and golden brown. Their shapes are innu-

[1]See Appendix II.

merable — branchlike, round, and so forth — depending, apparently, on the ordinary condition of the waters in which they live. Where water is usually calm, they take the form of brittle branches; but where there is a swell, they tend to cluster into more-massive shapes. Moreover, there are variations according to species and to the depth at which the madreporarians live. All these factors are responsible, in one degree or another, for the fantastic diversity of coral.

The relative immobility of the aquatic milieu beginning at about thirty-five feet below the surface allows coral to develop, both outside and within the reef, into forms of a fragility and delicacy of design that would be impossible out of water. In the air, such forms would collapse of their own weight. At much greater depths, however, it is equally impossible for coral to live. Its existence is bound up with that of unicellular algae that live in symbiosis with it and need light in order to achieve photosynthesis. These algae, which live in the tissue of the polyps, are called zooxanthellae.

An American research team, H. T. Odum and E. P. Odum, have discovered that there is another vegetable element in madreporarians: certain green filaments existing in the pores of the calcarious skeleton. Interestingly enough, if we add up the zooxanthellae and these "green filaments," we discover that coral contains three times more vegetable protoplasm than animal protoplasm ...

The extraordinary complexity of the world of coral is due to the fact that many other animals live cheek by jowl, as it were, with coral, and also contribute to the construction of reefs. There are, for example, a group of coralliforms — such as Millepora and Stylasterina — which also take on branched forms and secrete an exoskeleton. And other, and very different, life forms play a part in the make-up of this tropical marine jungle: a sea worm distantly related to the earthworm and belonging to the class Polychaeta (called a "feather duster" or Spirograph, it is topped by feathery plumes that trap tiny organisms); mollusks, such as the giant clam; various algae of green and pink which act as the mortar among sedentary animals; and thickets of venom-bearing anemones.

Given the richness and diversity of the living world of coral — a world so alien to our own — it begins to become clear that coral plays a considerable role in the life of this planet; a role much more important than is generally suspected. Coral, after all, is found in a portion of this

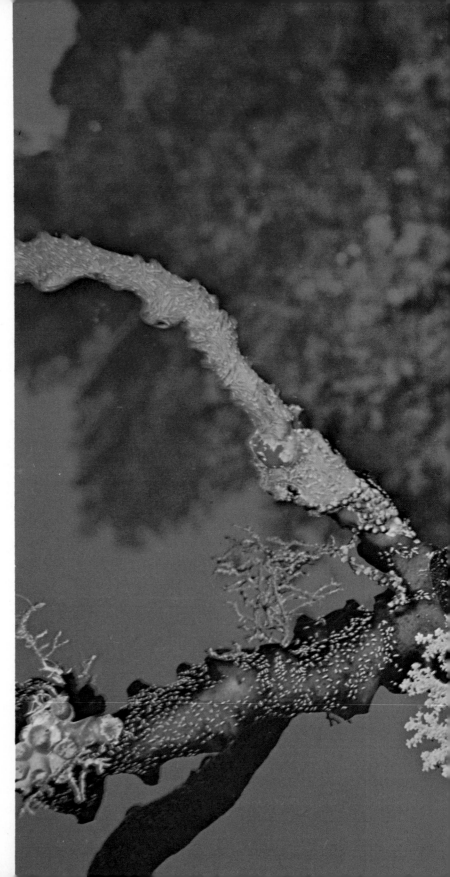

One of the most beautiful of coral fishes, *Holocanthus imperator*. It is swimming over alcyonarian formations of rare colors, shaded from pink to blue.

globe roughly twenty times the size of Europe, or twenty-five times that of the United States. It is not a world that we can afford to ignore.[2]

One evening, at a quarter after seven, I had the diving saucer lowered into the water. A team of us stayed down for an unusually long period with our floodlights, filming sea fans and the fish swimming among them. This was between, say, seventy-five and one hundred fifty feet. From one hundred fifty feet to three hundred feet, there were no more sea fans; there was a sandy bottom, and a wealth of coral. From three hundred to three hundred seventy-five feet, along a steep cliff, the coral formations were much smaller. At three hundred seventy-five feet, there was a vertical drop. Along its edge, we saw what appeared to be small, dark-red thickets moving about. These were starfish — the basket star, whose body is fairly small, but whose multibranched arms, when they are extended, resemble a tangled shrub several feet in diameter. Someone who had the patience to count the branchings found over eighty thousand terminal branches.

At four hundred twenty-five feet there was a small ledge. At five hundred feet we found branched sponges, and a flock of little crustaceans cavorting in a series of "molecular" motions. (This was the same species of small, curled shrimp that Laban had seen on an earlier dive.)

The cliff ended at six hundred twenty-five feet. Beyond, there were boulders and a stretch of sand and mud sprinkled with sea urchins (genus *Spatangus*).

At seven hundred feet, there was a very strong eastward current. We loosened our ballast and began the ascent to the surface.

On April 25 and 26, we were at Assumption Island.

Even before dropping anchor, I sent out a team in one of the boats. They radioed back almost immediately: "Jojo isn't here any more. But there are many other groupers. The bottom is about the same."

I anchored at about eight in the morning, in a good spot — in fact, an ideal spot for an underwater studio, where the depth varied from less than twenty-five feet to as much as one hundred fifty feet.

Jojo, of course, is the grouper who, under the stage name of Ulys-

[2] An average atoll, for example, contains about five hundred square kilometers of material, which is equivalent to 250 times that of New York City — or 15,000 times that of the largest of the Egyptian pyramids. Coral is a more diligent builder even than man.

ses, had been one of the scene stealers in *The Silent World*. He had become such a "ham" that we had to lock him up in the anti-shark cage whenever we were shooting scenes in which he did not belong. Otherwise, he would invariably come floating past the cameras at precisely the wrong moment. Even though we had no opening on this cruise for a grouper, we still would have liked to renew old acquaintance. We did, however, manage to meet, on friendly terms, another fish who has a bad reputation.

It came about in this way. Yves Omer and Dominique Sumian went down for the daily feeding detail, carrying a large bag full of pieces of meat. On the bottom, Sumian climbed up on a rock, and André Laban stationed himself a few yards away to film the scene.

In a few minutes, all three were surrounded by fish of every size. But Omer and Sumian did not suspect that the rock on which they were standing was the home of a giant moray eel; and the eel wanted to have his share of the food. Laban saw its head begin to emerge, and then part of its body. The two divers, however, had noticed nothing amiss until, with a couple of swift undulations, the eel made for the opening in the bag. It was a truly enormous beast, brownish and flecked with yellow. It advanced, its eyes fixed on the food — the other extremity of its body still in its lair. Its resemblance to a python, and the unknown quantity of its size, made its appearance as disconcerting as that of a shark would have been.

Yves Omer left the rock and, holding out pieces of fish, tried to lure the eel out into open water; but it immediately slithered back into its lair. Then, remembering the fish, it came out again. Yves held up a piece of fish, temptingly. The eel hesitated, and then, reluctantly, emerged completely, its long, muscular body magnificent in its graceful swimming motion. It must have been six feet long.

Everyone was still. The eel swam slowly up to Yves and took the food from his hand. It was almost as sensational as the results we had had with Jojo. Finally, Yves succeeded in doing what he had intended all along; he patted the eel's head without scaring it away.

If we had been able to stay there for two or three days longer, the eel no doubt would have come to recognize Yves and would have followed him about in the water like a dog on land. It seemed to us that it was easier to make friends with an eel than it had been with a grouper.

(Left) A diver petting a grouper hidden among the coral.

(Facing) One of the most dangerous of coral fishes, the *Pterois radiata*, whose long dorsal spines are venomous.

Whether or not it is difficult to tame this or that fish depends, I think, largely on the temperaments of individual members of a species. Like human beings, fish are sometimes nervous, skittish, frightened — and, as with human beings, fear sometimes makes them hostile and aggressive. I have noticed, however, that, in general, the older and the larger an animal is, the less "wild" it is. Perhaps it is because a large animal, being strong (or "secure"), is less open to fear. An eel of that size must feel that it is practically invincible in its own neighborhood — though we do not know the maximum size that an eel (or a grouper) can reach. We do not even know whether "death from old age" exists among such creatures. (Though there are many efficient grave robbers in the sea, such as the octopus, the crab, certain mollusks which devour

dead or dying creatures.)

We worked for two days, one 3-man team after another going down. The *Calypso* bobbed about like a cork on the surface, when it was possible to anchor securely; when it was not, she sailed in a circle around the diving area. I had made a list of subjects to be explored during our stay: turtles, groupers, sea cucumbers (the giant holothurians), and "volcanoes." But we saw not one turtle, nor a single sea cucumber. The groupers who were living in Jojo's old home would have been trainable, but the process would have taken four or five days.

We did, however, manage to solve the "riddle of the volcanoes," which had haunted me for years.

The volcanoes in question were not the awesome belchers of fire and smoke with which movie-goers are familiar. I had given the name, for lack of a better term, to a phenomenon I had observed a long time before. I had noticed that, on certain bottoms, there were small hills from which, from time to time, a jet of "smoke" — that is, sand — erupted. The cause of all this is an animal who lives in the mound of sand. That much I knew. But we had never been able to see, much less capture, that animal.

On one occasion, in 1955, a good American friend, Louis Marden of *National Geographic,* who is both a diver and a photographer, was aboard the *Calypso.* He attempted to photograph one of these volcanoes in eruption, which was easier to say than to do; for, each time he focused his camera on one volcano, another volcano would erupt. This went on so long that it began to look like an old Chaplin film. Finally I signaled Louis that I wanted to try. Then I pointed my index finger toward one of the mounds of sand, made some loud mumbling sounds in my mouthpiece — and the volcano erupted.

Marden was dumfounded. He wanted to know how I had done it, but I replied that it was a "secret technique." The funny part was that Marden was furious at me for not telling him. He did not even believe me when I swore (as was absolutely true) that the whole thing was nothing more than the wildest coincidence.

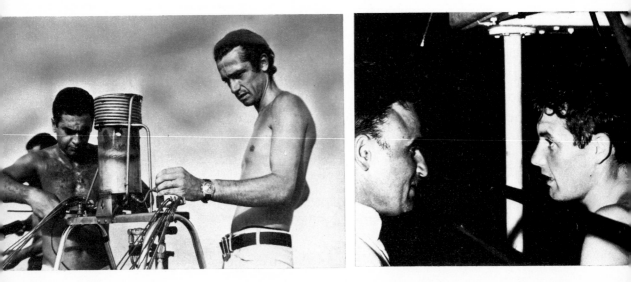

On this trip, I was determined to clear up, once and for all, the matter of the "volcanoes." Falco and Bonnici began filming several of them spewing out their clouds of sand. Then they shot some MS-222 into a mound and began digging. Shortly, they came up, triumphant, with their find: a small sand-colored crustacean.

We filmed the little creature in a series of close-ups, and, aboard the *Calypso,* we put him into the aquarium that we had used to observe the Heterocongers, or garden eels. As we watched, the animal, using his paws like tiny bulldozers, began to build a volcano in the sand. It was fascinating, and dizzying, to watch. Unfortunately, during the night, our treasure slipped out of the aquarium as the *Calypso* pitched and rolled, and we never found him.

Falco and Bonnici had spent a full day digging in mounds of sand before finding a single "volcano builder." But the entire sequence on film lasts only a few minutes.

Frédéric Dumas, along with Omer and Sumian, took care of the feeding detail, distributing chopped-up meat and fish by the pound to the marine inhabitants of Assumption. The result was an extravagant popularity of the divers among the large life forms of the reef. Two very large eels swam warily out of their holes and ate from Dumas's hand — which made his day.

(Far left) Dominique Sumian and Philippe Cousteau at work.

(Near left) Yves Omer prepares for a nighttime dive.

(Right) Michel Deloire and Albert Falco ready for a night dive, with the antishark cage.

Yves Omer feeds some friendly snappers (*Lutianidae*).

A Plectorhynchus swimming among the coral. He belongs to the *Pomadasyidae* family, of which the Haemulon, or grunt, is a member.

Raymond Coll feeding a bank of fish — what we call the feeding detail.

The Acanthurus, or surgeonfish, again — so called because of the two erectile spines, or scalpels, with which he is endowed. These spines are sufficiently sharp to wound the unwary diver.

Michel Deloire, for his part, discovered, at a depth of between twenty and fifty feet, a colony of garden eels. They were larger and less timid, and lived in shallower water, than those we had seen in the Maldives, and Deloire shot some beautiful footage of them.

Falco and Bonnici were back at their usual job of capturing specimens by the use of Quinaldine — a soporific that is specially formulated for cold-blooded animals of small size. They kept their catch in globe-shaped plexiglass aquariums — but the groupers in the area refused to play football with the aquariums as they had when we were filming *World Without Sun.*

We used our scooters to explore the area to the north of Assumption, and, thanks to these vehicles, such underwater "rides" became an entertainment and a pastime as well as part of our work. It took on many of the aspects of a horseback ride in the country. We had all the time in the world to look around, and to observe and note the changes of scene and the diversity of life forms that make the marine world so much more varied than the world on the surface. I noted the predominance of *Acropora,* the waving plumes of sea fans "planted" on the bottom — and a sizable blue-and-yellow butterfly fish, who swam along unconcernedly ahead of me, slowing as I slowed and accelerating as I accelerated. I stopped for a few minutes to observe a particular large sea anemone, which with all its tentacles spread, was exploring the surrounding water in search of a victim. I put my hand on the shell of a giant clam — which immediately snapped its shell shut with an audible "click." I saw sea worms, which are quite different from their rather somber and pitiful topside brothers. *Spirographis* — or feather-duster worm, which I have already mentioned — is particularly notable, for it carries a retractable patch of multicolored plumes at one end of its rigid stalk. The whole was like an enchanted garden out of the *Arabian Nights.*

At Assumption Island we had a nighttime dive, the purpose of which was to test our equipment in darkness. The divers were all in the water by 3 A.M. We saw many fish in the glare of our lights, but we did not manage to capture any, and so we contented ourselves with a stroll along the bottom, at a depth of about 125 feet.

Around us, beyond the circle of light that our lamps traced in the sea, was the coral jungle. The animals of that jungle, when caught in the brutal glare, started — and then froze, immobilized by this intrusion into the accustomed darkness. We saw parrot fish asleep among stinging coral ...

It is a strange and alien world, beyond the experience of humankind, wild, throbbing with life, an extravagance of color and of forms. There are laws here, and secrets; but they are not the laws and secrets of the world above.

It is during the time of darkness that coral is particularly active. One can see it as it is during the day, of course; but once night falls, its tentacles begin frantically reaching out for food, and its mouths, by the millions, begin to ingest its minuscule prey. The reef as a whole eats and digests. It is a being composed of many living and growing beings, and it is a study in life on a scale at once microscopic and gargantuan. It is difficult to imagine these millions and billions of tiny beings, these sedentary life forms, imprisoned within their own exoskeletons, who, with their explosive cells and their hooks and their poisons, trap, kill, and eat tiny victims — crustaceans, larvae, plankton, and even small fish. It is an entire cosmos, at the level of the infinitely small.

Madreporarians and hydrozoans eat in order to build those towers and walls among which we were riding on our scooters. But there is another contest that is of prime importance in the world of coral: the battle for a place in the sea. The life forms of a reef are constantly pushing and shoving one another, giving away and then recovering territory, gaining a millimeter of space here and losing one there, in an attempt to conquer and occupy the whole of the seas. It is a battle, and the battle reflects the needs and the power of living matter, which is both formidable and fragile.

Under our lights, coral tentacles wave about, forming halos around sea fans and on the downy branches of the madreporarians. Some of the *Alcyonium* swell up in the darkness, sometimes quadrupling their size to form plump, transparent, pink tree shapes in which their mouths are clearly visible.

The deeper we go, the more fragile are the sedentary life forms. At about 125 feet we no longer see reef-building coral, but much-more-delicate creatures: palm branches of *Acropora* and leafy discs of the solitary coral *Fungia*. It is true, nonetheless, that a single species of coral can have a very different appearance, according to the depth and move-

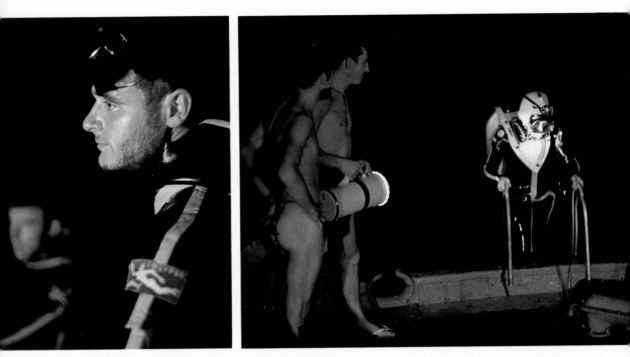

Serge Foulon
about to make a
nocturnal dive.

A nocturnal dive in the Red Sea — with the usual danger from sharks.

Fishes, startled by our floodlights, react by trying clumsily to escape.

Yves Omer feeds an eel and manages to
lure it into open water and to pet it.

ment of the water. It can be branched, or elongated, or massed into a single ball. Obviously, such flexibility, however much it may contribute to the beauty of the coral world, does little to simplify the job of the observer. *Madrepora cladocora*, for example, is on record in seven different shapes (or morphoses, as they are called).

These nighttime dives into the coral world teach us a great deal by showing us a new aspect of what we see during the day. For marine life exhibits, in those magic hours of darkness, the fullness of its wealth.

On such occasions, we make use of a full complement: fourteen men in the sea at once, of whom six are divers outfitted in our new diving suits with lights built into the helmets. Falco and Bonnici each have a 1000-watt spotlight. Maurice Léandri is to stand off to one side and light up the shooting area with two 1000-watt floodlights. Dr. Leenhardt and René Le Bosco, still farther out, are in charge of the cables and wires. Raymond Coll and Raymond Ammadio, in a boat on the surface, are responsible for communications with the *Calypso*. With Robert Gilles, our director, are Deloire with the 9-mm. camera and a 350-watt spot, Dumas with the wide-angle camera, and Laban with the still camera. It was the first full-scale filming operation of the expedition, and the first total confirmation of the techniques thought out aboard the *Calypso*.

On April 29, we dropped anchor at the island of Pemba, near Zanzibar. Since March 18 we had been limping along on one engine, at a speed of not over six knots. I wanted to see whether it would not be possible for the divers, by themselves, to change the propeller shaft. I knew, of course, that we would not be able to find a replacement until we reached Mombasa; but it was necessary that I know beforehand if the divers could remove the two pieces of the broken shaft without creating a leak. It took us a whole day of work to find out that the task was impossible. But it was not a wasted day, by any means. The divers, working under the hull, discovered a treasure-trove of marine life: fish with what appeared to be horns on their heads, and an unusual species of red and gray starfish, armed with stingers, which seemed carved out of wood and then painted. They also saw giant sea cucumbers, and a green crustacean five or six inches long that resembled a praying mantis and had eyes that could be divided into four parts. In addition, it had two false eyes on its head. This extraordinary creature was brought aboard by Omer and filmed in an aquarium by Barsky.

On the same day, we experienced one of the unending series of surprises that the sea holds for those who court her: we were inundated by a veritable cloudburst of insects. They were flies of monstrous size, black, and aggressive. Our doctor was astonished. He had never seen — or heard of — anything like them.

On May 5 we arrived at Mombasa, just before the monsoon season began. We therefore had to reach the Red sea as quickly as possible. I have unpleasant memories of the Indian Ocean at that time of year, for no work can be done during the monsoon. The *Calypso* also has unpleasant memories. Twice — in 1954 and again in 1955 — we had been very badly battered about when we stayed a bit too long in the vicinity of the Seychelles, and the trip from those islands to Cape Gardafuy was an experience that I was not looking forward to repeating.

It took two days in port at Mombasa for the starboard shaft to be changed. We took advantage of the delay to visit an animal preserve in Kenya, and then weighed anchor and headed north, toward the Red Sea, happy and secure now that we could again travel at our normal speed of ten and one-half knots. It was then, in the last few days before the beginning of the monsoon, that we finally saw a few whales. Falco was able to implant a harpoon in the blubber of one of them, and we followed it for a whole day, recording its exchanges with the other whales of its group. Eventually, however, the harpoon worked loose, and we lost contact.

At almost the same time, and in the same area, we were able to see and to film the so-called whale shark *Rhineodon typus* — a very rare species of shark which I had seen only twice before in my life. The whale shark is properly a shark and not a whale, and it is the largest of the species — indeed, the largest of all fishes — and sometimes attains a length of sixty-five feet and a weight of fifty thousand pounds. Beyond that, it has the characteristics of other sharks: the same fixed round eyes, the distinctive dorsal fin. This encounter has already been reported by my son Philippe in our book *The Shark*, and I shall limit myself here to remarking how impressive, and even frightening, a sight this monster is, despite the fact that it is relatively docile (as sharks go) and feeds only on plankton, schools of small fish, and squids. It is a true mountain of flesh and muscle, animated by a mysterious and enigmatic intelligence.

An underwater television circuit allows those on the *Calypso* constantly to keep an eye on our divers. We also keep in touch by means of an ultrasonic telephone.

Despite its overwhelming presence, this particular whale shark seemed friendly enough, and it even allowed Raymond Coll to hitch a ride on its tail.

These encounters, as worth while as they were, delayed us to the point where the monsoon was almost upon us. The Indian Ocean had become a sea of lead, with gray waves moving under a lowering sky, before we sailed into the Gulf of Aden — where we sighted another school of whales. Even here the weather was threatening, and it continued to be so until we reached the island of Perim, off the coast of southern Arabia. As soon as we had passed through the Bab el Mandeb Strait and entered the Red Sea, the water took on the familiar color of intense blue, although ominous yellow clouds still floated across the sky. For the whole of the monsoon season, we would be prisoners in the Red Sea. And for a month we were to be victims of the khamsin, an Egyptian wind that specializes in putting sand everywhere and in everything, from one's engine to one's mouth.

FIVE

Coral Traps in the Red Sea

Sailing the Calypso *between barrier and fringing reef.*
Sunken ships clothed in coral.
A dying reef, killed by oil, garbage, and debris.
Precontinent II revisited.
Caught in the Six-Day War.
The hot-air balloon.

On May 26 we left Djibouti for Port Sudan, sailing along the Arabian coast to reach the Farasan Islands, a sprinkling of coral islands that contain what is no doubt the greatest density of marine life in the world. I wanted to see the Farasan area again to judge for myself whether this stretch of coral had been affected by the decline that seemed endemic in all the reefs we had visited in the Indian Ocean. We were hoping we would not be greeted by the sight of fields of dead coral, as we had been in the Maldives. These stretches of deserted bottom from which all life has fled, where one sees only gray sand broken by the branches of shattered madreporarians, are like a devastated forest empty of birds. If one loves the sea, it is the stuff of which nightmares are made.

The coral formations of the Red Sea are very different from those of the Indian Ocean. The reef structures that we had visited in the Maldives and the Seychelles and at Cosmoledo were all atolls, islands, and archipelagoes. In the Red Sea, madreporarian corals are seen in another of their aspects. They do not exist there in isolated massifs, but in a complicated coral system that stretches the length of the coast — a labyrinth running from north to south for several miles. These madreporarians growing along the coast form what is called a fringing reef, or if the water is shallow, a level reef. Here, in the Red Sea, this line of coral is duplicated, a short distance away, by a parallel construction: the barrier reef.

It is safe to say that no ship's captain in his right mind would attempt to sail between those two walls of coral. It is our job, however, to do what no one else would do. If we wanted to explore the world of coral, we had to take certain chances — which in this case meant navigating among coral formations that might, at any moment, rip holes in the *Calypso*. I do not mean to make it sound more dangerous than it actually was. I have had, after all, some sixteen years' experience in just that sort of thing.

I must confess, moreover, that I rather enjoy navigating the *Calypso* in and out of this maze of coral corridors and dead ends. It is a challenge, both to me and to the maneuverability of the *Calypso*. Marine charts, unfortunately, are useless. The blank spaces in the charts of this area are not very comforting or very helpful, and the slightest error can send the *Calypso* onto a coral projection. Our ship is sound — but even so.

I wanted to begin our stay in the Red Sea by diving down to sunken ships. I know many such, but I am never tired of visiting them. Some shipwrecks are clearly marked on the charts. What makes them interesting to me, however, is the fact that sunken ships are usually a focal point for animal life, because the vessels offer both shelter to fish and a framework on which sedentary forms can build. There is no problem in finding food in such places, but there is a problem in finding space. The hulls of sunken ships, therefore, are preserves teeming with life; and this is true especially in warm water, where coral covers and transforms such hulls into the skeleton, as it were, of a living thing.

We spent a whole day on three sunken hulls off the eastern end of the island of Jebel Zuqar. One of them — the most beautiful of the three — had been completely stripped, but it was covered with coral and it offered shelter to a large number of multicolored fish, which made it of sufficient interest to be the subject of a certain amount of film footage. It was a "ghost ship," to all appearances: covered with limestone exoskeletons. There were mollusks everywhere, and a fairly large number of pearl oysters. The divers brought up a few of the latter, but found not even the trace of a pearl. For my part, I was sufficiently rewarded by the spectacle of this once-great ship, a captive of the inhabitants of the sea. To find pearls in addition to that would have been "to gild refined gold, to paint the lily."

In the past thirty years, my companions and I have seen many ship-wrecked vessels, both in the Mediterranean, where they seem becalmed in a fog and where their metal ribs are often exposed, and in the coral seas, where they seem crushed and reconquered by the ocean's vitality. I am always moved at the sight of a hull lying at the bottom of the sea. To me, it seems that a ship in that situation has entered into the "great beyond," into another existence, into a world of shadows. For ships, we might say, there is indeed a life after death.

One of the projects we intended to undertake on this expedition was the exploration of a shallow area about twenty-one miles from the volcanic island of Jebel Teir. The depth there was about one hundred feet, and the area was an island of the same kind as Jebel Teir — but an island that had never risen to the surface.

There was a delay, because the depth finder was not working. Marcelin, in a state of outrage, quickly set to work to repair it. While we were waiting, however, "Uncle" — Jean Philippe Adrien Plé, as he is known on the beach — studied the charts and the radar report and declared, "We'll sound by hand. If it's a hundred feet, let's drop anchor." I let him do it. He let down 110 feet of line, and still did not touch bottom. At that moment, however, the depth finder began working and revealed that the water immediately around the *Calypso* was 140 feet deep — but that, beyond that closely circumscribed area, the depth was four thousand feet. We were, it seems, directly over where we wanted to be.

We put down a buoy and took soundings in the area. There were no hundred-foot shallows, but there was a long and narrow plateau at 140 feet. It was what we French call a *guyot*, but what American mariners know, perhaps more descriptively, as a flat-topped seamount. It occurred to me that this plateau had probably been at the surface of the water in some bygone age. Was it perhaps a coral reef, or the crater of some extinct and submerged volcano?

We lowered the anti-shark cage and a television camera. On the screen there appeared the dim reflection of a flat bottom broken by a few rises, some coral — and the inevitable sharks. I decided to go down with Falco in the diving saucer to explore this flat-topped seamount, while successive teams of divers went down with the anti-shark cage to do some filming. It was my first saucer dive since my automobile accident and, happily, my back did not bother me at all.

The saucer came to rest. The bottom here was as flat as it had appeared on the television screen. The area reminded me strongly of the photographs we had shot on a similar seamount in the Atlantic in 1959. There were sharks, as always, some of which were unusually large and apparently well fed. Beautiful beasts, on the whole. There were schools of pompano (*Caranx*, or jack), and a multitude of such fishes as one would normally expect to see along a coastal reef: doctorfish and Moorish idols, among others.

Shortly, a strong current began to move us eastward. There was no point in trying to fight it, and we began to move rapidly down the incline. Once we had reached the shelter of the overhang, however, the water was again calm. There, we photographed two handsome "Japanese gardens." One was in a tunnel that had been cut, or worn, through a column of rock which seemed so fragile that the slightest movement of water might make it crumble. I suspect that, if we had run into it with the saucer, twenty tons of rock would have gone sliding down the incline.

I asked Falco to circle the reef on its north side, staying at a depth of about 350 feet. This was exciting enough in itself, for each time that we came around a ridge we were struck by a current going in the opposite direction, and we could get out of it only by going down deeper or going up. It was an exercise in three-dimensional navigation that Falco — and I — found somewhat trying.

So far, we had seen nothing to distinguish this sunken reef from those on the surface. Then, all of a sudden, the appearance of the bottom changed. We had entered a semicircular depression about seventy-five to one hundred feet across, its bottom covered with black sand and sprinkled with the debris of polyzoan life forms, which gave the place a sinister and unearthly appearance. Then everything fell into place. I was suddenly convinced that we were in a crater of which only half, or perhaps two thirds, was left. It is possible that the missing part had been

A coral maze, the walls of which are covered with life forms.

lost through an explosion, as often happens to submerged volcanoes when they cool too quickly. The bottom of the crater was, I estimated, between five and six hundred feet deep, and in it swam a crowd of large fish — especially sharks and tuna. It was an impressive sight, and it is one that film, unfortunately, cannot wholly capture or convey; for the scene was too large, and the water not clear enough — and, to make matters worse, the cameras jammed. More than ever, I thought longingly of the photographs shot on the flanks of a similar formation. On the plateau, as on the north, east, and west slopes, there had been clean sand bearing the ripple marks of sponges. On the south slope — a cone of volcanic ash. The similarity was too striking to require comment.

Before rising to the surface, we used the underwater telephone to contact the *Calypso*. We were told that the diving teams had already gone down and come up again. We dropped our ballast and, a few minutes later, we were back on the bridge of the *Calypso*.

I had the feeling, as always on such occasions, that our role as pioneers and explorers of the sea is a strange one. I sense that we are privileged beings for whom it is possible, almost by a miracle, to observe the vast, dramatic, and mysterious world that lies beneath the surface of the sea — a surface which, seen only from above, appears as an impenetrable barrier shimmering in the sunlight of the tropics. I am also constantly aware, however, that, regardless of how long we stay under water or how much area we cover, we can visit only an infinitesimal portion of the sea. It is remarkable, of course, that we can see what is happening six hundred feet below the surface: but that is nothing when compared to the vastness of the oceans. How narrowly circumscribed are man's ambitions!

On Monday, May 29, we explored the island of Maf Zuber. The sole inhabitants seemed to be an army of crabs — ocypodan, or swift-footed, crabs, they are called — the number, constant activity, and aggressiveness of which were both fascinating and disconcerting. Like conquerors, or superior beings, they ignored us completely and went about their business. The island, a strip of sand and beach rock, was theirs, and they crawled over it from end to end, apparently in a vain search for food. How do they survive? No doubt, they eventually go into the water to find what they need to live.

To the south of Maf Zuber, there is another small island that I wanted to visit. The reason is that it is the most unusual bit of land in the Red Sea. It is only a pile of beach rocks, heaped onto a level reef. There is not the slightest bit of vegetation on this stretch of dead coral, and it is the epitome of barren deserts the world over. The island, however, is not entirely without its uses. It is covered with tombs, including those of children, all of which are made in the shape of small boats. The tombs are connected one to the other by footpaths of sand, which have been carefully lined with pieces of rock. We saw an area covered with flat rocks, lined up vertically, as if to commemorate the deaths of men whose bodies were not there. Perhaps they represent men who were lost at sea.

There are several low shelters or lean-tos on the island, placed in such a way as to protect one from the sharp wind. And there are vestiges of human presence. But all is still and deserted.

Anguish and mystery are almost perceptibly present in this coral city of the dead. The waves break constantly and uncaringly, and the wind howls, and the sun beats down mercilessly on this pile of broken coral and empty shells. Sea gulls circle overhead, uttering short, angry screams and waiting impatiently for us to leave.

Was the island once inhabited? Who are these dead? Are they victims of the sea, or perhaps pilgrims who drowned while en route to holy Mecca? Or it may be that it is a place of prayer and burial for local fishermen.

At one o'clock in the afternoon, I anchored the Calypso in eighty feet of water about 650 yards off the northern tip of the island of Mar Mar. We knew this place well, having visited here in 1951 and 1955. It is a sandy, crescent-shaped bar, running southeast — northwest, on which there is not a single tree and not a drop of fresh water. The only sign of vegetative life is a few patches of wretched-looking grass. The sun and wind are pitiless and unrelenting.

Yves Omer, Bernard Delemotte and my son Philippe went ashore. They were to spend five days there, photographing this desert isle so typical of the Red Sea. On the shore there were ocypode crabs, and gannet nests here and there on the ground. This proximity of nests to the sea made for vicious and continual combat — witnessed by our landing party — between the birds and the turtles that came up out of the sea at night to devour the young gannets.

Philippe, Delemotte, and Omer, in addition to photographing the island, were to make a series of dives along the perimeter. At one point, however, their inflatable boat was caught in vicious eddies at the northern tip of the island and carried into the waves, where it was tossed about so violently that it literally bent in half. By some miracle, they were able to right themselves and make for the shore — although they were already about a half mile from land and in constant danger of being swept out into the open sea by the current.

Despite this misadventure, they carried out their task. The coral, they reported, was built vertically, at a depth of about fifty feet, and resembled deep furrows plunging into the dizzying blue of the bottom. Omer and Delemotte discovered a colony of sand sharks living in holes in the coral wall. They tried to lure them out into the open to photograph them, and, when nothing else worked, they resorted to pulling them out by the tail; whereupon the sharks would immediately dart into another hole. It was impossible to film these fearsome-looking, but timid, monsters.

Off the southern tip of the island, the men discovered a steep cliff, in which there was a grotto about forty feet deep, which they explored under the cold stare of other, more extroverted, sharks.

Off the southwestern side of Mar Mar they found a small plateau about seventy-five feet below the surface of the water. At their approach, they had seen perhaps a hundred eagle rays quickly bury themselves in the sand. Teased and prodded by the divers, the rays emerged, their "wings" beating and throwing off grains of sand, which looked like flecks of pure gold. The image they presented was that of the great bird after which they are named as it rises in flight.

The team brought back the news that I had been dreading: the coral at Mar Mar was on the decline. It was much less abundant and colorful than it had been during our previous visits. I had to see for myself, however, and I went down — only to find large areas where the coral was not only declining, but dead. The entire reef, in fact, seemed slowly moving toward extinction. The cause — at least here, among the islands of the Farasan Archipelago — is only too obvious. En route to

Despite its ferocious looks, the spotted eel is one of the animals that the *Calypso's* divers have succeeded in taming. Yves Omer and Frédéric Dumas have petted many of them.

these desert islands, which lie off the main sea lanes, one comes across great masses of garbage floating in the sea: bottles, metal containers, masses of plastic sheeting — and most often the whole is covered with oil. Man has made a garbage can of the sea. But it is a garbage can in which the trash does not stay put. Everything that is thrown overboard by passenger liners and tankers and freighters is taken by the current and brought to these coral islands. And there it stays, destroying the coral, which needs clean, clear water to exist. For the Red Sea is a closed sea, and there is no way for this debris of civilization to move out into more open waters.

During our exploration of Mar Mar, no one was idle. On another reef — this one less threatened by civilization because it is farther to the center of the archipelago — our movie makers were at work filming a group of parrot fish. These large blue and green specimens were remarkable for the presence of a bump on their heads and for their truly parrot-like beaks. They "graze" on coral (as I have already mentioned) and eject it in the form of sand — an operation for which their parrot beaks seem eminently suitable. For two days, Falco, Bonnici, and Coll filmed the grazing and subsequent ejection of coral bits. It was a rather spectacular undertaking, and the parrot fish proved themselves to be ready actors. They are shy creatures by nature, but they quickly overcame their reticence in the presence of the divers and continued their meals and their digesting as though they were alone. Before long, in fact, they became "hams" as much as Jojo had ever been, swimming back and forth in front of the camera as though they knew exactly what was going on. It has often occurred to me that fish may know more about us than we know about them.

After filming the parrot fish, we were preparing to leave when I decided that I had to have one more close look at the effect of pollution on the coral in the area. I had the saucer lowered off the north-north-eastern point of the island, and went down to a depth of about 350 feet. There in one of the valleys or depressions that are common to this region and that are themselves another seventy-five or eighty feet deep, I looked around. On the bottom, the sand was so white that it literally lit up the water, and I could see that along the walls of the valley the true madreporarian corals were scarce and lusterless. On the other hand,

A diver on the bottom inspects animal colonies of various forms and colors.

there seemed to be an abundance of black coral — from which one may conclude that black coral has more resistance than the madreporarians to impure water.

Black coral, under water, appears maroon rather than black. It grows in thicketlike formations, and the larger branches are sometimes between one and two inches in diameter — so large that specimens can be cut only by using a saw. In the Arab countries, black coral is highly valued for its power as a protection against sickness and evil, and it is commonly used to make amulets and beads. For divers, its value consists in its rarity — and its interest in the fact that it is an "urticant," or stinging, coral. On one occasion, Coll had taken hold of a branch of black coral while wearing gloves, and so was protected. Once on the surface, however, he took off his mask and absent-mindedly rubbed his eyes with the gloves. The next day, he was blind; and it was several days before he recovered.

After leaving Mar Mar, we noticed that the farther northward we went, the less healthy the coral seemed. Its deterioration, in fact, was so marked that we could not avoid noticing it. The reason is that the Gulf of Suez (toward which we were heading) is a dead end, and that although the currents and the wind are constantly agitating the water, they do not rid it of debris. Most of the islands of the Farasan, therefore, have become receptacles for this debris and have been poisoned by oil slicks. The coral everywhere is surrounded by filthy water and covered with a revolting greenish gluelike substance. Its total extinction seems only a matter of time.

The worst damage appeared to be in the waters off Jidda (which is the port of Mecca). At that time, of course, the Suez Canal was still open to traffic, and there were a large number of tankers and freighters in the Red Sea. Today, the tankers must go the long way, around the Cape of Good Hope; and it is possible that, on some future visit, we will find the water clean again and the coral renewed — at least temporarily. The crucial question is whether coral is capable of reviving and renewing itself. Its life is precarious, and its existence depends upon a more or less fortuitous combination of circumstances. Years of observation and experience with coral have taught me to be skeptical.

I might mention, in passing, that those years of observation and experience were inspired, when I was still a child, by the books of Henri Monfreid, a Frenchman who wrote a whole series of adventures stories about pearl fishers, pirates, slaves, and hashish smugglers. It was Monfreid, in fact, from whom I got the idea for the observation deck on the bow of the *Calypso,* from which I am able to see, from above, the labyrinth of reefs through which I am steering at any given moment. (One of Monfreid's stories told of an Arab boat that escaped from pirates by putting children up on the mast to observe the reefs and to shout navigating instructions to the captain.)

This fiction-inspired observation deck has proved its worth many times over. It makes it possible for the *Calypso* to maneuver in and out of coral formations. In very tight spots, we keep several men on duty there at once — and I'm often up there myself. Our purpose may be only to observe the spectrum of blues and greens of the water — shadings that allow us to determine, with a variable degree of accuracy, the depth of the water at a given spot. Very dark blue, for instance, is a good sign; it means the water is very deep. Dark green means that we can pass. Bottle green, however, indicates the presence of a reef, and tells us to be careful. A light, almost yellow green is a danger sign, indicating that the water is very shallow. There are times, nonetheless, when visibility is poor, say because of the position of the sun; and at these times we have to depend more on intuition than on the color of the water.

These hazards are implicit in our mission in the Red Sea, which is basically to explore this coral area, where so many ships have sunk; an area that extends for hundreds of miles and is virtually unknown. One of the main things we intended to do was to study the condition of the coral, and to explore the banks and barrier reefs that stretch from north to south, both on the Arabian side and on the African side.

In the world of coral, with its mazes and crenelated towers, its sculptured walls and its grottoes, there live an enormous population of sedentary fish. The collective life of these inhabitants is what determines the laws, the celebrations, and the tragedies of the reef-jungle. It is an elaborate ballet in which the dancers face death with every pirouette.

Deloire gave us an account of his dive that morning: "There was a cliff of about seventy-five feet, which ended at a plateau. The vertical wall itself was marvelous to see, and on the plateau there were crowds of all kinds of fish: butterfly fish, Moorish idols, parrot fish — everything. I was watching them when a shark jumped out of nowhere into a school of mackerel, throwing himself around from right to left with his mouth wide open. It was like nothing I had ever seen before; and the shark was so fast that I couldn't even see if he was catching anything."

As a means of self-defense, several species of reef fish live in schools. This works rather well, because a predatory fish must usually isolate an individual fish if he is to catch anything to eat. He is therefore confused by a large number of fish moving together in what appears to be a solid mass.

Coral massifs constitute a fairly well-defined area of habitation for a large number of fish species — species found nowhere else than in coral waters. Such fish are particularly adapted to life among the reefs. They are flat and often round — like discs — and have very mobile fins, by virtue of which they are able to turn quickly in any direction and therefore to hide immediately among the coral formations. This maneuverability is, for them, literally a matter of life and death.

Their colors and the beautiful patterns with which they are marked make coral fish the most striking creatures in the sea. Many of them change color as they grow older or as the seasons change. Sex also determines color. Parrot fish may change color three times in their lives, and males and females are often quite different in coloration. This, of course, makes it very difficult for ichthyologists to tell one species from another, and often the same species has been thought to be several different species. At one time, more than three hundred "species" of parrot fish were listed — a number that has now been reduced to less than one hundred.

The magnificent colors and patterns of coral fish are not without a purpose, as I have already indicated. Coloration is one form of protection, and pattern — stripes and dots — may serve to confuse and distract an attacker and allow the intended victim to blend in with the coral. That explanation, however, is not entirely convincing. The imperial angelfish (to take one example), striped as it is in blues and golds, is quite conspicuous, and its coloration does not serve as camouflage even against the brilliant background of the coral world.

Another, and very interesting, explanation has recently been offered by Konrad Lorenz, an eminent zoologist. The function of coloration among coral fish, Lorenz says, is to enable the members of one species to recognize one another as, so to speak, brothers-in-arms. Thus, coloration and pattern would be intended for the information of one species rather than for the confusion of another. This is entirely possible, for, on a reef, every fish has his "turf," or territory,[1] which he defends fanatically against every other fish of his own species. In the same way, coloration may be connected with sexuality, since it may serve as a warning to rivals of the same species.

On the whole, however, I think that the striking patterns and colors of tropical reef fauna serve several purposes: Many fishes apparently have distinctive markings so as to be recognized, and therefore avoided, rather than to be inconspicuous; and in such cases, the conduct seems aimed at the intimidation of foes rather than at appearing to be as inoffensive as possible. The dragonfish, for instance, when threatened,

[1]Further on, in the discussion of groupers, I will deal with the importance of "territory." Suffice it to say here that it is basically a "living space," which marine animals defend with the same alacrity as do land animals.

spreads its "fans" and shows its stings — a demonstration that must have some significance for other fishes.

In this sense, the color, markings, and other characteristics of fish are "signals" directed both at members of the same species and at members of other species. They serve to attract one sex to the other — but also to discourage rivals, and to indicate to them that such and such a territory is already occupied, or a particular place already taken.

This "social life " of the coral world is an area of which we know very little, and of which we can gain an understanding only if we approach it as an inseparable whole. Signs, territories, hierarchies, rivalries — all these are subordinate and interdependent parts of a precariously balanced system that it has taken millions of years to work out. Its infinite complexity, of course, is what makes it so fascinating. But man is just beginning to be aware of that complexity. He is just beginning to suspect that the daily life of the smallest coral fish (for example, that of the *Heniochus acuminatus*, or pennant coral fish) is as complicated as

Certain species of starfish — this one, for example, which is an Acanthaster — eat coral. Acanthasters have greatly increased in number in the past few years and they have caused considerable damage to coral reefs. (The specimen shown here has its arms folded.)

that of an office worker who has to contend with the intrigues of his associates, the whims of his employer, the moods of his secretary, and the ambitions of his union. Both fish and man, in such circumstances, must have recourse to a series of stratagems, discussions, and confrontations. And each will, in all probability, try to get away with with as much as he is able. For all life forms have this in common: that they must survive, and survival is not easy.

On June 1, we put into Port Sudan, where we found the *Espadon* shining like new.

Port Sudan was, and is, the only practical port on the Red Sea; the only one where one can obtain services equivalent to those available in European ports. There is a dockyard, and a supply of replacement parts. The pilots, the merchants, and certain of the craftsmen and technicians are English.

The city itself is interesting enough. Situated near coral waters, it is at the latitude most favorable to our work. To the north, up to the island of St. John, there is a string of fringing reefs along the coast. Ten miles out, this is paralleled by a barrier reef, and between the two there is a channel, about nine hundred feet deep, which is perfectly navigable. To the south, there is another coral maze, the Suakin Archipelago. We may say that Port Sudan is the African capital of the coral waters.

On June 2, at four in the morning, we set sail for Shab Rumi, and by six forty-five the *Calypso* was there, at that huge and beautiful lagoon which had been the site of our experiment with Precontinent II (also known as Conshelf II). For six weeks, men had lived under those blue waters. The sight brought back many memories — memories of our work, of the success of the operation, and especially of our phenomenal struggle with the enormous lead weights that we had had to use as ballast for our underwater buildings. It was here, too, that we shot *World Without Sun*. The coral reef here is completely isolated in the sea, and a large part of it is barely at water level.

This time, however, we were here alone. There was no freighter like the *Rosaldo* and its crew of Sicilians that had accompanied us on the occasion of Precontinent II. Indeed, there seemed hardly a trace of our earlier presence. A metal footbridge that we had built on the reef — and that we naturally called "the Bridge over the River Kwai" — had disap-

On this desert island, crabs feed on the eggs of seafaring birds.

Bernard Delemotte tries to make friends with a mother who dares not leave her family.

The observation point from which we always watch carefully during hazardous navigation.

peared into the sea. Somehow, it was comforting to think that the sea
had erased every vestige of our adventure.

However comforting it may have been, it was not wholly accurate.
Falco, Deloire, and I dived down to the site of our underwater village of
1963, and while it hardly looked like a habitable site at this stage, it was
nonetheless there. The garage for the saucer seemed in good shape; even
its coat of yellow paint had held up. The tool shed was also intact. The
house in which the oceanauts had lived had been dismantled, of course,
and removed at the end of the experiment.

A feather star, seen from the bottom. In front are coral pinnacles and red sponges.

But the bottom itself was a disaster. It was covered with the debris from the experiment — cables, iron bars, fragments of sheet metal, and fish cages. It looked like a junkyard on the outskirts of a city. And naturally, there were comparatively few fish, except for a school of trigger-fish who regarded us with consummate indifference. Where, we wondered, were all the wrasses, the groupers, and the snappers? No doubt, divers often come here from Port Sudan to see the site of Precontinent II; and no doubt they bring their guns.

Coral was everywhere. On the cables and the iron bars and the fish cages there were growths of pink coral as large as a man's fist, all of which had come in a space of four years. (Parrot fish are particularly fond of this pink coral.) It seemed especially plentiful around portholes from which we had removed the glass. Everything made of iron was transfigured into an alien form. Our sheds were now the habitations of sea fans and madreporarians and alcyonaceans of every color.

It seemed the perfect opportunity to gather data on a controverted question — the rapidity of coral growth — and Gaston found an acropore on one of the cables jettisoned from the *Rosaldo* which, in four years, had grown to a diameter of almost eight inches.

At Shab Rumi, we shot the best sequences on the reefs of the Red Sea. To begin with, I had drawn up a provisional map for the guidance of the cameramen, showing the areas where we would dive. In the southern sector of this area we found the same abundance of fish that we had seen on earlier visits. Circling about in extraordinarily close-knit schools were barracudas and mackerel; and the barracudas sometimes seemed so densely packed as to form a solid wall as they swam; with their sharp teeth protruding, they looked like a crowd of voracious pike. I do not recall ever having seen so many barracudas in one place before. A wall of fish would be followed by another solid wall; and sometimes two walls of different species would meet head on — but then they would pass each other without fraternizing. At one point, in the middle of a cascade of fish, a shark, five or six feet long, swam lazily, apparently indifferent to his surroundings.

There also were small groupers everywhere. And at night, hundreds of doctorfish suddenly turned up, in tight ranks, all marked with a white dot near the tail, where they carry their "scalpel," or defensive spine.

The *Calypso* during this time was at anchor in a sheltered spot within the atoll, and we could carry on several projects at once. One team, therefore, comprising Falco, Deloire, and Coll, set up an underwater studio in order to film "bulldozer" crabs. We wanted to have a record of them, not only in action, but also within their burrows. To begin with, we used a microsuction to remove the sand from around the burrows; and then we realized that the burrows were not merely tunnels or holes, but endless labyrinths of passages, reminiscent of the Roman catacombs. It was impossible to uncover the entire system with our suction.

We call these particular crabs "bulldozers" because they are always engaged in scooping out an alley or roadway in front of their burrows, which they line with a barricade of bits of coral and shell. I never tire of watching them at work. They go at it with a single-minded devotion and a diligence that is rarely seen on dry land.

These crabs have an interesting home life. Two crabs, one male and the other female, always live in the same hole. Each hole or burrow has a watchdog, in the form of a goby. This tiny fish's job is to warn the crab couple at the approach of danger. He takes up his post at the opening of the burrow and, if he notices anything that might be dangerous, he immediately flees into the hole. The crabs will not come out as long as their watchdog does not signal that the coast is clear by taking up his outside post again.

The bulldozer crabs are normally found at a depth of less than twenty feet, but occasionally we find burrows as deep as forty-five or fifty feet.

We dived one night at Shab Rumi, and this time we intended to observe the behavior of fish at night rather than the beauty of coral with extended tentacles. We were able to take advantage of the fact that fish at night are blinded, and momentarily stunned, by bright lights: we filmed angelfish and shot footage of parrot fish sound asleep among the stinging coral of the area.

At night, some fish sleep and some do not. Many are so inactive that one can catch them by hand, simply by reaching out carefully. But it is not always easy to know if a particular species sleeps or not, in the regular sense of that term, for there are degrees of sleep in the fish kingdom. Some species sleep very lightly, and, no matter how quiet we try to be, they wake up. This was true of the angelfish and butterfly fish on this occasion, who immediately began swimming slowly around the divers' lights.

It is at night, above all, that we feel we are uncovering the secrets of a world that is unknown, mysterious, and without defense against us in the darkness. Without defense? Not quite. Sharks seldom sleep. Most of them never sleep, so far as we know. And a few large ones, attracted no doubt by our lights, swam out of the darkness to join us. There was no way to get rid of them. Sharks, because of the sensory cells scattered over their bodies (and especially on their heads) in large numbers, are

A group of Holocentrums, with an unusual yellow marking whose purpose is unknown.

better equipped than the diver to operate in dark waters. That is not to say that sharks have "night vision." They see no better than we do at night. But they have senses, other than sight, that we lack, and these senses allow them to know what is going on in the water at night. We do not know the exact nature or function of these senses or organs, but we have measured their scope and the nature of the information that sharks receive from them: vibration of the water, hydrostatic pressure, taste, chemical analysis, sound, odor, etc. It is, on the whole, a range of aquatic perception much more extensive and effective than our own. Sharks are far better equipped than we to perceive the least change in environment and to distinguish degrees of sensation. And still, we sometimes call them "primitive" animals.

An alcyonarian formation on the bottom, above which swim some *Myripristis* and damselfish.

As soon as we left the coral reef, at a distance of no more than thirty-five feet the water became very deep. In those blue depths were the schools of large fish. Shab Rumi was the ideal spot, it seemed, for a large-scale film project. The water was very clear, and there was an abundance of fish of all kinds — mackerel, wrasses, doctorfish. On June 3 our divers went down, therefore, with their new underwater equipment. We filmed them as, in fan-shaped formation, they met and passed a group of large mackerel. Spontaneously, the two groups — men and fish — turned around to meet and pass once more, a maneuver that they repeated several times, as though it were an exotic ritual dance or a delightful game. The sea, one might think, conferred a common instinct on every living thing in it, native or visitor, fish or diver. The shooting was a spectacular success.

The next day, a Sunday, we finished our filming and weighed anchor to sail for Port Sudan. Once there, we realized that the tension between Egypt and Israel was about to erupt into open war. I hurried to the office of our agent in the city — a Greek entrepreneur named Contomichalos, who had lived in Port Sudan for years — to ask him to arrange passage for me to Paris. For, given the state of things in that area, I had no idea whether the *Calypso* would be allowed to pass through the Suez Canal.

The next day, June 5, war broke out between Egypt and Israel; and late in the morning, we learned that the Sudan had also declared war on the Egyptian side. There were demonstrations in the streets of Port Sudan, and two of our men, who were ashore, were stoned by the crowds.

Contomichalos, our agent, had arranged a seat for me on a noon plane to Paris, but the flight was postponed to five o'clock, and then to seven o'clock in the evening. War or no war, everyone in Port Sudan had to take his siesta until late afternoon. In the meantime, the atmosphere at Sudan Airways was very hostile. Contomichalos did what he could, but he, being a foreigner, was in the same boat, as it were, that I was.

Finally, shortly before seven, I arrived at the airport once more, with my papers in order and a confirmed reservation. Falco and Dumas were with me, and they remained in the airport until my plane took off. The flight was delayed once more, however, by an unusual incident. Three Fokker planes of Mistra Air — the Egyptian national airline —

(Right) A Holocentrum
enters an opening in the
coral — and finds himself
face to face with a diver.

(Below) Our former fish
house at Shab Rumi.
After four years, what
remains of it has been
covered by coral.

showing not a single light, landed one after another on the runway. There were no passengers and no stewardesses: only soldiers, who hurried up to the Sudanese airport officials and, shouting unintelligible (to me) Arabic words at them, were offered, and accepted, cups of coffee. At that point, my plane finally took off.

The *Calypso* was headed for Suez, where it anchored in a roadstead alongside the *Espadon*. The latter ship was now manned by a skeleton crew of only two men.

It was not a pleasant situation. No one was allowed ashore, and it was impossible to have water and food supplies brought aboard.

The Egyptian authorities did allow our men to put ashore some of our equipment — the scooters, cameras, film — to be sent to France. But the boxes were machine-gunned by Israeli planes while they were still on the wharf, and everything was destroyed.

On July 14, the oil refinery at Suez was bombed, and shell fragments fell like rain around the *Calypso*. Zoom, our dog, was terrified and hid in the hole, his jowls trembling with fright. It took hours of coaxing to get him out again.

Since July 14 is also the French national holiday, the *Calypso's* crew had planned a fireworks display, which they carried out late in the evening. It was a waste of time. Surrounded as the ship was by burning tanks of gasoline, the rockets were all swallowed up in a cloud of dense black smoke that hung overhead.

We realized then that the *Calypso* was sitting in the middle of the battlefield. Nonetheless, we did not give up hope. I, as well as the men still aboard, was convinced that we would soon be able to continue northward and, somehow, get through the Canal. The trip did not seem any more dangerous than skirting in and out of the coral reefs of the Farasan Archipelago. "There are sunken ships in the Canal," the authorities told our men. "Well, then," our men replied, "we'll go around them."

Everyone was outraged that the Egyptians would not allow the *Calypso* to go through. As soon as I returned to the Suez, on July 15, I tried everything I could think of, and even begged the French Ambassador for help. To everyone who would listen, I pleaded, "Just let us try!" Obviously, I did not convince anyone. But I am still certain that, if we had been allowed to proceed, we would have gotten through the Canal.

A few days later, when hostilities ended, word was received that the Canal would remain closed indefinitely. I therefore arranged for all aboard to be relieved, in three stages, so that they might visit their homes. (Maritime law requires that a crewman remain at sea no longer than six months at a stretch.) At the same time, we took on board our new crew members. I say "new," although these were mostly young men whom I knew and who had, in fact, already sailed on the *Calypso*. They were not beginners, in any sense. Even so, we would have to do a certain amount of "breaking in" — and for this I was counting on our chief diver, Raymond (Canoë) Kientzy, and on several of the older hands.

Next, my son Philippe left for the United States, where he was to learn (in Sioux Falls, South Dakota) how to pilot a hot-air balloon. We had ordered one such, and it was supposed to be delivered to us at the end of August, at Massawa. It was to prove very useful, both in reconnoitering passages for the *Calypso* through the atolls and in filming sequences on turtles when we reached the island of Europa.

Once the exchange of personnel had been completed, the expedition continued — this time, toward the south — with a full store of water and supplies. On July 23, we anchored off St. John, a small island with a lighthouse, midway between the Strait of Jubal and Port Sudan. Canoë Kientzy wanted to try out our new team members right away and to see their first reactions to sharks. As usual, we had no problem in finding the sharks. They were all around us, swimming very calmly, indifferent to the presence of the divers. Our new companions were equally calm, and everything came off very well. This team, we concluded, was a worthy successor to the old one.

The following day, we stopped at Abington, seventy miles to the north of Port Sudan. Abington is a circular reef that rises vertically from a great depth. When we dived, we were astonished to see this tiny island rising abruptly from the Red Sea, like cathedral spires out of bottomless depths. Around Abington, we discovered a great cliff under the blue water of the surface, which plunged downward in thirty-foot stages until it disappeared into the darkness beneath. And in that mysterious and somber depth we could see the dim forms of sharks turning slowly. The "drops" in the cliff were absolutely vertical, broken only by tufts of black coral. To swim above that emptiness, along a cliff composed of living beings, is a disconcerting experience. Moreover, we had to be on the alert for the first signs of rapture of the depths. I called an end to the dive before it became dangerous.

The next day, the new team went, in its turn, on pilgrimage to Precontinent II. Canoë found the shark cage that had been left there, and he organized a night dive off the southern tip of Shab Rumi for the benefit of the new men who had not yet dived at night in the Red Sea.

Canoë became a member of our team after having been a diver in the French Navy, where he spent some time with the commandos in Indochina. Then he left us for a while to go off treasure hunting on his own, for Canoë hunts treasure the way other men play golf. On the basis of a mysterious tip, he had gone to the Caribbean in search of a sunken ship said to be filled with gold. And, to make sure he was not wasting his time, he took a dowser, or diviner, along with him, who, with his wand, was supposed to find doubloons and pieces of eight in the sea.

As it turned out, Canoë's trip was a great adventure, but not quite the one that he had expected. One night, his small sailboat was anchored over the presumed site of the treasure ship, and Canoë and his diviner were sleeping the sleep of exhausted divers. A wind arose and began moving the boat out, over the maze of coral reefs in the vicinity but without touching a single coral formation. Anyone who knows the reefs in that area will know that nothing less than an act of Providence could have prevented a catastrophe. And yet, when Canoë and his associate awoke the next morning, there was not even a scratch on the boat. But Providence was not as generous with its gold as with its protection; and Canoë eventually returned, without a trace of bitterness, to his old job with us. He still dreams of galleons and gold.

The *Calypso* arrived at Massawa during the afternoon of August 3, with the temperature hovering around the 120° mark. The heat was almost insupportable. The worst sufferer by far was Zoom, who whimpered so pitifully every time he walked on the deck that his two-legged friends took to carrying him about in their arms.

A large yellow feather star on a coral formation. These animals are able to move through the water by means of rhythmic motions of their feathery arms.

SIX

A White-Haired Wreck

Exploring coral-covered hulks.
Dealing with sharks.
Diving in a salt lake.

"We can't film this," Deloire declared. "The water is too troubled. What's more, there's a layer of some sort of white filth from the surface down to thirty-five feet. It's impossible to see anything down there. It would be like trying to take pictures in soup."

My son Philippe had returned from the United States, and his enthusiasm was too strong to be affected by feasibilities. "It's absolutely the most beautiful ship I've ever seen," he said. "It's huge, and literally enveloped in a cloud of fish — including some beautiful barracudas. I think the ship was probably scuttled, because everything has been removed from it; it's been cleaned out, from top to bottom. Even the propellers are gone. And it's covered with animals, like a fleece. It's fantastic. A real ghost town. Or maybe the palace of the Old Man of the Sea."

We had left Massawa that morning and, making directly for the Dahlak Archipelago, we had entered the inner circle of Dahlak Kebir Island. The lagoon is a body of water seven to eight miles in diameter, connecting with the Red Sea by a narrow inlet. (The Arabs call it *Mousselfou*, but we French know it as the "Goubet Zoukra".)

It is interesting to note that within the Goubet Zoukra, the water is about five hundred feet deep, while along the shore of the island itself it is less than three hundred feet. The Goubet, therefore, is a sort of depression in the sea. It is possible that it is a submerged crater, but I do not think so. The bottom immediately around the island is composed of a mixture of sedimentary earth and shale, none of which shows any trace of volcanic origin. It resembles, in other words, several other depressions on the continental shelf all along the African coast. We used the diving saucer to explore one of them to the north of Port Sudan, and another to the south of Abington Island. The origin of these depressions is a mystery, at least to me, and I can offer no explanation for them. Possibly they are somehow related to the famous "blue holes"[1] of the Bahamas.

We had no sooner entered this enormous lagoon than we saw a short piece of rusted metal protruding from the water — the mast, it turned out, of a very large Italian ship sunk during World War II.

I immediately sent out an exploration team composed of Philippe, Michel Deloire, Canoë, and a few others. There is always a crowd of volunteers when it comes to an underwater "walk," and particularly when it is a matter of investigating a sunken ship. Except for my son, however, everyone seemed pessimistic when they returned to the *Calypso*. All agreed that the hulk was really enormous. It lay at a depth of one hundred to one hundred twenty-five feet, and it was covered by a thick shell of madreporarian corals, mollusks, and sea fans, all of which had multiplied, it seemed, with extraordinary exuberance. So far, so good. But there were problems, and the principal one was the lack of light. For the first thirty-five feet below the surface, as Deloire said, the water was opaque and acted as a curtain, so that light could not penetrate into the clearer water below.

The solution, it occurred to me, might be to use floodlights; but I wanted to see for myself what the situation was. I got ready to dive, and asked Paul Zuéna to come along and to bring a Ruggieri light with him. These portable floodlights were invented by an ingenious Italian of that name and were designed for use under water. We had used them before in filming and had obtained spectacular effects. I would have been very surprised if a Ruggieri were not able to solve our problem on this occasion.

We reached the site of the wreck and went down along the mast. I had a cold at the time, and so I descended slowly and cautiously, even

---

[1] These "blue holes" — which were visited by the *Calypso* in June 1970 — are submarine grottoes, dug out of limestone, the vaults of which have collapsed. Our divers were able to bring up a stalagmite, from which, it is hoped, scientists will be able to reconstruct the history of these "holes."

before I began to feel pressure in my ears. It was a wise precaution, for before I had gone down ten feet I noticed that I was having trouble maintaining my equilibrium. All the more reason to be careful.

The water was white, as the exploration team had reported, and quite rough near the surface and even for a good distance below. I took the time, however, to examine at leisure the plentiful fauna attached to the metal mast. It was almost all soft and rather slimy, and drew back or contracted when I touched it. Not very appetizing; but at least there was nothing that had stings or other disagreeable marine weapons.

Paul Zuena, who was in perfect shape, politely waited for me as I continued my slow downward progress. Finally, we stood on the forward deck of the freighter. At this depth, the water was sufficiently clear for us to be able to see for a distance of about seventy-five feet. But the light was unearthly, filtered as it was through the layer of white on the surface, and it was difficult to distinguish colors or to see objects in detail. The sight, nonetheless, was incredible. Here were specimens of every sedentary animal that I had ever seen — washed of their colors by the bizarre light from above.

Before the mast were the windlasses, and I noted that their rusted cables were neatly rolled on the spools.

The whole of the forward deck, and all the portside of the hull (I could not see the starboard) was a field of countless white coral pinnacles, like blind men's canes, but surmounted not by a handle but by a pig's-tail twist. Philippe was right; it was indeed like a fleece, or like a mass of long blond hair. And everywhere among these strands I saw huge pearl oysters.

All the wood on the ship had been devoured. There was no deck covering, no hatch covers, no doors or window frames. The use of wood for these things indicated that it was a fairly old ship, probably built, in my opinion, before 1940. At the foot of the bridge, I noticed that there was no bell; but I did not go forward far enough to be sure that it was actually missing.

Next, I went down along the hull, on the portside, to the level of the lowest gangway, and entered the ship through a rip there. Then, five or six feet from me, I saw a shadowy form, distinguished by a great, white-

A grouper is frightened off by a diver's friendly advances. Despite this inauspicious beginning the grouper will be tamed easily enough.

lipped mouth. It was a giant grouper — which we French call a *loche* but which is not the small freshwater fish of the same name — weighing all of two hundred fifty pounds. I pointed him out to Paul, but the grouper, annoyed by all this attention, swam majestically into the hole and disappeared.

Amidships, we began to climb about on the ship's skeleton, and I signaled Paul to turn on the Ruggieri light. It worked very well indeed. Then, cautiously, I began to move from one beam to another, remarking that many of the steel plates were so rusty that they were beginning to look like metallic lacework.

I felt a tap on my shoulder, and Paul indicated that his breathing apparatus was leaking and that he would have to go up. Together, we began floating slowly toward the surface. I offered Paul my mouthpiece, but he refused; his own seemed to be working better now. We surfaced a few feet from our boat and quickly were aboard the *Calypso,* whereupon, almost immediately, Deloire's team went down to film the wreck. It had been a beautiful dive — but Paul was overcome with remorse at having "spoiled" it.

Paul is precisely the sort of young man that we are proud of having trained aboard the *Calypso.* He provides not only expertness in diving, but also good companionship and the ability to live well, and even gracefully, in quarters as cramped as those of the *Calypso.* He is one of the "new ones," who have been trained during the course of this expedition. The older men share with these more recent additions to our team their marine experience, and also their views on life and the world. Such was the custom a century ago among seamen, I am told, and I am delighted and proud that the men of the *Calypso* have chosen to carry on the tradition of the sea. Paul Zuéna, for example, was trained by Maurice Léandri; and Maurice was trained by Captain François Saout, who had commanded the *Calypso* on several expeditions.

That same night, we returned to Massawa, where the heat and humidity were as stifling as ever. It would have been unbearable if we had had to stay in port at this time of year, in August, not only because of the temperature but also because of the khamsin. We made it tolerable for ourselves, however, by going out every day in the waters around Massawa and diving in the anti-shark cage. We called this "Opération

La Balue" — after a French cardinal of the same name whom Louis XI shut up in an iron cage for eleven years. We at least had sharks as visitors, while Cardinal La Balue was allowed no visitors at all.

Aboard the *Calypso,* we rarely hear the word *requin* (shark). Divers prefer to speak of sharks as *les barbus* — the bearded ones; or as *balaises* (which has no English equivalent, or, for that matter, any particular meaning in French), or as *Jean-Louis.* The name Jean-Louis is a traditional one for sharks, and is of long standing in the French Navy.

It is hard to pinpoint the reason why we prefer these circumlocutions. It may be superstition, or it may even be a mark of respect for these redoubtable beasts of the sea. Or, more likely, it is simply the "in" language of an exclusive society. It is impossible for thirty men to live at close quarters and to share dangers and projects every day without evolving some kind of special vocabulary for themselves. A clever psychologist, no doubt, could divine our darkest secrets from the words that we use aboard the *Calypso.*

In the same vein, I should tell you that we are addicted to naming animals that we meet in and on the water; and, above all, animals that we take on board, feed, and train. A whale calf that we liked was christened Jonah (naturally), for we were certain that he had indeed been in a whale's belly. And our two sea lions became television stars under the names of Pepito and Cristóbal. This preoccupation with naming animals reflects, I think, an effort to make these animals members of our group. This is especially true in the case of animals with whom contact is difficult, and training even more difficult, and to whom our men must accord a certain amount of patient affection. The very act of giving a name to an animal is a sign that contact has begun and that the animal is regarded as a member of the group rather than as an outsider; as such, it has a psychological impact upon our men. (There is no record of whether it has any effect upon the animal.)

Dealing with animals often has a peculiar effect upon men. When we were filming sequences for our movie on sharks, it was necessary, from the nature of the work, to take certain risks, and everyone realized it. After a short time, Dr. Millet, our ship's doctor, noticed that a peculiar psychosis had taken hold of our divers and cameramen. It was not fear, or dread, but rather a heightened state of excitement and enthusiasm. For some reason, everyone wanted very badly to get down in the water among the sharks. Everyone had to have his daily quota of sharks. And all felt so strongly about it that it was impossible for me to ask them to do a little less diving. In retrospect, I think the reason for this strange attitude — in my own mind, I called it "shark fever" — was a need to show the sharks that man was their master. In fact, day after day our men went down and demonstrated clearly to the sharks that man could be a formidable rival for domination of the sea, and that what he lacked in physical gifts he more than compensated for by spirit.

On August 6, the weather was bad. The khamsin was still blowing with a vengeance. The sea had a yellowish cast, and the water was cloudy. After a brief call at the port of Abu Marina, in the Suakin Archipelago, we sailed northward for a time, following the line of the Farasan Archipelago, where the reefs were thickest. Then, returning southward again, we passed through the Suakin. Thus, we had traversed the coral borders of the Red Sea, along both the east and the west banks.

I am not much given to describing décor, natural or otherwise. So perhaps I will be forgiven if I explain what I find so fascinating about the Red Sea — which is no doubt my favorite spot on earth. It is not the coral reefs themselves, but the underwater scenery as seen from the observation deck of the *Calypso*. This labyrinth of crescents and half-moons, surrounded by water in varying shades of blue, this maze through which the *Calypso* must delicately pick its way, is an astounding and awesome sight. Nothing else conveys so strongly an image of the chaotic forces of creation when left to themselves. It is a microcosm of the universe, superficially anarchic but subtly ordered in accordance with laws of which we have only the vaguest notion. All this is much more striking when we take it all in from the surface, with one sweeping glance, than when we are crouched before a coral reef to examine a fragment of that cosmic image.

Certainly, there is an element of wonder also at the level of the infinitely small, and an astonishment at the presence of organized life in an organism that can hardly be seen. On that scale, however, the imagination of man is not inflamed, nor his mind awed.

I know the ocean well. It is always present in my mind, and vivid in my memory. I can truly say, however, that I have before me all its vastness and its wealth when I see, from the height of the *Calypso's* deck,

Exploring the ship that we called "the white-haired wreck." Coral pinnacles have sprung up everywhere, and blind man's canes cover the decks of the wreck.

reefs rising like gothic spires from the unmeasured depths. Then, as far as the eye can see, there are massifs and trees of coral, set in the blue or green velvet of the sea and separated from one another by fine enamel-like basins of sand. Then I am content, and it is only with difficulty that I can tear myself away from that sight. At times, I spend days guiding the *Calypso* through this wonderland, from one narrow opening to the next, at a speed of only two or three knots, filling my eyes with the splendor of it.

On August 7, still in bad weather, we dived in the vicinity of Dahl Gab, another island of the Suakin group. At about seventy feet we came across a group of sharks, none of them less then ten feet long. I counted seven of these monsters. They seemed very sure of themselves and of their role as kings of the sea. Nonetheless, they were wary, watching us from the corners of their eyes and only very slowly beginning that maneuver of encirclement that reminds one of Indians about to attack a wagon train.

Forewarned, as they say, is forearmed, and we decided to use the anti-shark cages in our project. What we intended was to "mark" the sharks; that is, to attach to each one a small metal tag on which was engraved the address of the *Musée Océanographique de Monaco*. The whole procedure is similar to the marking of migratory birds, and it is done for similar reasons. The catch, of course, is that we were dealing not with small, harmless birds with limbs to which an identifying ring is easily and quickly attached, but with unfriendly beasts who, very likely, would become man-eaters at the slightest provocation. The method we use to overcome this difficulty is to attach the tag to a small harpoon, which we then shoot into the shark by means of a harpoon gun. The crux of the operation is to put the harpoon in precisely the right spot; for, to assure that the tag is permanently attached to the shark, the harpoon must be lodged exactly at the base of the dorsal fin. To hit this bull's-eye, it was necessary for a diver to leave the cage — which was attached to the underside of a small boat — at least briefly. At each shot, the target shark would give a great start. I was terrified that, at any moment, there would be what we euphemistically call "an accident." All the more so since sharks are especially aggressive when it seems that their prey is cornered, as we seemed to be in our wire box. As soon as one of the divers emerged from the safety of the cage into open water, he would become the object of their attack. Pablo Ruiz, one of the divers, was set upon by a shark at the very moment that he left the cage to go to the surface, and only the quick reflexes of Jean-Paul Bassaget saved the day. Bassaget was in the runabout, watching the operation, when he saw the shark lunge toward Pablo. Grabbing a shark billy from the bottom of the boat, he dealt the beast a blow on the nose that sent him scurrying back to his friends.

The shark billy is one of our own inventions, dating from our first expedition into the Red Sea in the early fifties. It is simply a stout piece of wood with a handle at one end and a cluster of small nails at the other. It is effective in turning an attacking shark, but only if one acts quickly and firmly. The user must also judge the blow in such a way as to avoid injuring — and consequently enraging — the shark. (The nails are not intended to wound the animal, but only to prevent the stick from sliding off his skin.) Essentially, the shark billy is used to push, rather than to beat, the shark away from its intended prey, and its function is similar to that of the chair that is used to train lions and other great cats.

We remained in the vicinity of Dahl Gab until August 10. On the eleventh, we headed for the island of Tai Mashiya. The only inhabitants of Tai Mashiya are a species of white tern known as sea swallows, and we found that a new generation of these handsome birds had just been hatched. The young were still covered with down, and the mother birds were admirably brave in protecting their offspring. They remained with them until we were literally standing above them.

Monday, September 4, we began searching for, and quickly found, a sunken hull at Cape Si-Ane, in the Strait of Perim. The ship, of considerable size, was at the bottom in about a hundred feet of rough water. Canoë and Philippe went down first, and on reaching the wreck, they were met by a giant grouper of such incredible size that they were momentarily taken aback. The grouper fled and was never seen again. Unfortunately, neither Canoë nor Philippe had thought to bring a camera. (The so-called giant grouper has a rather flat head, and reaches a weight of as much as six hundred pounds. It is said that one can swallow a man in one gulp — but I know of no such case.)

The sunken ship was about 350 feet long, and it contained an extraordinary abundance of marine life — among which were other groupers, six or six and one half feet long; but none, unfortunately, of the size that Philippe and Canoë had seen, which they estimated to have been eleven feet long. There was a great sea turtle, which must have weighed at least two hundred pounds, and a large number of barracudas and small sharks. There were also parrot fish, busily grazing on coral.

The hull of the ship was covered with a layer of coral never less than several inches thick, so that it was impossible even to make out the ship's name. We surmised, however, that it was a freighter that had been sunk during World War II, for there was an enormous hole torn in the hull, and one of the masts had been broken in two and lay in pieces on the deck.

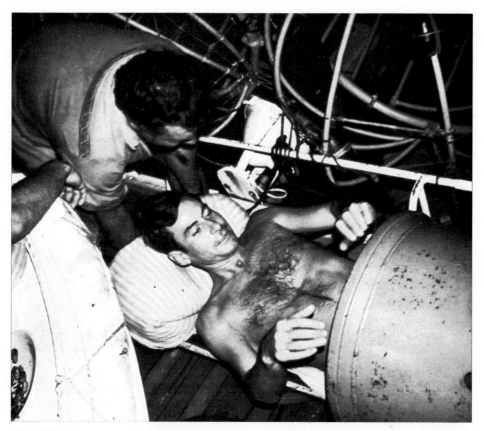

Michel Deloire, our movie cameraman, stayed underwater for a little too long; he has just spent eight hours in the decompression chamber, which is very narrow and not comfortable.

We attempted a night dive to the wreck, but the water was too troubled for us to be able to film satisfactorily.

A short distance out of Port Sudan, there is a very different kind of sunken ship. It is the *Ombria*, a large freighter, about four hundred feet long, and its hold still contains its last cargo of munitions. It is lying on its portside in shallow water, with its starboard davit protruding above the surface. What is most striking about the *Ombria* is that it is practically buried in coral. It has become, in effect, part of the reef on which it lies. At certain points, it is impossible to tell where the ship ends and

(Left) An interior view of "the white-haired wreck," showing alcyonarian formations in the holes of the hull. Their brilliant colors are revealed by our floodlights.

Continuing their exploration of the wreck, our divers discover extraordinary formations of colonial animals — mostly pink alcyonarians mixed with orange sponges.

André Laban, the engineer in charge of the minisubs, is also our resident artist. He has had several exhibitions in Los Angeles. He dives with his easel and his brushes.

marine life begins. The whole of the ship has been taken over by sedentary animals, for whom the great problem in life is not one of finding food but of finding a space where they can attach themselves. The *Ombria*, and ships like her, offer additional living space to these creatures, and for that reason the hulls of ships sunk in tropic seas usually abound in marine fauna of this kind. On this particular ship, there were madreporarians everywhere, as well as many large mother-of-pearl formations and masses of coral fish. On the portside, black coral grew, surrounded by quantities of pearl oysters. Looking aft, we could see the *Ombria's* great bronze propeller silhouetted against the water. Laban, who, in addition to his talents as a diver and violoncellist, is a painter, set up his easel on the bottom and painted a view of this striking, but somehow sad, sight.[2]

On September 5 and 6, we were at Shab Arab, some thirty miles east of Djibouti. The reef there is submerged and lies at a depth of from twenty-five to forty feet. We had to put out a buoy and work out a map grid with the *Calypso's* sounding device.

Canoë swore that he had never seen so many sharks in one spot. Since we were going to remain in the area until October 24, we concluded that he would have occasion to see even more. We were right. On September 12, we counted more than a hundred swimming around us at one time. And on that same day, Philippe was bitten on the finger by a small shark.

On the twenty-second, on an island not far from Djibouti, we tested for the first time the American-made hot-air balloon that Philippe had learned to pilot, and that he called "the poor man's helicopter."

We inflated the balloon without mishap, by means of a propane heater we had on board, and then we all admired its vivid stripes of red, white, and blue against the African sky. Philippe climbed aboard, taking a camera with him. The balloon began to rise majestically. We stood watching it, rather enviously; and then it came down precipitously, dip-

[2] Laban has had two highly successful exhibitions of his underwater paintings at a Los Angeles gallery. On both occasions, some patrons of the gallery expressed astonishment at the prevailing "blueness" of the scenes Laban depicted. We often tend to forget how alien and strange the underwater world is to people in general.

ping Philippe in the sea. It rose again, hesitantly, and again Philippe was dunked.

The poor man's helicopter proved at first to be mainly a spectator sport, and everyone except Philippe was vastly amused. Later, it would even be useful in our work, although it remained difficult to handle because of a thermal inertia that is aggravated in warm climates by atmospheric layers of varying temperature. Philippe, however, was determined to master the balloon, and he did so in short order — but not without a few accidents. A few days after the first attempt, he succeeded in launching it from the rear deck of the *Calypso,* keeping it fastened to the ship by a cable while it was aloft. All went well until the balloon had been retrieved and the plug pulled to deflate it, at which point it collapsed suddenly and drowned everyone in a sea of nylon.

There is a salt lake in the neighborhood of Djibouti, called Lake Assal, which it seemed to me would be interesting to visit for a dive. The lake is much frequented by tourists, but no one, I think, has ever bothered to look below the surface of the water.

We traveled to Lake Assal by helicopter, in two stages, through the courtesy of a detachment of French soldiers stationed at Djibouti, and landed on the shore of the lake. We immediately suited up and waded eagerly into the water. But we could not submerge. The water was so saturated with salt that our usual ballast — lead weights suspended from our belts to neutralize the floatability of the human body — was insufficient. We therefore gave all the belts to Philippe and Serge Foulon and, thus equipped, they managed to get beneath the surface. (Foulon, with his ordinary equipment, weighs slightly over two hundred pounds. To enable him to get below the surface, we had to add another sixty pounds of ballast.) Philippe filmed Serge against a background of beautiful gypsum crystals that had formed at a depth of thirty or forty feet. Later, they tested the water for salinity in different parts of the lake and found that there was considerable variation. The salinity apparently results from the evaporation of sea water.

Sea water reaches Lake Assal by filtering through rocks. In searching for the exact spot of the water's entry, we found, to our astonishment, a school of coral fish. They are probably the only coral fish in the world who live in an inland body of water.

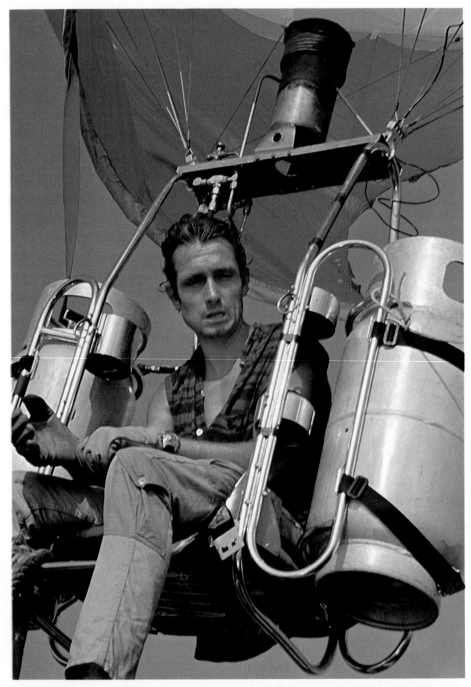

(Above) Philippe Cousteau at the controls of our hot-air balloon, of which he is the only qualified pilot. The balloon proved very useful in guiding us through coral formations when it
seemed that the *Calypso* was hopelessly trapped.

(Right) The balloon descends slowly to the sea. It will be hauled aboard the *Calypso*.

Despite our ambitions with regard to Lake Assal, we had to cut short our visit. Because of the intense heat, we were all covered with prickly heat from tip to toe. Serge and Philippe discovered that their dive, which had begun so auspiciously, very soon ceased to be an adventure and became a martyrdom. The intense salinity of the water aggravated their heat rash to such a degree that we had to hose them down with fresh water before they could obtain any relief. But the surrounding countryside was so wild and so beautiful, with its bleak mountains and its sparkling beach-bordered lake, that it never occurred to any of us to complain of the blazing sun — nor even of itching skin.

On October 1, we dived again at Dahl Gab. Canoë, using an underwater rifle, killed a mackerel; and immediately, a shark, sensing food, zoomed out of the depths below, straight for Canoë and his prize. Canoë barely had time to pull himself out of the way. Philippe, however, was directly in the shark's path as it shot past Canoë, and there was no time to move. Acting on pure instinct, he put the only thing he had between himself and the onrushing shark: his camera. The shark smashed into it, veered away, and then vanished. The whole drama of a narrowly averted tragedy occupied no more than a few seconds in time; but to us, who were watching it, it seemed an eternity.

The same night, we decided to film an underwater sequence off the eastern end of the island. In this operation, Philippe and I used a heavy steel anti-shark cage that had already served in the filming of *The Silent World*. Other divers used newer cages, made of aluminum and much easier to handle. Just as we were ready to begin, however, the wind rose and the sea became too rough for us to use our camera. I therefore suggested that we move to the other side of the island, which was more sheltered. Moving our steel cage is a difficult chore, and Philippe suggested that we simply have it towed by the *Calypso* — with him inside. I agreed that the cage should be towed, but I absolutely refused to allow him to remain in it during the operation.

As we moved to our new location, the wind rose again and the water became even rougher. With an audible snap, the tow cable broke and the cage sank beneath the waves and disappeared into the depths. If Philippe had been in the cage he would, no doubt, have been able to get out simply by opening the door. But it is equally certain that he would have emerged into the middle of a troop of sharks already overexcited by our presence.

Two near-tragedies seemed to me sufficient evil for the day.

As the *Calypso* cruises along, we gather near the prow to watch the water in the hope of spotting sperm whales, dolphins, and other large marine animals.

SEVEN

Life Around the Coral Reefs

Exploring the waters of Coetivy,
the Glorious Isles, Madagascar, and Ste. Marie.
Mirror experiments with a grouper.
The ecological equilibrium of coral massifs
and surrounding fauna.
The sea anemone and clown anemonefish.
Delivery of the "Sea Fleas."

The grouper puffed out his cheeks, stuck out his lower lip, and made a disagreeable face. His gill covers waved slowly in the dimness of his grotto. Then his armor-plated head advanced toward me with an unmistakable expression of curiosity. He showed no sign of fear. If anything, he was angry. I am familiar with the symptoms: dorsal spines erect, head lowered like that of a bull about to charge. It was not an engaging head, even in the best of circumstances, with its bony skull, smooth and convex as a shield, and its tiny, staring eyes.

I could not help wondering what was going on in that massive skull. What idea can a grouper have of a human being? That question has troubled me for many years, since I first began to dive; since Philippe Tailliez, Frédéric Dumas, and I used to feed groupers in the Mediterranean before they were all chased away or killed by underwater hunters.

At that time, we had tried to strike up a friendly relationship with them; but our advances had almost always been repulsed. I think, however, that our good intentions had been based on a sentimental misunderstanding. Divers are always proud when they succeed in approaching one of these relatively large marine animals without frightening him away. If they succeed — and it is relatively easy to succeed — in feeding him by hand and in petting him, they imagine that they have somehow created a bond of affection between themselves and the grouper.

In the Red Sea we found handsome pink groupers spotted with blue — the same species as Jojo, the hero in *The Silent World.* One of the favorite subjects of debate aboard the *Calypso* was the level of intelligence among groupers. Opinion was sharply divided. Some of the divers — Delemotte and Bonnici, who knew and loved groupers — believed that these fish were capable of a certain kind of affection, or at least of sustaining a certain relationship with a human being. Some of the other men aboard were more skeptical — Falco, Coll, and Canoë. They were convinced that what appeared to be affection in a grouper was really a symptom of voracity; that is, that groupers loved the food that humans provided rather than the humans that provided food.

This controversy sprang up with renewed vigor during our stay at Coetivy, where coral is puny and scarce but groupers plentiful.

It was at the end of October, in splendid weather, that we reached this small island, which lies to the northeast of Madagascar. Coetivy is so low and flat that, seen from a distance, it appeared to be merely a group of coconut trees emerging from the surface of the water. It is, in fact, a rather enchanting place, surrounded by beaches of clean white sand. There are about a hundred inhabitants (of mixed, but chiefly Arabic, origin), and it is the traditional copra mill of the region. The only village is on the west side of the island, in the plantation area. Although Coetivy is a British possession, the chief (coconut) planter is the French consul, a M. Delhomme.

Coetivy is the regular port of call for a Ceylonese ship that comes once a month to take on copra. This occasion — which is greatly looked forward to by the residents — is the island's only contact with the outside world.

Coetivy is home also to a species of wild donkey. The animals, which are very abundant, are rounded up once a year and used in the copra harvest, and then let go again. This obviates the necessity of feeding them all year, between harvests; but, as one can imagine, the services they render during the harvest are characterized more by whimsey than efficiency.

The one great event within the living memory of most Coetivians was the arrival of the island's single truck. Everywhere, we were told the story of its arrival and of the Herculean effort (there was no crane, of course, and no wharf) that was deployed to get it ashore. The entire population was mobilized to get it onto the beach, and it is an exploit of which Coetivians are justly proud.

One end of the island extends into the sea in the shape of a beautiful coral reef, which connects with a small neighboring island called Lys. Both islands rise — like the Seychelles — from a flat, rather sterile, plateau. On the bottom to the west, there is an immense flat area where the water is almost thirty-five hundred feet deep — too deep for coral, but too shallow for the great creatures of the deep. Our dives, therefore, were disappointing.

For this reason, we would have been willing to cut short our visit, despite the warm welcome the islanders had extended to us. Our ship's doctor, however, had too much work on the island for us to do so. Part of our job is to bring medical assistance to any place that we visit — and especially to isolated places such as Coetivy. Dr. Millet was the first doctor the Coetivians had seen for four years, and they immediately set him up in what they rather pretentiously called "the infirmary" — which was a hut, and a very poorly equipped one. Then the inhabitants presented themselves, one by one, with that mixture of wariness and blind faith that characterizes people unaccustomed to a medical presence.

First, as always, came the children, screaming and crying in their parents' arms. Then the women came, embarrassed to the point of catalepsy by their extreme modesty. And finally the men came. For several days and nights, Dr. Millet did nothing but attempt to alleviate some of the suffering of these people, who were the victims of an isolation that seems to encourage diseases now almost unknown in the West — parasitic and tropical diseases, particularly.

The social life of the Coetivians presents some points of interest, particularly in those structural aspects that we might call "medieval." One of the most important personages on the island is the local buffoon, who, by his jokes and gestures, plays a role analogous to that of a king's jester in Europe. This man regularly staged impromptu performances in the village square, where his antics, Dr. Millet said, showed signs, at first glance, of being pathological. Examination, however, proved the man

(Above) Our divers never weary of exploring the crystal waters of this wonderful world.

(Left) At the bottom of one of the Seven Lakes: a dead tree is covered with Saprophytes.

to be afflicted with tertiary syphilis in a very advanced stage. The poor clown was, in reality, only sick. And, unhappily, given the state of medical care on Coetivy, his disease was incurable.

From the ninth to the eleventh of November, we were at Diégo-Suarez, on Madagascar, where we had some work done on the hull of the *Calypso*. When the water was drained out of the dry dock, we noticed that a large porcupine fish — one of those bizarre tropical fish covered with spines — had been stranded, and we took it aboard. The divers tried to tame it, but, good treatment and offers of food notwithstanding, they were unsuccessful. At the slightest motion or noise near its tank, the porcupine fish would swell up like a balloon (which is its standard reaction to danger) with its spines in their best defensive posture.

We took advantage of our time in port to organize several expeditions on land. The first was to one of the numerous lakes of Madagascar, where crocodiles are worshipped. When we arrived, however, there was not a single crocodile to be seen. The chief of the local village explained that the crocodiles would not show themselves unless we offered a proper sacrifice. And, as it happened, he had a buffalo for sale that would do very nicely. We bought the buffalo, and the chief promised to take care of the details of the sacrifice. Then we were shown some floating objects in the middle of the lake, which, we were assured, were crocodiles. To us, they looked more like logs; and we began to have the feeling that we had been had. We said nothing, however, and left for the next leg of our expedition. On the way back, however — the next day — we decided to make a stop at the same village. We found the entire population in the midst of an uproarious feast, the principal dish of which was our crocodile sacrifice. The chief, with open arms, and without a trace of embarrassment, welcomed us to the celebration, and the whole affair was liquidated in the best possible spirits.

The next expedition was more difficult. We went in search of fossils on the banks of a river on the northwest coast of Madagascar, a place that was very difficult of access and in an almost deserted region. We were traveling in two vehicles, and both managed somehow to take the wrong turn and get lost. Finally, we had to abandon the vehicles and continue on foot. We walked for several hours and finally reached the lake, which, as it happened, was clouded over with swarms of mosquitoes. We had also run out of water, and the lake water itself was not particularly appetizing. Dr. Millet, in fact, forbade us to drink it; but we did so anyhow, and survived to return to the *Calypso* with a great many excellent marine fossils.

The most important and successful of our expeditions to the interior, however, was to the Seven Lakes area. In that instance, we brought along our diving equipment and underwater cameras.

The Seven Lakes lie at the foot of the Lisalo Mountains. They are thirty or forty feet deep, and are fed by the melting snows of the mountains. The water is virtually free of salt, and so pure that it contains hardly any organic matter at all. For that reason, the water in which we were diving was extraordinarily clear. But water of such purity contains little food for aquatic animals, and, consequently, the Seven Lakes are practically sterile. About the only living thing we saw was a colony of fragile saprophytes attached to the branches of sunken trees. It was a stark scene, which contrasted dramatically with the teeming life to which we had grown accustomed in coral waters.

By now, repairs had been completed, and we left almost immediately for the Glorious Isles, off the northwest tip of Madagascar. These splendidly named islands — two in number — are a French possession *(les Iles Glorieuses,* we call them). They serve as a meteorological base for the observation of hurricanes.

Arriving early in the morning, we dropped anchor near the larger of the islands and immediately sent a party ashore. They found there three natives of the former French colony of Réunion, whose job it was to man the meteorological station. And these three were the only inhabitants of the island.

This little speck of land is what travel folders describe as a "tropical paradise." It is rimmed with perfectly clean, broad beaches of dazzling whiteness, which are lined with coconut trees. At one end of the island, a coral massif forms a cape, on which is the meteorological station, built in a grove of coconut trees. There are woods of a tree known in the region as *filao,* and sand dunes provide a variation to the flatness of the land. The island is also interesting zoologically — for here the birds build their nests on the ground, while the rodents live in trees.

There have been attempts, of course, to exploit the island commercially, particularly in the form of coconut plantations. We found the remains of the workers' camps; and, as always, there were two small, ageless cemeteries under the palms.

The area was as much a paradise in the water as on land. The weather was beautiful, the water was clear, and there was an extraordinary wealth of marine life — mackerel and wrasses especially. On the bottom, composed of that sparkling white sand that is one of the beauties of the island, we found a splendid coral maze. As we were inspecting it, we discovered that we were being studied, in our turn, by a huge sea turtle hidden under a madreporarian coral formation. We tried to stroke its neck — an absurdly human gesture which the turtle no doubt found revolting, for it turned and swam away, slowly and disdainfully. The coral here was grouped in massifs, and each massif was separated from the others by a short interval. The butterfly fish, of which there were many here, occasionally attemped to go from one of these coral formations to another. When they did so, however, they had to reckon with the local tyrant — usually another butterfly fish or an angelfish who, determined to maintain his authority, would attack the intruder and force him out into the open water.

The ecological equilibrium of each one of these massifs is apparently the result of a very complex series of relationships between their inhabitants. It is the same riddle of the social life of marine animals that I have mentioned before, and that continues to haunt me. I never tire of observing these tiny universes inhabited by sedentary fish of various colors, into which, from time to time, an alien predator intrudes, turning that universe upside down and demolishing the local power structure.

We found the coral here to be as varied as, but less vivid in color than, the coral in the portion of the Red Sea that has not yet suffered from pollution. Man comes here very rarely, and so the coral world is still intact.

On the side of the island that faces the open sea, a lined reef, which is covered with tufts of coral and groves of sea fans, slants slowly downward toward the deeps. There are beds of giant clams everywhere, and the great, half-open shells clam shut when one reaches out to touch them. Farther on, groupers stare curiously from their lairs as we inspect large trees of coral.

The island has a lagoon, the gently sloping bottom of which is covered with the same white sand. Even here, the abundance and diversity of marine life is exceptional. We find mackerel, unusually large wrasses, and the usual school of butterfly fish.

The larger island, on which we had landed, is about two miles long and a mile wide. The smaller, however, is only a half mile long and perhaps six hundred yards wide, and it is quite different from its sister island. The two are connected by a coral plateau. We wanted to visit the smaller island, but the plateau seemed too shallow even for our runabout. Philippe, Serge Foulon, and Dr. Millet, however, tried it. While they were on the other island, the tide went out, and when they returned to the beach they found the boat sitting gracefully on a coral pedestal. The only way to return to the larger island was to walk across the plateau — carrying the boat. At every step of the walk (which took four hours), the madreporarians ripped mercilessly at their feet. It will be a while before any of them forget their visit to the Glorious Isles.

The small island, they reported, seemed endowed with a strangely tragic atmosphere. It is a mere pile of shale; yet, it was obviously inhabited at one time by some sort of Robinson Crusoe, who had built a shelter of stone and planted a tree. The tree by now had grown to such a size that it had half-demolished the house. We were silent for a moment thinking of that hermit — the survivor of a shipwreck, probably — who had thought to plant a mango tree in his front yard, and then had gone, leaving his island to the rodents and the crabs.

During the length of our stay at the Glorious Isles, we worked steadily and systematically at observing and recording the marine life in the waters surrounding the islands; and at the same time, we worked at establishing a harmonious relationship between those life forms and ourselves. Every day, Bernard Delemotte went down to the bottom with great quantities of food. It was an outright exercise in demagoguery, or in bribery. Mackerel, wrasses, and butterfly fish surrounded him by the hundreds. It reminded one of the pigeons of New York or Paris when someone arrives with a bag of bread crumbs. At times, the fish were so thick that we could not see Delemotte at all. And every day the fish became bolder and bolder. Delemotte, to see how far they would go, put a couple of pieces of food inside his mask. The fish at first circled his head curiously, and then began staring into the mask. And finally they started throwing themselves furiously against the plexiglass visor.

Here, as at Coetivy, there were many groupers, and I decided to take advantage of the friendly atmosphere to perform an experiment. There was some equipment, however, that I needed, so the *Calypso* made a short trip to Diégo-Suarez to purchase a large quantity of mirrors. Finding mirrors in Madagascar is not like buying them in New York or Los Angeles. It takes a certain amount of genius. Fortunately, Bernard Chauvellin, our quartermaster, is well equipped in that area. He has no equal in being able to turn up the most unlikely objects even in the most underdeveloped countries. And, in this case, he uncovered just what we needed: a number of very large mirrors of the kind generally used on dressing tables. We returned with our treasure to the Glorious Isles, where the unsuspecting groupers were waiting.

I wanted the mirrors for an experiment regarding the "territorial problem" among groupers. I should explain that many land animals are

A grouper staring at his reflection in a mirror held by a diver.

known to be subject to a "territorial imperative," by virtue of which they regard their immediate surroundings — their living space — as a sacred and inviolable possession that they defend against all comers, even if it costs them their lives. This is as true for the nightingale as it is for the rhinoceros. We know very little, however, about the territorial imperative among fishes. There have been experiments under controlled conditions in laboratories and in aquariums, of course: but the definitive experiment must take place, I think, in nature — that is, in the sea. A coral reef seemed a particularly suitable place; and groupers particularly good subjects, for they are sedentary and have lairs from which they never stray very far.

A grouper raises his dorsal fin. He thinks he has seen a rival.

I have observed in the sea that exercising the territorial imperative in practice is most often a matter of intimidation rather than of outright force. Combat, in fact, is comparatively rare. There is a confrontation, and a volley of challenges and threats; and then the intruder usually swims off. In the case of a grouper's territory, other fish are sometimes allowed to trespass — but only if the grouper-proprietor gives permission. This, the grouper sometimes does; for groupers are basically capricious animals.

Why the mirrors? We knew already, from experience, that a grouper usually mistakes its own reflection for another grouper; and, if it is a matter of trespass, it attacks its own image in the mirror. (Mirrors, being fragile, are difficult enough to use on the floor of the Indian Ocean; but it is even more difficult to get a grouper to invade the territory of another grouper on cue.)

On our first try, using a medium-sized grouper as the subject, our mirror proved too thick and the grouper was not able to break it when he charged. (Breaking it, of course, is important; the grouper is then victorious. Otherwise, we would have a frustrated and neurotic grouper on our hands.) On the second try, the mirror proved to be too thin, and we broke it against a projection of coral. The next mirror was smashed into a million fragments by a ridiculously tiny grouper who had no business there in any case, and who, moreover, would not look good on film. At this point, I called a temporary halt to the experiment, before every mirror aboard the *Calypso* had been smashed.

We began again the next day, this time with our cameramen present with their equipment. But, given the diminishing supply of mirrors, I thought it best to have another rehearsal. We managed to find a grouper of the right size who became angry enough, at just the right moment, to break two mirrors. In the face of such good will, I decided to take the experiment a bit further. This particular grouper had his lair, a grotto, but he had also taken over an adjacent tunnel leading to the grotto, as well as the area immediately outside the main entrance.

We therefore surrounded the grouper with four mirrors, enclosing him in a circle of "invaders." He went from one reflected image to the other, glaring at each one for a moment — and then he charged. He was a brave grouper, and a victorious one, for he smashed all the mirrors. It would be a stunning sequence.

And then we noticed that the cameras had jammed.

We began again. Four more mirrors were brought down and installed in the grouper's den. But by now Michel Deloire and Raymond Coll had been in the water for four hours, and they were exhausted. The grouper also had had enough, and he seemed as discouraged as the divers. Finally, however, his instincts prevailed, and he attacked once more. Once more, he conquered. And then he began eating the mirror fragments. The next day, we found the grouper floating belly up on the surface. Unfortunately, even a grouper cannot digest glass. Deloire, particularly, was very sad.

All in all, we spend four weeks on the reef. They were four weeks of continual astonishment at the biological wealth of the area, at the intensity and density of life there. And, before leaving, we had to capture some of those life forms in order to send them to the *Musée Océanographique de Monaco* for study and observation.

The most difficult part in a scientific "fishing expedition" is to take specimens without injuring them, or even frightening them unduly. For that reason, we use — as I have already explained — a soporofic (MS-222) prepared by our medical officer, which we shoot into a reef by means of a special pistol. The fish in the area then go to sleep, and we can take those that we want.

As specimens are gathered, they are placed inside a globe-shaped aquarium we use to transport fish both under water and aboard the *Calypso*. Because of the aquarium's shape, the fish are not likely to be spilled out as the *Calypso* pitches and rolls in rough weather.

On this occasion, we were able to take some rare specimens. In a square yard of bottom, there were fish for which amateur collectors would have paid large sums. They were of the most vivid colors and markings — bright blues and golds and yellows, and an infinity of spots, bars, and stripes.

As we were collecting specimens, I noticed a paradoxical situation: Our plastic globes were aquariums within that vast natural aquarium which is the coral reef. The globes, being transparent, were practically invisible in the water and, even from a short distance, the fish within them seemed to be in the open water. They were distinguishable, however, because once they woke up they behaved abnormally; their swimming space was circumscribed by the walls of the globe, and they therefore either swam about in an unnatural way or simply remained still. This, of course, did not escape the notice of other fish, especially those of the same species, and they quickly came over to investigate.

Next, the predators arrived. At first, they were only mildly curious. Then, when they perceived that the fish inside the globe were in a state of panic, their indifference quickly changed to excitement, and they attacked.

A large grouper seemed to be wondering how to take advantage of the situation of the specimens within the aquarium. He had noticed that there was something unusual about their behavior; and, in the coral

Many coral fishes
live in bands or
schools, since
numbers are their
only defense against
predators. The latter
become disoriented
in the presence of
large numbers of
small fish and are
confused as to their
target. These
handsome fish are
called *Ostorhyncus
fleurieu*.

jungle, I have noticed, that is equivalent to a sentence of death. As soon as a fish gives any sign that he is in trouble, he is lost. Our specimens, therefore, were advertising their helplessness and inviting attack. The grouper obliged; but he struck the globe with such force that he was momentarily stunned. Frustrated and enraged at the presence of food within sight but out of reach, he redoubled his attacks, smashing his head against the plexiglass sphere until he succeeded in knocking it loose from the rock to which it was attached. Then he proceeded to play a game of solitary volleyball with it, butting it about until we rescued our specimens and took them safely up to the *Calypso*. Whereupon, peace was restored on the reef.

That evening, the wardroom was the scene of another chapter in our perennial discussion of groupers. Raymond Coll's opinion, like my own, varies according to circumstances and according to our most recent experiences. Neither one of us has yet reached any firm decision regarding the intelligence, or the affective dispositions, of these creatures.

"Of course," Raymond says, "it seems to be the easiest of all the fish to tame. It follows you around like a dog. But, apart from that, groupers seem to have a mean streak a mile wide. There was one grouper today who followed me around so devotedly that I decided to pet him. And then he attacked me. It's possible that we were in his territory at the time. In any case, he was swimming very slowly toward me, and I began swimming very slowly toward him. I stopped; but he continued swimming — faster and faster until it was obvious that he was charging me. Instinctively, I put my arm in front of my face, and he got hold of my elbow with his jaws and wouldn't let go. I finally shook him off, but he had torn my diving suit and broken the skin, but not seriously."

Frédéric Dumas also had been attacked by a grouper. And, of course, I knew of other instances. But generally groupers are inoffensive creatures. Even so, the very next day Raymond Coll's grouper was back, trying to bite everyone in sight. But this time we were forewarned, and we handled the creature as one would handle a snarling dog. It's possible that this particular grouper had had bad experiences with divers who were here before us.

"Actually," Falco said, "there are only two fishes who, in my experience, are capable of a special, if somewhat ambiguous, relationship with man. One is the grouper, and the other is the triggerfish."

Coll — who has a tendency to attribute human virtues and vices to fish — interrupted: "Triggerfish are nice," he said, "but they're alto- gether unreliable. Everyone knows that their favorite food is the giant clam. Well, I once opened a clam and offered it to a triggerfish — and he bit my finger. I think that groupers and triggerfish have this in common, that they are both just plain mean. Another time, Delemotte and I were swimming by some triggerfish who were fanning eggs. We didn't look at them, and they went out of their way to attack us."

Acting on Coll's story, we got the idea that it would make an inter- esting sequence to show a triggerfish attacking a diver. But it did not work out very well; or rather, it worked out too well. Delemotte was very badly bitten. For the next try, therefore, we wrapped his hands and arms in heavy bandages.

From all this, one might get the impression that a triggerfish is a fearsome adversary. So it is. But it is an unusual "monster," being only fifteen or twenty inches long and gaily spotted and striped. What ac- counts for its ferocity is the peculiar milieu in which it lives. In the coral world, weakness is synonymous with death. Individual fish, and entire species, who turn and run, rather than fight, do not last long. The de- fenseless and the timid are quickly eaten. Thus, marine life forms very often show a degree of courage which, by human standards, is heroic to the point of being ridiculous. Triggerfish are particularly ferocious while their eggs are incubating. The female stands guard over her nest and defends it against all comers (including divers) regardless of their size, with a vigor and disregard for her own safety that it would be difficult to match with any land animal. The need to propagate the spe- cies takes precedence over the instinct for survival, and the mother trig- gerfish will attack without hesitation even when it is obvious to her that the only result will be her own death. The courage of the triggerfish, however, is dictated not by any innate heroism, but by the necessity for an ecological balance within the reef. Despite the mother's protection, only a small number of triggerfish survive into maturity — just the num- ber that the reef can support.

Delemotte, who has had some experience with triggerfish, assures me that the fish's jaws — which I know are strong enough to break the

(Facing page) Bernard Delemotte carrying the giant syringe and the plastic globe that he uses to capture rare fish.

(Left) A grouper attacks the captured fish.

(Below) Bonnici injects a soporific into a coral massif.

shell of a giant clam — can inflict a serious bite. And as Delemotte says, "It hurts." Nonetheless, the triggerfish, when it bites a man, does not tear off pieces of flesh.

Still, I would not like to leave the reader with the impression that all triggerfish are necessarily "mean" — Coll to the contrary notwithstanding. In 1963, during the Precontinent II experiment, when several of our associates lived for a whole month at the bottom of the Red Sea, their most faithful companion was a triggerfish of which Pierre Guilbert had made a pet. This triggerfish knew Pierre to the extent that he could distinguish him from the other divers, and he would follow him everywhere in the water. When Pierre was inside, he would knock on the window, and immediately the triggerfish would come. Then he would swim around to the entrance and beat against it with his fins until Pierre went out with food for him.

In dealing with fish, as with all other animals, we must resist the temptation to make value judgments. Fish are what we make of them. I still believe that the triggerfish of the Glorious Isles, which we qualified as "disagreeable" and "hostile," simply had not had time to get used to us. Their defensive reactions were perfectly normal and understandable. I am convinced that they would have "come around" if we had been in the area just a few more days.

While at the Glorious Isles, we had the opportunity to film a clown anemonefish[1] in the exercise of that peculiar relationship that it maintains with a sea anemone.

Sea anemones are often quite beautiful, and quite poisonous. They all have the same general form, which is columnar. The tentacles that surmount the column are extended when the anemone is feeding, and retracted when it is frightened. These tentacles, which are used for stinging and feeding, bear an intricate complex of cells. The stinging cells, or nematoblasts, are capsule-like and lidded. Inside is a rolled filament covered with hooks. The filament is hollow and connects with a venom gland. At the slightest contact or stimulation, the lid opens, and the filament is shot out, and the hooks lodge in the flesh of the attacker, who is paralyzed by the venom injected through the filament. The tentacles then stuff the victim into the anemone's gastric cavity. The wounds

[1]Not to be confused with the ordinary clown fish, which is a species of triggerfish.

they inflict are very painful, and the poison is sufficiently strong to paralyze a fish four or five inches long. Indeed, small fish, along with crabs and free-swimming organisms, form part of the sea anemone's regular diet.

I had a particular reason for being interested in sea anemones. These animals played a part in an important discovery made aboard the oceanographic vessel of Prince Albert of Monaco. In 1902, two eminent French physiologists, Paul Portier and Charles Richet, discovered how to produce anaphylaxis[2] by injecting the poison of the sea anemone (actinotoxin) into the ship's dog, Neptune. This was enough to arouse our interest in the disagreeable ways of the sea anemones of the Glorious Isles.

The relationship of the sea anemone and the clown anemonefish is a very special one. An ordinary fish is affected by the sea anemone's poison, but the clown anemonefish is not. Moreover, the clown anemonefish is not only immune to the poison, but lives, literally, among the sea anemone's tentacles. This is his protection against attack from outsiders. Even the grouper leaves him in peace when he is with his anemone host.

It is not certain just why the clown anemonefish is immune to the sea anemone's poison. One may conjecture that he pays for this immunity to attack by stroking the anemone's tentacles (as he has been observed to do). Just as he pays his rent by catching, and bringing back to the anemone, prey that the anemone could not catch alone.

The common life of the clown anemonefish and the anemone is a fact of long-standing observation. We, however, were able to film, for the first time, a clown anemonefish in the act of feeding the anemone host. Our method was simple enough: We put some pieces of fish into the water near the anemone, and the clown anemonefish immediately saized them and took them to the anemone, which ate them forthwith. The bits of fish also attracted a few groupers and snappers — with which the clown anemonefish fought. When the larger fish were at the point of overwhelming him, he fled back to his refuge among the anemone's tentacles.

It is noteworthy that the clown anemonefish, while the best known "guest" of the sea anemone, is only one of a dozen species of damselfish

[2] The heightening of the sensibility of an organism to a particular substance by means of the (earlier) injection of a small amount of that substance into the organism.

Raymond Coll becomes the target for the attack of a triggerfish. The fish is defending the eggs that she has laid among the coral, and the size of her enemy does not discourage her.

who can exist in this odd relationship. In addition, the goby has been observed, in aquariums, to take up residence among the tentacles of an anemone.

This period was a time of intense work for everyone aboard the *Calypso*. Even so, we took the time to explore the bottom in the entire area, and also to get to know the island itself and its inhabitants — that is, the three men of the meteorological station.

The station owned a small tractor with a trailer, which was used to carry the coconuts the men gathered. The men there were kind enough to let us use the tractor for a tour of the island, as a means of recreation and a change from our incessant diving. Our destination on this tour was a small forest of coconut palms located in a shallow valley, but we were in no hurry to get there. We followed a road — the only one on the island — along the north shore to a creek, where we found two parallel

The most beautiful of the Chaetodons is called *ornatissimus*. It feeds by pecking at coral.

rows of coconut trees leading into the interior of the island. These trees were too evenly spaced to have grown there naturally, and we concluded that they had been planted years before. At the end of the small avenue afforded by the trees, we found a cemetery hidden among a grove of palms. The tombs were scattered about in no particular pattern. On the headstones there were names and dates — the names of natives of the Seychelles who had, many years before, attempted to found a colony here and who died of thirst. Overhead, the palm fronds waved and sighed. We returned several times, and each time we were struck by the tranquillity, and the inescapable sadness, of the scene.

We also had occasion to make several trips between Madagascar and the Glorious Isles. We were waiting for our new diving saucers — which we had christened "the Sea Fleas" — to arrive. They were aboard the freighter *Ville de Brest*, we had been told, which was to dock at Tamatave. But the freighter was behind schedule. We therefore decided to stop over at the island of Ste. Marie, off the east coast of Madagascar. The island itself is a former whaling port, and very beautiful; and, to complete the picture, the bottom around it proved to be an excellent studio for our underwater cameramen. At first, because of a strong wind, we dived on the leeward side of the island. The bottom was muddy, but there was an abundance of fauna, in the form of starfish, tropical fish, and so forth.

The situation seemed worth the work and trouble of a nighttime dive. And indeed it was. We witnessed a veritable migration of sea urchins. While on the bottom, we noticed what seemed to be a cloud of mud rising from the floor of the sea. As the cloud came closer, we realized that we were watching schools of sea urchins of several species in motion — advancing towards us at a speed we clocked at 450 yards per hour.

We had already noticed, in the Red Sea, that mollusks and urchins move about at night. At Ste. Marie, however, nocturnal activity seemed particularly intense. Starfish and shellfish accompanied the urchins in their travels. Happily, we were able to film the whole thing — the first time that anyone has been able to do so. In the glare of our lights, the great starfish, mixed in among the sea urchins (for which they have a special fondness), show up as bright red.

The sea urchin resembles a doorknob covered with spines. The spines are movable and produce a painful, though not fatal, wound. Some species use these spines as a means to walk along the bottom, while others move about on small, tube-like feet. Underneath the spines there is meat, which other fish would consider a rare delicacy, if only they dared take it. But the urchin is too well armed for them to try.

The sea urchin, like the sea anemone, has a close friend in the damselfish, or blue reef fish, who hides among the urchin's spines. Indeed, damselfish and urchins seem to be inseparable. Even when the urchins migrate and reassemble farther out to sea, their little blue friends follow them and claim their former places among them.

By way of experiment, we tried to break up that relationship by chasing away the reef fish and then confining several sea urchins within plastic globes. The reef fish were overcome with panic and, as soon as we removed the globes, they darted frantically into the protection of the urchins' spines.

It is a delight to browse among the infinitely varied splendors of a coral sea — but the men of the *Calypso* have little time for leisurely contemplation.

Our divers usually are responsible for several tasks at a time — photography, the gathering of specimens, identifying fish, and observing the sea's ecology, biology, and geology.

(Left) A half-open actinian. The fish is a *Fissilabrus*.

(Below) A sea anemone with a clown anemonefish *(Amphiprion)* among its tentacles.

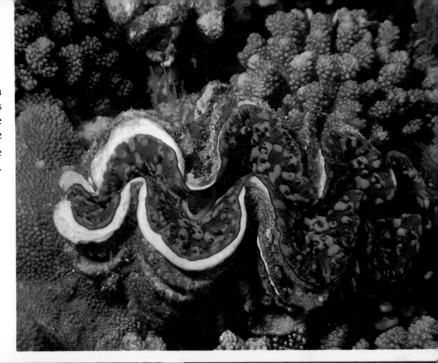

(Right) A partially open giant clam, showing its marbled flesh. The giant clam is the largest of the mollusks.

(Below) Sea anemones have extremely venomous tentacles, which are capable of paralyzing small fish.

In all, we spent three days at Ste. Marie, and very profitable days they were. We were especially happy to be able again to film some specimens of *Periophthalmus koelreuteri* — the mudskipper, which we had already seen along the African coast. In the latter case, we had observed them perched on the mangrove roots; but here they stayed out of the water for considerable periods, sitting on rocks.

It was raining when we finally arrived at Tamatave to accept delivery of our "Sea Fleas," and we worked for hours, drenched, to get them aboard the *Calypso.* They had been built to fit exactly into the hold, with a tolerance of only one inch. So it was a rather exacting job.

We tried to be at our best, which was not very easy under the circumstances, for the arrival of the saucers was something of an occasion for the Tamatavians. It seemed that everyone in Tamatave had heard that we were loading; and every man, woman, and child with time to spare gathered on the dock to watch us work. They were curious; but their curiosity was mingled with a good deal of sympathetic understanding. In fact, the people of Madagascar in general seemed enormously pleased that *their* island and *their* port had been chosen for delivery of the minisub, and that it had come to rest on *their* soil before plunging into the sea. Photographs were taken by the hundreds, and almost before we knew it the *Calypso* was swarming with representatives of the local press. Thereafter, it became impossible to keep anyone off; but I confess that we did not try very hard, for we were unable to resist the exquisite courtesy with which they requested permission to come aboard. The "sea fleas," of course, were the sensation of the day, narrowly followed by the anti-shark cages. Almost everyone in Tamatave seemed to have a supply of stories about sharks, which they were able only with the greatest difficulty to resist telling.

Despite this auspicious atmosphere, we were unable to do much diving at Tamatave. The weather was not good, and the sea was rough. Nonetheless, our memories of Tamatave are filled with the images of the splendor of tropical flowers — bougainvillaea, particularly — and of tropical fruit, of which we had been deprived for so long.

Tamatave is noted for its lush beauty, the friendliness of its inhabitants, and the great number of sharks that live in the neighborhood. Among the natives, these sharks are said to be particularly vicious; and, for once, rumor seems to be justified. There had been two "accidents" just before our arrival. A young girl had been attacked by a shark and had lost a leg; and a Japanese seaman, in attempting to swim from ship to shore, had been mauled within sight of the Nautical Club of Tamatave. Another Japanese seaman had courageously attempted to save him, but he had been able only to recover the body of his friend.

We were somewhat surprised at these horrible, and nonetheless true, stories. For several months, both in the Red Sea and in the Indian Ocean, we had had to do with dozens of sharks, and without the slightest "accident." It is true, however, that, as professional divers, we run less risk than ordinary swimmers, simply because we take fewer chances. Whatever the case, these recent incidents did not keep us from diving once or twice. We did not see many sharks, and those we did see were not especially aggressive. It may be that we had caught them in whatever passes for a good mood among sharks.

A Tetraodon, which seems covered with diamonds.

EIGHT

The Depths:
The Second Frontier
Testing the Sea Fleas.
A change of crews.
Watching a coral reef die.

I was alone in one of our new diving saucers — Flea No. 2. After passing the 350-foot mark, I had slowed my descent. Now, at slightly less than seven hundred feet, the total pressure on the saucer was about twelve hundred tons. The metal hull was beginning to turn cold, to contract, as I continued downward into the dark water through a forest of sea fans. I began to feel a damp chill to the marrow of my bones. Somehow, it had been easier to use the old SP-300. It held two men: a pilot and a passenger; one was at the helm, and the other observed. And it was helpful to exchange comments with someone.

The fact that the Fleas were one-passenger vehicles, however, had advantages. Since they were smaller than the SP-300, we could house two of them aboard the *Calypso* — which meant that one could be used to film the other. Moreover, it was safer to use the two Fleas than the single SP-300, for the new saucers were equipped to latch on to one another and, if necessary, to tow one another to safety in case of a malfunction or accident.

On this occasion, Canoë Kientzy was in Flea No. 1, the other saucer. I could see it through my porthole, a few yards away, its round chassis painted a bright yellow, its lights illuminating the nearly vertical wall of the cliff. As I watched, the other saucer seemed to vibrate violently for a moment, and then stabilized itself again. Canoë was coping with the job of controlling his Flea's motion both horizontally and vertically — a difficult exercise which requires dexterity, judgment, and nerves of steel. For the Fleas were proving themselves to be capricious. We still had much to learn about handling them. And Canoë and I were both trying to learn.

The Fleas had been designed by our team of scientists and engineers according to my specifications, and built by Sud-Aviation. Each one is an autonomous unit, containing equipment for propulsion, navigation, and security. They are small craft, a little over three feet in beam and six and one half feet long and weighing two tons. There are two water-jet engines in the forward section, and the electric motor, which activates the engines, is enclosed in a fiber glass compartment on the outside of the hull. The batteries are also on the exterior. In this way, the pilot is in no danger if the motor should catch fire, or if the batteries should short out.

The Fleas were designed for a double purpose: for underwater scientific observation, and for underwater filming. The recording of underwater scenes on film plays an important role in the advancement of marine knowledge, and today it is a large part of oceanography. For that reason, I had insisted that the Fleas be equipped with sufficiently large portholes (of three-inch-thick plexiglass) to provide a wide field of vision.

In order to keep down the size of the Fleas, we had made certain accommodations. For one thing, a pilot guides the Flea lying on his stomach, holding a remarkable all-purpose lever by means of which he starts and stops the motors, accelerates or slows; starts the sonar, the tape recorder, and the two cameras; and turns on the lights. The lever can also send the ballast of 125 pounds of mercury forward — which, in turn, will cause the Flea to go into a nose dive.

Canoë and I talked by sonar telephone. When we were both ready to rise, I notified Laban, who was waiting for us on the surface in a runabout, that we were coming up.

I had scheduled seven days of testing for the Fleas — to check out the hulls, the motors, the batteries, the valves, and the navigational instruments. It seemed that I had overestimated the time necessary for this. Everything seemed to be working perfectly. As we rose to the surface, Canoë and I congratulated one another. We felt that we had just been paid in full for six years of hard work in the design, construction, and "ironing out" of the Fleas. And we were enthusiastic about the possibilities that they would offer in our work.

(Right) Gaston, who is in charge of the maintenance of the diving saucers, is also a coral enthusiast.

The launching of a diving saucer (minisub) from the *Calypso*. The whole operation takes only a few minutes.

A diving saucer — which we call the "sea flea" — and a suited diver meet on the bottom. The vehicle and the diver have about the same mobility, but the saucer is able to go down to about two thousand feet. Sea fleas have no propellers and are moved by jets of water. They are equipped with two powerful deep-water cameras, which allow them to record views of marine landscapes that have never before been seen, let alone captured on film. The sea fleas are the revolutionary tool by means of which we have been able to cross "the second frontier" of the deep — a frontier which man, equipped only with scuba equipment, cannot cross otherwise. Some of our television films contain sequences shot aboard the sea fleas. They have already been helpful in revealing a few of the secrets of the deep.

According to the procedure we had worked out, the divers were in the water waiting for the Fleas to approach the surface. As soon as we were within sight, the divers attached slings to them so that the vehicles could be hoisted onto the rear deck of the *Calypso* almost as soon as they broke the surface of the water. Canoë and I were therefore in the wardroom almost immediately, comparing notes on the performance of the new saucers.

The next day, Falco went down with Flea No. 1. Laban was in contact with him through the sonar telephone. "Everything seems to be going well," Falco reported from time to time. At about nine hundred feet, however — after an hour in the water, which was a third of the time we had allotted for the test — Laban reported that communication with Falco had been broken off. The sonar was not working. It was possible that the Flea itself was not functioning and that the engines had stopped. There was nothing to do but rely upon Falco's good judgment and *sang froid*. Eight eternal minutes passed with not a sound from Falco. Then the Flea appeared on the surface to the starboard of the *Calypso*. Falco even had the presence of mind to perform the last test on the agenda: to release the inflatable belt that had been designed to keep the Flea afloat in a rough sea.

As we had suspected, the saucer's battery had discharged, so that the Flea had no power at all.

Anyone who has ever worked on the sea knows the law of the deep: if anything can go wrong, it will. If it is not the wind, or the current, or the waves, it must be a mechanical failure. And that, of course, is precisely why we have trial runs on all our equipment.

The motor was dismantled and, all night long, the engineers were at work analyzing and repairing what had gone wrong. At such moments, there is no distinction between divers and technicians, between "teams" and engineers. Everyone works for a common goal.

At dawn, both Fleas were ready to go down again. This time, Laban was in No. 1, and I was in No. 2. At 7:04 we began to work our way down the check list; and at 7:23 we began the descent. No incidents, and no problems. Everything was working perfectly. This was Laban's first time in a Flea, and he handled himself, and the new saucer, like a veteran.

Laban is one of the most complicated and hard to understand of the *Calypso's* regular crew. By training and profession, he is that most respectable of technicians — an engineer and a chemist. There was nothing in his background to make one believe that he was destined for the life of a wanderer over the seas of the earth. Nothing, that is, except a total dedication to the search for beauty and to its expression in artistic form. He plays the violoncello, paints, and dives. If he is enthusiastic about the Fleas, it is because he sees in them a platform from which to view scenes of extraordinary beauty and unearthly splendor.

Laban is as uncommunicative as he is dedicated. If he has something to say, he prefers to say it by means of music or painting. Like many of our companions aboard the *Calypso,* he is fond of solitude and of meditation. When someone speaks to him, he turns his shaven head and stares directly at his interlocutor. If he must answer, he does so, but briefly and softly, with gentle emphasis.

One day Laban picked up a stray dog and brought it aboard the *Calypso.* There was some speculation about which one of the two had adopted the other. There was a strange bond between that pair. They were entirely devoted to one another, and they shared a common outlook on life; but each considered himself and the other to be totally free. Pasha, as Laban called the dog, would come and go as it wished while we were in port. One day in Marseilles he strolled aboard a freighter about to sail for Tunis, and we thought we had seen the last of Pasha. But six months later Laban stepped off a ship in New York — and there was Pasha, waiting for him on the dock.

After the final testing of the Fleas, in which Canoë Kientzy and my son Philippe each handled one of the vehicles, we sailed for the Geyser Bank, off the northwest coast of the island of Madagascar. The sight of it was enchanting even before we dropped anchor. The varying colors of the water as we approached the coral reef were as rich as those of stained glass — bright green, changing to emerald hues above a stretch of sand, and the whole surrounded by the ink blue of the ocean.

We were in the water as soon as the anchor touched bottom. The water was shallow — one side of the Bank is at water level, while the other goes down to a depth of sixty-five feet or so — and spectacularly clear and clean. Farther out, the bottom continues on to greater depths in a series of cliffs, like a gigantic staircase. There were fish everywhere, especially mackerel more than three feet long and weighing at least thirty pounds. The fauna here were not timid; probably they had never been in contact with human beings before.

The Geyser Bank is uninhabited, and few vessels — even small boats — ever go there. The charts are imprecise concerning its whereabouts. Moreover, the madreporarian massifs make navigation hazardous — though not so hazardous, so far as we were concerned, as some of the reefs of the Red Sea. We discovered that our own chart was inaccurate concerning the Bank, showing it to be a whole mile from where it actually was.

I was fascinated by the place. It seemed made especially for us. Its surface is uninhabitable and without resources. There is not sufficient earth to grow even a single plant. Only a few projections of stone-hard coral break the surface. No one could possibly live here; no one, that is, except divers. Ships avoid the area as dangerous and hostile. Only we, it seems, know how the sea, in its depths, can be warm and welcoming, rich and beautiful. In those primeval waters, I feel that we have been compensated for all our efforts, and that our interminable explorations have been justified. No doubt, others will come after us. I hope they will take into account, and respect, the biological equilibrium of this maritime Eden. For I know from experience how delicate that balance is, and how easily it can be upset.

We sent out a small boat, with a diver, to circle around the Bank, while other divers went down to inspect the slanting bottom on the west side. They found innumerable groupers, and a large colony of sharks.

Up to then, the weather had been beautiful. But now the sky clouded over, the sea rose, and the wind began to howl. It seemed that only at the Glorious Isles were we able to find the kind of weather we wanted, and the kind of protected anchorage we needed, as well as beautiful and healthy coral reefs.

The end of the year was now almost upon us, and it was time for a large part of our crew to return to France. Five months at sea, especially for men with homes and families on dry land, is a long time. We therefore put into Diégo-Suarez, where we were met by my son Jean-Michel. Jean-Michel, throughout the course of this expedition, had the thankless job of finding and contracting for the *Calypso's* supplies and, in cooperation with Air Madagascar, of arranging whatever air transporta-

An illustration of the infinite diversity of life in tropical waters. To the left, the "bouquets" spread along the extremity of the stem are Hydrozoans. The little pink tufts are Coenopsammia. On the wall are encrusting algae and Madreporarians with porous skeletons.

tion we needed. He had diligently compiled a list of places and things he thought it would be interesting to film. It was through his efforts that the Fleas had finally reached us. And it was thanks to him that, on December 20, a large number of our friends were able to return to France for the holidays. Dr. Millet, for his part, decided to spend Christmas and New Year's in Réunion. The rest of us remained in port at Diégo-Suarez, waiting for the arrival of our new team.

It was while we were waiting at Diégo that there occurred what we refer to as the Boubouli episode.

Boubouli was a native of the Comores, a group of French islands to the northwest of Madagascar. Some time before, he had approached us and begged us so pitifully to be allowed to join the crew of the *Calypso* that we couldn't find it in our hearts to sail without him. We had therefore taken him on as a sort of handyman. The truth is that he was handy at very little; and whatever he did manage to do usually ended in catastrophe.

One Saturday, before going ashore in Diégo-Suarez, we asked Boubouli to adjust the tap in the shower. The water had been shooting out with such force, and in such quantities, that the deck was often flooded.

The next day, a Sunday, a group of government officials visited the *Calypso,* followed by the inevitable entourage of school children and curious natives. We were all on deck, extending the hospitality of the ship to our visitors, when a great shout came from below. René Le Bosco rushed up to inform me that I now had a foot of water in my cabin and in my office. "And," he said, "it's rising."

Boubouli had done his very best to fix the shower. He had cut off the water, adjusted the tap, and then turned the water on again. But he had neglected to close the tap in the shower.

There were only nine of us aboard at the time. Four of us stayed with our visitors, and five went below to try to repair the damage as discreetly as possible. They sponged, pumped and bailed, trying to stay out of sight, while the rest of us pretended that nothing unusual had happened. Our guests, for the most part, were polite enough to pretend along with us. All except for the children, who, in the midst of our scientific apparatus and technical explanations, amused themselves by speculating on how fast the crazy foreigners' ship was sinking.

On December 28, we took aboard our new crew and a new captain, Captain Roger Maritano. By December 31, we were celebrating New Year's Eve on the open sea, for which occasion the wardroom had been lavishly decorated with fish nets and sea shells. We happened, at the moment, to be directly over Leven's Bank, which is about one hundred feet below the surface. I decided to drop anchor. Everyone was agreed that we must start the new year with a dive. Bonnici and Sumian insisted on being the ones to go down, in the middle of the night, but in the anti-shark cage. When they returned, they were clutching a giant sea fan — which became, rather belatedly, our Christmas tree.

Our feasts and celebrations may seem a bit strange to those who live and work on dry land. They serve their purpose, however, in tightening the bonds of companionship and mutual understanding that hold us together aboard the *Calypso*. As I've already said, to me the most precious thing in our adventure on the sea is the light that is shed on human qualities. Every man of our team reveals what is best in himself; and the result is a marvelous diversity of temperament, character, and sentiment.

Just as not all our men came to us for the same reason, so, too, not all of us go about our work in the same way. Gaston does it with quiet humor, and makes us a present of an undersea oasis. Laban does it with heightened sensibility. And Delemotte, with an intuitive sense of what is most effective with marine animals.

There are others who hold a particular place aboard the *Calypso* and who contribute to the special *esprit* that reigns there. Among them are Jean-Paul Bassaget, Bernard Chauvellin, and Philippe Sirot. All three are divers, and all three are constantly animated by the desire to better themselves and to live more fully. They thrive on physical effort, and also on dangers, difficulties, and responsibility. For them, adventure is not merely a word, or a pretext to do whatever they wish. They live adventure, and in it they find the freedom that they need and, indeed, the meaning of their lives. Among our cameramen is Jacques Renoir (great-grandson of the famous painter Auguste Renoir), whose talent becomes more obvious with each film he makes. Moreover, he has added considerably to the joy of life aboard the *Calypso* by his personality and intelligence.

These are not the only ones, of course. It is a great happiness for me to think that many young men have overcome the disappointments and disillusionments of their early years and "found themselves" by means of a common effort, a common life, and common dangers, as members of the *Calypso's* team.

Many of those who come to us are sensitive men, men who have not found happiness or peace in leading an ordinary life. And that is what makes them valuable to us. I cannot help thinking that the men of the *Calypso* resemble, in many ways, those of Jules Verne's *Nautilus* — men who had been wounded by life on land, and who thereafter put their trust in the sea.

On New Year's Day we were again at the Glorious Isles, where we finished shooting the sequence of the triggerfish defending her eggs. There was one mishap: Raymond Coll, careful as he always is, was bitten by an outraged mother.

On January 5 and 6 we visited Bassas de India, which is a perfect atoll, a belt of coral that barely reaches the surface of the sea and is unmarred by a single coconut tree. It is simply a speck of emerald in the sea; a rather dangerous speck, for it has no buoys and is very badly shown on the charts.

I had thought that we could find a sheltered anchorage within the lagoon, and I sent boats ahead to scout out an easy passage. While waiting, Bonnici, Chauvellin, and I took one of the inflatable rafts along the reef. When the reconnaissance party returned, they reported that there was only one relatively safe passage into the lagoon, and even there a swell was running. Even if we were successful in entering through it, I was dubious that we would have an easy time when we tried to come out again.

Bassas de India is an old atoll, with only a few mounds of coral showing above the surface of the water. There is not a blade of grass, and not an open space large enough to pitch a tent. There are very few such atolls in the Red Sea or the Indian Ocean. Coral generally builds banks, or fringing reefs. And this atoll is in the process of dying.

Atolls can disappear in several ways. They always move vertically, ascending or descending. If they ascend, the coral above is killed by sunlight when it rises above the level of the water. It happens sometimes

An *Aliqueres centriquadrus*, a fish living in tropical waters, which belongs to a large family commonly found in the Mediterranean.

that the lagoon is gradually filled by coral, living or dead (as at the island of Europa, which we visited shortly afterward). In any case, it has always seemed to me that there must be a natural term to the multiplication of coral; there must be a point of saturation in the collective life of polyps.

Now, however, a new factor has come into play, which works havoc with nature's equilibrium and kills all coral indiscriminately. And that factor is pollution. Coral, as I have already said, can flourish

only in very pure water; and, I must repeat once more, the sea the world
over is now the garbage can for the detritus of human civilization. And
so, Bassas de India is disintegrating. We found enormous stretches of
dead coral in the water, indicating an advanced stage in the death struggle of an atoll.

It serves little purpose to describe once more these dead areas of the
sea, so similar to abandoned gardens filled with disintegrating bits and
pieces of form and color. Where once there was life, we now see only
fragments of limestone in the process of turning into gray sand. Now it
is impossible to find a single parasol of *Acropora* or the golden plume of
one sea fan. Even the shells of the dead mollusks are dull, and in the
early stages of dissolution. Everywhere we read the same message: a
world of wonders has been destroyed.

Until the present time, all Charles Darwin's observations and conclusions with respect to coral were valid. Henceforth, they have no
meaning, for an artificial instrument of death has abrogated the law of
the survival of the fittest.

People are less aware of, and less alarmed by, pollution of the sea than by pollution of the air or of the earth. It seems that the danger in the first case is less immediate. Such an attitude is easy to understand. Anyone can see the clouds of death that hang over our cities. The same holds true of the pollution of our rivers and streams and lakes. Anyone can see the trash and filth covering them, and the dead fish competing with industrial waste for a place to float on the surface of them. But few people have the opportunity to see the world of coral in the Indian Ocean or in the Pacific.

Our obligation, for all that, is absolute. We must bear witness to what we have seen; we must explain, to anyone who will listen, exactly what is happening to our seas; and we must hope that our message will hit home. Perhaps our strongest hope lies in the people of the United States. Americans are more familiar than Europeans with the beauties of coral. Measures have already been taken to protect the coral complexes of Florida from further damage, and an underwater preserve has been created, at Key Largo, which is similar in concept to that of the national parks of America. It comprises some eight thousand acres, and is situated about twenty-five miles from Miami. It was named after a famous biologist, John Pennekamp. That preserve, however, may well symbolize the complexity of the problem we face. For the moment, it is protected from damage; but how long can it be protected from pollution?

I am haunted constantly by the thought that so few people, up to now, have been able to come to know the world of coral. It has taken us almost twenty years to discover and to learn to appreciate the beauty of that world. And there are millions of men and women who do not even suspect the existence of that incredible wonderland of the tropical seas. It may be that our television films will awaken in them the desire to see for themselves these variegated corals, sea fans, giant clams, and sea stars. But what if they come too late? What if that world is poisoned, dies, and disappears, before these people have the opportunity and the joy to see it for themselves? What if the precarious equilibrium that exists among marine life forms is shattered before the scholars and researchers are able to study and understand the coral world? If this happens, it will have been the fault of our generation; and the generations to come will surely never forgive us.

Ideas spread slowly, and it is difficult to persuade man of the harm that he is doing. Consequently, he is causing pollution faster than he can become aware of it. It has long been clear to me that man is unwilling to admit that this ever-increasing pollution of the sea can be, and in the long run will be, extremely harmful to the rest of the world. We humans tend to think that our need to exist and to multiply is sufficient reason and justification for anything that we do; but surely it must be possible for us to live and to multiply without destroying what is good and beautiful in creation. All that is required is a minimum of understanding of what is involved, an abundance of good will, and great respect for life in all its forms. (And, I might add, a few international rules and regulations would do no harm.)

NINE

Cyclone

Battening down the Calypso.
*A crew is left on Europa Island with
swarming mosquitoes and attacking birds.
Two cyclones strike the* Calypso.

On January 9, after a brief stay at Mayotte, in the Comores, we were within sight of the island of Europa. For almost a month, we had been sailing in bad weather. The sea was rough and choppy, a moving mass of white-topped waves of gray, meeting a leaden sky. We had not expected otherwise, for this was the normal weather of the season in the Indian Ocean, and there was nothing to do but wait it out. There was little noticeable change from day to day; it got no better, but it got no worse. There was no indication of anything unusual in the air — or in the weather bulletins — and I was preoccupied with the possibility of finding good anchorage at Europa.

Europa is in the Mozambique Channel, about three hundred miles from the east coast of Africa. It is a small island, only some six miles in diameter — a measurement that includes a brackish and shallow lagoon and wide beaches of white sand. These beaches are a favored spot for the love-making and egg laying of sea turtles.[1] Our purpose at Europa, in fact, was to film the rendezvous of these amorous turtles, who weigh

[1] See Appendix IV. We had been told of Europa, as a mating site for turtles, by Jacques Stevens, a diver and cameraman who had already shot a film there.

Cyclone Flossie is near, and the *Calypso* is badly shaken up. We try to reestablish communications with our crewmen on the island of Europa, who are short of food and equipment.

as much as 450 pounds and who come from as far away as Mozambique, Madagascar, and even from the Gulf of Aden. Some of them swim as much as a thousand miles to participate in the activities at Europa.

Europa, in addition, is a weather-watch station, with four men permanently assigned there. Their job is to keep watch for cyclones. Like their associates on the Glorious Isles, all four are natives of Réunion; for Europa is a French possession administered from Réunion. Their life is unusually austere, for everything that they need must be brought – at considerable expense – from Réunion. Europa itself has no resources beyond a few coconut palms, some frigate birds, and a few black goats whose ancestors escaped from their human masters and reverted to the wild. These is scarcely any vegetation to speak of, and no fresh water at all. Europa is, in a word, a bleak and sterile bit of coral. It is also the site of one of the Indian Ocean's innumerable cemeteries.

Shortly after dropping anchor, we sent ashore a landing party comprising Falco, Coll, Dr. Millet, and Pierre Goupil. They radioed us almost immediately that the weather-station attendants had told them a cyclone was imminent: Cyclone Flossie.

Moreover, they added, there had been still another unpleasant surprise on Europa, in the form of swarms of mosquitoes so bloodthirsty that the men who had stayed on the beach had had to bury themselves in the sand to escape being eaten alive.

There was one spot of good news along with the bad; there were indeed sea turtles. A good number of them had already arrived and were in the shallows around the island. In fact, the mating had already begun.[2] We therefore decided to begin shooting as soon as possible.

Before devoting ourselves to the turtles, however, we had to take precautions against the turn of events in the weather. (The meteorological station now told us that there was not one cyclone approaching, but two: Flossie and Georgette.) The first thing to do was to lighten the *Calypso,* which was heavily loaded. Flea No. 1 was put into the hold.

[2]The sequence of events in this phenomenon is rather mixed. At this time of the year at Europa, there are some males and females mating, some females laying eggs, and some young turtles already hatching after incubating in the sand. We were therefore in the enviable position of being able to film any sequence that we wanted, from the mating cycle through the birth of the baby turtles.

Flea No. 2 was loaded with pig-iron ballast and made ready to be put into shallow water, if need be. The Galeazzi tower had its electric circuitry removed, and it, too, was prepared to be lowered into the water, from which it would be retrieved, along with Flea No. 2, after the cyclone.

Meanwhile, one of our cameramen, Lionel Legros, spent part of the night under water, filming turtles in the shallows of Europa. By the time he had finished and climbed up on the beach, however, the wind was beginning to rise; and only a few minutes later it turned into a furious gale accompanied by rain. Our men's camp was turned upside down. The tent collapsed, and equipment was scattered about. The only solution was to bury everything in the sand, as the wind howled and the rain fell and one great wave after another broke against the beach. In the light of the moon, which appeared from time to time among the clouds, the sea appeared extraordinarily high, and there were swollen clouds low above the water.

As though they were not being sufficiently punished by the wind and water, a new trial broke upon the heads of our four Jobs. Like the victims of some Hitchcock melodrama, they were suddenly attacked, for no apparent reason, by an enormous flock of birds. Perhaps the creatures had been aroused by the coming cyclone. In any case, they threw themselves upon our team with wing, beak, and claw; then, rising together high into the air, they attacked again with renewed determination, uttering shrieks of rage or terror. The men attempted to fight them off with pieces of driftwood but had little success; and soon they were too exhausted to do more than cover their eyes and hope for the best. It was a nightmare scene, played to the accompaniment of the crashing surf and screeching wind. Then, as suddenly as they had come, the birds were gone. An epic gust of wind swept them violently into the interior of the island. The ensuing semi-silence was eerie, almost threatening; but the birds did not return. The men of the *Calypso* had had their fill of excitement for the night.

Early the next morning, Falco, Coll, and their companions radioed that, since the weather made it impossible for them to remain on the island, they would return to the *Calypso*. They proposed to circle along the interior of the reef toward the north, and to rejoin the ship by crossing the bar in the inflatable raft.

Our small boats in the water, trying to get through the waves breaking on Europa's coral reefs.

Dawn had not yet broken, but I could see the white foam on the waves at the passage through the reef. It seemed to me to be dangerous to try to cross in darkness, particularly in such a rough sea, and I persuaded them to wait for daylight. Finally, around five o'clock, I told them that they could chance it, if they still wished to do so.

Into the raft they loaded their cameras, food supplies, film, tent, and diving equipment, and began looking for the passage through the reef. Aboard the *Calypso*, we held our breath as the raft, dwarfed by the white-flecked waves, bobbed about like a cork. They found the passage. Then, by a miraculous combination of luck and good judgment — and a

(Above) The *Bombard*, hauled to shore with a line, has managed to get through the breakers.

The *Bombard*, entirely closed over, brings aboard our nonswimming Canadian cameraman.

momentary break in the waves — they shot like an arrow through the narrow opening. A spattering of applause greeted them as they climbed aboard the *Calypso*.

A short time later, there was a period of relative calm, and I decided to take advantage of it to send another team ashore. There was no telling how long it would be before another such opportunity would present itself; and the longer we waited, the greater was the risk that we would miss the scenes that we had come so far to film. And so, Falco, Naguy, Goupil, Laban, Coll, and Bonnici took to the raft again, and succeeded in making it safely through the passage. To keep the weight of the raft to a minimum, however, we had had to send them off without food or equipment, with the understanding that, if the weather held, one of the men would return later for supplies. In the middle of the afternoon, therefore, Bonnici returned, reported that newborn turtles were beginning to emerge from the sand, took aboard the raft as much in the line of food and equipment as he could carry, and left immediately for the island. By now, however, the weather had worsened again, and the sea was becoming increasingly treacherous. The light raft was tossed about until it came dangerously close to the reef. One particularly violent wave dashed the outboard motor against a protrusion and tore it off. It sank to the bottom in the shallow water of the level reef, from which Bonnici was able to retrieve it — with considerable damage to his hands from the coral. The situation, nonetheless, was desperate. Aboard the *Calypso*, we concluded that Bonnici would never be able to get out of it by himself. To make matters worse, it could be only a short time before his relatively fragile boat would be torn apart either by the sharp coral or by the increasingly violent sea.

The only solution was to send out another boat. The decision had no sooner been made than Chauvellin and Maurice Léandri were in the water. We watched anxiously as they made their way toward the passage. Just as they were about to enter it, however, a giant wave took their boat and tossed it violently onto the reef. Somehow, Léandri succeeded in freeing it and getting it into the open water again. Now Chauvellin climbed into the water with a towline, and swam through the coral toward the bar. When he had reached the latter point, he stopped swimming and allowed the waves to carry him toward the beach. Falco was by now in the water, and managed to grab hold of Chauvellin as he was swept past, and the pair of them made their way, by holding on to the coral, to Bonnici's boat. The line now connected the two boats, and Léandri began pulling Bonnici's raft — which was already full of water — toward him. At that moment, two giant waves broke, one after the other, over the men and their boats. For what seemed an eternity, everything was hidden by the sea. Then they reappeared, still moving slowly along. Léandri's outboard motor had not even been flooded, and he took advantage of a short period of calm to bring his own boat, and Bonnici's, safely back alongside the *Calypso*.

Such actions demonstrate the qualities of the men of the *Calypso*. I am convinced that few seamen or divers could have survived, without casualties, in the circumstances that we experienced, and would experience, before Flossie and Georgette were over.

I have already spoken of Falco, Chauvellin, and Bonnici; but I would like to say a word about Maurice Léandri, whose competence and coolness on this occasion saved the day. We are particularly proud of Maurice because he is something of an adoptive child of the *Calypso*. His older brother, Octave — whom we call "Titi" — was the *Calypso's* first mechanic, and it was Octave who brought Maurice aboard when the latter was hardly more than an adolescent. Maurice then trained under Captain François Saout, who commanded the *Calypso* for several years and who was a remarkable educator as well as an expert in matters maritime. No doubt it was that long — and sometimes rough — period of apprenticeship that had enabled Maurice to perform as he did on this occasion.

Although Maurice, Bonnici, and Chauvellin were now safely aboard the *Calypso*, there was still a part of our team on the island. That night, the weather was so fierce that they were obliged to ask for shelter at the weather station.

By now, we realized that the time had come to prepare ourselves for the worst. The wind seemed to be increasing in velocity with every passing hour and had shifted to the north. Our position had become impossible to maintain, and I decided to change anchorage. We proceeded at low speed in search of a more sheltered — or less exposed — location. Europa, however, being flat and round, offered no such shelter, and there seemed to be no relatively safe anchorage in the area. Meanwhile, the wind seemed to be changing direction from one moment to the next,

Launching a small craft in a rough sea — a difficult job.

(Left) The *Calypso* struggles against the approaching cyclone.

and, moving slowly, we tried to turn with it as the *Calypso* tossed and turned and shivered.

It was now impossible to keep the *Calypso* on course around Europa. I therefore decided on a rather desperate solution. We would pull away from the island and try to maneuver in such a way as to get behind the "front" of the cyclone, where there is usually a semicircular area of relative calm. Our only guide, of course, was the information we could gather from periodic weather bulletins received on our radio.

As we headed away from Europa into deeper water, the color of the sea became indefinable. It was not metallic, nor yellow. Instead, the air and the water seemed to melt together into a substance like thick fog. The angle of the waves was such as I had never seen before and have never seen since. Although they were not particularly high — twelve to fifteen feet — their insides were practically vertical. It was as though the *Calypso* were smashing against one stone wall after another, and I decided that we could not continue to subject her to such punishment for very long without running the risk of serious damage. We therefore turned and headed back toward Europa.

On January 21, back at Europa, we found it impossible to hold a position. With the anchor scraping along the bottom, it was all we could do to use the *Calypso's* engines to keep ourselves from drifting away at the mercy of the sea.

Our main problem, however, was not the sea, but that of getting supplies to our men on Europa. After much discussion, we brought out the smallest of our boats and filled it with food and water. Then, using a procedure that had already been tried and found successful, we attached a line to a rocket and fired the rocket onto the beach. At our end, the line was attached, in turn, to a heavy nylon rope; and the rope, of course, was tied to the supply boat. The men ashore then hauled the boat toward the beach. There was no necessity for a passenger, and the boat could go over the reef instead of through the passage.

The operation was successful, but the waves had gotten so violent that we had to stop after the first boatload. It might be possible the next day, we thought, to send ashore the heavy equipment.

On January 22, the weather station warned us that Flossie was heading directly for us. It seemed best not to remain in the vicinity of

Maurice Léandri (on the left) and Dominique Sumian.

Europa, but before heading out once again, it was necessary for us to leave more supplies for our men on the island. Once more we used the small boat, as we had on the previous day, to transport food and water, and some equipment for filming and recording. All in all, five trips were made without mishap. We even sent across a container of gasoline by floating it through the waves. On the last crossing we had to figure out a way to send a plexiglass dome, which was to be used in filming the birth of the turtles. It was too large to fit into the boat, and we had to tie it across the beam. It took Chauvellin and Bonnici a half hour to get it in position and fastened; and then the wind ripped it off. They tried again, this time successfully — but at the price of having their hands cut almost to ribbons by the dome's sharp edges.

Flossie had now passed. Despite the violence of the weather in the vicinity of Europa, we had been spared the worst of the cyclone. There was still Flossie's sister, Georgette, to contend with; but, according to all reports, the danger seemed remote, for that cyclone had bypassed us

Albert Falco in the midst of the breakers, trying to haul one of our craft ashore.

and was heading for the African coast. As it turned out, Georgette did indeed hit the coast, leaving twenty-three dead; and then, on January 23, she turned around and, to the astonishment of our local meteorological experts, made straight for Europa. The sea once again boiled furiously around us, the sky was of an incredible blackness, and the wind was an incessant tempest of sound.

It was obviously impossible to remove our team from the island at this point. We radioed them: "Bury yourselves in the sand and wait it out. We are going to try to reach Tuléar and find a protected anchorage."

But it was not to be that easy. I had no sooner started up the engines of the *Calypso* than the starboard propeller shaft broke.

Our prospects were not very bright. The sea was rough in a wind of thirty-five knots. And yet, if we wanted to be able at least to maneuver in the storm, someone would have to go down and disengage the broken shaft, for the starboard propeller and the end of the broken shaft were jammed against the rudder. If the propeller shaft could be replaced, then perhaps we could make Tuléar on a single engine.

Chauvellin, Bonnici, and Falco manage to establish a communications route on a level reef where large waves are breaking. The cyclone becomes even more threatening.

We immediately set about the job, installing a double pulley, with steel cables, on the after deck of the *Calypso*. The cable was lowered and fastened around the shaft, and the shaft was then disengaged and put back into place. It was not a very complicated operation in itself; but with conditions as they were, the stern of the *Calypso* was rising and falling precipitously the whole while, and the divers had to tie themselves to the shaft and the ship itself, and duplicate all its movements as they worked. Even so, they were sometimes brutally pounded against the *Calypso's* hull. Coll, Bonnici, and Chauvellin were at it from 11:15A.M. until 1:30P.M. — a feat that is memorialized by a television film I had made of the whole operation.

Finally, in midafternoon, we left for Tuléar. On one engine, our speed was six knots — which was roughly the traveling speed of Georgette, which was behind us. With an enormous sense of relief, we limped into Tuléar with Georgette still slightly in the rear.

There was no question, of course, of finding a replacement at Tuléar for our broken shaft. I was anxious, however, at least to be rid of the useless propeller, which seemed to be acting as a brake. As soon as the *Calypso* was moored in the Tuléar harbor, therefore, everyone went down, in an attempt to remove the starboard propeller. Bonnici, Coll, René Jaubert and René Le Bosco worked like demons, but they were unable to succeed.

And then Georgette was upon us.

She came so suddenly that the *Calypso* had to pull out to a more secure anchorage, leaving part of her crew ashore. I had worked out an anchorage plan, however, which held us solidly despite the ferocity of the wind and the sea. We used two anchors, one large and one small. The smaller was placed in front of the larger and attached to it. This procedure — known as "backing" — worked, and prevented drifting, by the expedient, as it were, of anchoring the anchor.

On January 27 the wind was at seventy knots, and it contained so much water that it acted almost as a solid object, stripping paint from the hull and superstructures of the ship and ripping off the radio antenna.

In the port itself, the barges (which are used for loading and unloading freighters) broke their lines and were swept out into the open sea — a couple of them barely missing the *Calypso* in the process.

My son Jean-Michel had gone ashore for supplies as soon as we had docked at Tuléar, and he had been left there when we were forced to leave the harbor. He was a witness to the damage caused by the cyclone. Tiles, torn from the roofs of houses, swept murderously through the streets. The inhabitants, however, did not become frightened until they saw the coconut palms of the city beginning to break. A coconut tree can literally be bent level with the ground without breaking. When they begin breaking, therefore, it is an indication of a meteorological catastrophe.

The streets were entirely flooded, and automobiles everywhere were inundated. High-tension wires fell into the streets, and many people were electrocuted. All communications with Tananarive, the capital of the island, were out, and there was no telephone service at all. (Jean-Michel, however, was able to communicate with us by walkie-talkie.)

The captain of the port, an old friend named Michel Appert, was untiring in his efforts to keep damage at a minimum. He even went out in a small launch and succeeded in freeing the barges which, under the action of the sea, were beginning to demolish the jetty.

On January 28, the worst seemed over. The wind was down to thirty-eight knots and the weather seemed less ominous. We therefore made for Europa as expeditiously as possible, with one propeller useless. On arriving there, we learned that winds of one hundred knots had been clocked. The weather station's anemometer had been jammed. Coconut trees had been broken in two, and the black goats had been picked up like leaves and tossed about in the air. We saw them — at least the lucky ones — all over the island, stunned, staring blankly at the devastation about them.

For almost forty years now, I have lived on the ocean. I have dedicated myself to the sea, and wholly consecrated myself to it. I have explored depths that, until then, were unknown. I have had good days and bad days. I have dived in waters of incredible transparency, and I have experienced the violence of waves like those at Europa, which tore the *Calypso* from its anchorage and battered its aging carcass with elemental fury. But, despite all the dangers, all the fatigue, all the sacrifices, I have never regretted the choice I made. The sea, in the final account, always brought me more joy than pain. And that was true in this case also; for I had the pleasure of seeing us all together again — our entire team, gathered under a blue sky, on a blue sea. Once more, the sea had refused to exact a price for our audacity and our curiosity; and once more I was grateful to her for her generosity.

There is a saying in French: *fortune de mer*. In English, we might say, "the luck of the sea"; but in French it has a much broader meaning. It means the dangers of the sea, and its whims and even its treachery; but above all it means, quite literally, "fortune" — the interior wealth which a seaman must learn to deserve. And our fortune is the common good of our whole team.

During the days of the hurricane, we had been witnesses to one of the great dramas of the sea, and to one of the traditional dangers of life at sea. We had been compelled, like seamen everywhere since man launched his first ship, to fight for our lives against the fury of the ocean. It was an adventure, and a classic one.

I should add that, as seamen, we are different from those who have preceded us. Storms and calms control not only our lives *on* the sea, but also our lives *in* the sea. We have much more to learn in the sea than on it, and ours is a three-dimensional world of water. From that standpoint, we are a new race of seamen. We must learn to take care of ourselves among the waves and winds on the surface, as mariners have always done, but also in the darkness and among the dangers beneath the surface of the water. To us, the complete seaman is the one who is perfectly at home both on and under the surface. And I think the time is near when no one will be able to call himself a seaman unless he is both.

TEN

Deepwater Dives
Into the Ocean's Past

Finding the ancient sea level, marked by coral.
Diving deep.
The Galeazzi tower.

Despite the interruption of cyclones Flossie and Georgette, our film on the turtles was well under way. Falco and his team had been marooned on Europa for ten days, and, the weather notwithstanding, they had been able to do a good deal of work.

Now that the sea was back to normal around Europa, I took the opportunity to verify a hypothesis that we had formulated several years previously and that, in my opinion, had been corroborated in the course of the present expedition.

In 1963, while diving in our saucer in the Red Sea, the Gulf of Aden, the Indian Ocean, and the Gulf of Oman, we had taken note, at a depth of between 350 and 375 feet, of a so-called *Lithothamnion* walk or pathway. This walk was almost continuous and formed a porchlike overhang at the top of the vertical undersea cliff.

We could not help speculating at the time that this phenomenon marked a fossil level of the oceans, one that probably coincided with an ice age during which the level of the water was lowered. According to that theory, the level of the Red Sea and of the Indian Ocean would have been at one time about 350 feet lower than it is now.

In the course of our more recent dives in the Indian Ocean — especially in the Maldives and at Europa — we turned up evidence that proved, at least to our satisfaction, that that water level had actually existed. What we saw, in those instances, was not merely a walk or a porch, but a veritable underwater seashore. There was a sandbank sloping gently to the foot of a vertical cliff. The cliff itself was riddled with numerous grottoes — all of which opened in the direction of the dominant swell. From this, we concluded that they had been dug, or excavated, by the waves.

These grottoes were sometimes small and sometimes large. We had explored one that was fifty feet deep on Powell Island, in the Maldives, from the ceiling of which we took a splinter for analysis in order to determine the approximate date of the nearby coral formations. That date, we decided, would correspond to the time at which the fossil level began to be submerged by the rising waters.

Jacques Stevens, the diver and film maker who had told us about the turtles of Europa, had also mentioned a particular grotto there that had a ceiling at least 175 feet high. Since we wanted to explore the cliff about one hundred feet below the level of the grotto, as well as the grotto itself, it was necessary for us to make what we call a helium dive. That is, we filled our tanks with a mixture of 50 per cent pure helium and 50 per cent air. The purpose of this procedure is to avoid that peculiar state, which is an occupational hazard of all divers, called rapture of the depths.[1]

This phenomenon is due at least in part to the entry of nitrogen, under pressure, into the blood. The effect is a physiological malfunction to which even the most experienced among us are subject once we pass a depth of, say, 160 feet. (The depth varies, however, according to the individual diver.) The most common symptom is a euphoria, similar to alchoholic inebriation or to the effect of certain drugs, which renders the diver oblivious to his own limitations and those of his equipment.

The addition of helium to one's air does not eliminate the danger altogether, but replacing some of the nitrogen in one's breathing mixture with helium makes it possible to go considerably deeper — to about three hundred feet — before "rapture" begins to take hold.

On this occasion, therefore, the use of helium would allow us to retain perfect clarity of vision and of judgment during the dive to the grotto and below. On the other hand, it would make it necessary for us to spend a longer period of time in decompression — that is, in a gradual return to the atmospheric pressure on the surface. The time necessary

See Appendix I.

for complete decompression, in this case, was one hour and forty minutes.

Divers normally use a decompression chamber to achieve the desired results, and, on the *Calypso,* the Galeazzi tower serves this purpose. It is lowered to a depth beyond eighty feet. Air is supplied from the surface by means of a large pipe, and the divers enter through a hatch in the bottom of the tower.

On this occasion, we used a team of seasoned divers, for the first deepwater dive requires particular care. They suited up on the after deck of the *Calypso*: Falco, who had had much experience with such dives; Coll, who began diving when he was sixteen; Bonnici, who had proved his expertness on innumerable occasions; and Deloire, our cameraman, for I wanted the entire dive to be filmed. Everyone was calm and smiling.

The *Calypso,* happily, is fully equipped for deepwater dives. We have large triple air tanks, for such dives require more gas than usual. These tanks — which are actually three tanks bound together — are quite heavy; so much so that it was necessary to offset their weight by adding sections of rubber-covered cork. Le Bosco, Chauvellin, and Bassaget had to help their friends to strap on these tanks; they were too much for one man to handle alone.

Deepwater dives require careful preparation and special (and expensive) equipment, but they are well worth the trouble. This is particularly true when the purpose of the dives is scientific observation. Diving saucers and remote-controlled devices and automatic cameras are all very well; but only man can see, touch, judge, and understand. Man is the witness par excellence, in the sea as well as on land.

It was also necessary to anchor several buoys before starting, so that the stem of the *Calypso* would be steadied on the edge of the reef and the stern would be away from the submerged drop parallel to which the divers would descend. Once the ship was in place, we let down the Galeazzi tower, which was to serve as a decompression chamber, to a depth of ninety feet.

Our preparations were complete, and there was nothing visibly amiss. And yet, I could not rid myself of a feeling of anxiety. Even though I had directed every step of the preliminary work myself, and even though I had complete confidence in every member of the diving

On a shining sea, the island of Europa, seen from the air, looks like a marvelous ring of coral.

(Right) Falco using the underwater telephone to maintain contact with the Galeazzi tower and with our deep-sea divers.

(Below) The launching of the Galeazzi tower. The tower serves as a decompression chamber for our divers as they come up.

team, I knew that I would never be really at peace so long as my friends were down there, working 350 feet below the surface. I know from experience what a diver goes through once he goes beyond two hundred feet — the cold, the overwhelming sense of isolation even in the midst of his companions. He is walled in by silence and haunted by the fear that, if anything should happen, he will not be able to make himself understood to those around him. The surface seems far away; and if, despite all our equipment and all our precautions, there should be a mechanical failure, the pressure at that depth would crush a man.

The divers were now getting into the water. Since they were breathing a mixture of helium and air, they had to go down very quickly. At the surface, the breathing of that comparatively rich mixture results in underoxygenation. It is not until a diver reaches a depth of thirty-five feet that he begins getting a normal amount of oxygen. At ninety feet, the team passed the Galeazzi tower. At that point, a second team went down. These divers were equipped with ordinary diving gear, and they went no deeper than the tower. Their function was to remain at that level so that help would be readily available, if needed, when the first team arrived at the decompression chamber during their ascent.

By then, the deepwater team had reached the grotto and were beginning the filming. This is not an easy operation. The divers and the cameraman must be able to maneuver easily while handling floodlights (which work from cables running up to the *Calypso*); and they must be able, at the same time, to take samples of anything interesting for further study at a laboratory specializing in the measurement of feeble radioactivity.

So far as the actual filming was concerned, the project had been planned in detail by the cameraman and the divers beforehand. Moreover, they are all so accustomed to working together that they co-ordinate every movement almost instinctively.

In these dives, the cameraman goes first — Deloire in this case. He was followed by Bonnici. who was carrying twin floods of 1000 watts each; and then by Coll, who was to be the "subject" of the film on this occasion. Above them, at the level of the tower, Sumian and several other divers were lowering the electrical cables from which the lights worked. And, on the surface, more divers were ready to go down if they were needed for any reason. In all, twelve men were immediately involved in the filming project.

Deloire, as lead man, was the first to enter the grotto, so that he might film the others, as they came in, from a vantage point in the rear of the grotto. The divers must learn to sense where the camera is, and they must move in such a way as to remain as much as possible within camera range. The area in which they can move about is therefore narrowly circumscribed — a factor that is complicated by the presence of electrical cables everywhere and by the fact that visibility is very poor — particularly in a grotto, which is actually a shallow cave.

In every deepwater dive, caution is the order of the day, for at such depths the least false move can result in disaster. But in this case, as in so many others, the results were well worth the effort. The film disclosed that the walls of the grotto, bathed in the light of the floods, were covered with blue sponges, brilliantly colored algae, bryozoons, hydrozoons, and red and yellow sea fans.[2] Deloire, by lying on the floor of the grotto, was able to capture an extraordinarily beautiful scene of the vaulted entrance outlined against the water outside. A lilac-colored alcyonium was on the ceiling in exactly the right place to turn the scene into a study in perfect composition. Such opportunities, and such scenes, can be found only in the sea, and only in deep water; they are wholly alien to conditions on the surface.

The diving team carried out the scientific part of their mission as they were filming. There, at a depth of almost two hundred feet, they observed exactly the same morphological and geological characteristics we had already seen in the grottoes of the Maldives. This was of some significance, for it lent support to our theory regarding a fossil level in the Indian Ocean. Europa and the Maldives are a considerable distance from one another, and the team's observations enabled us to surmise that the change in water level, which formed the basis of our hypothesis, occurred throughout the whole of the Indian Ocean.

In any event, there is incontestable evidence of the existence of that earlier, lower level in this grotto — evidence that, hundreds of thousands of years ago, when the atoll was still young, the surface of the water was here, at the level of this grotto; and that at one time the area that is now so far below the surface was covered with living madreporarians, their tentacles waving, their mouths devouring their prey. Now, at the present depth, they are all dead; our divers removed and brought back several remnants of their skeletons from the ancient wall of the grotto.

[2] Madreporarian corals, which are ubiquitous elsewhere, do not exist at these depths.

Our deep-sea divers are helped by their friends, in ordinary diving gear, in removing their heavy equipment. Then they enter the Galeazzi tower. The net bag contains specimens of coral found in deep water. Decompression time on the *Calypso* will be an hour and forty minutes.

(Facing) Alcyonarian formations, sea fans, and black coral at the entry of the grotto.

After filming and inspecting the grotto itself, the team moved downward, with the camera still in action, to the foot of the cliff, at a depth of some 350 feet. Then the sequence was finished. It was a few minutes after eleven in the morning; and now the ascent began.

I knew, of course, that we had taken all possible precautions. Yet, it is during the ascent after a deepwater dive that I am most on edge. There are things over which we have little control. A cable might break, or a valve go wrong, endangering the lives of the four men for whose safety I am responsible.

The divers reached the Galeazzi tower without incident, and the first part of the ascent was over. The operation was still delicate. The interior of the tower is so small that divers cannot enter while wearing the large helium bottles. The divers stationed around the tower — they wear suits of bright yellow, so that they may be seen easily — must remove the deepwater divers' equipment. The bottles are then placed in special cradles on the exterior wall of the tower. The divers take a last gulp of the air-helium mixture, release their mouthpieces, and swim to the entrance of the decompression chamber. Once inside, they close the interior and exterior hatches. One of the divers — Falco, in this instance — adjusts a valve designed to maintain pressure at the level necessary for gradual decompression. When that is done, the divers signal, by telephone, that the hatches are closed and that pressure has been adjusted. Then the tower — which weighs four thousand pounds — is hoisted onto the after deck of the *Calypso*. The worst is over, and I begin to breathe more easily.

Falco and his friends remained in the decompression chamber for one hour and forty minutes, during the last half hour of which they breathed pure oxygen in order to rid their systems of any helium or nitrogen they might have absorbed. The whole procedure is carried out under the supervision of the ship's medical officer.

Falco, Bonnici, Coll, and Deloire all emerged in fine shape and in good spirits. We, and they, were ready to begin again the next day.

The chief problem in the project was the result of our intention of filming the entire dive. We had to spend several days filming numerous continuity sequences and scenes that we could not film during the actual dives for fear of compromising the safety of the divers: the entry into the tower and the process of decompression, for example.

The job was further complicated when, on February 3, the anchorage of the *Calypso's* prow slipped. We had to take time to put the ship back in its proper position relative to the underwater cliff, and to work out a new system of secure anchorage. Then we went back to diving, so as to familiarize as many of our divers as possible with the helium technique and with the use of the Galeazzi tower — and to gather more specimens of deepwater sedentary animals.

The whole day of February 5 was spent shooting scenes with the tower. On the sixth, we took a last deepwater helium dive with our cinematographic equipment. And on the evening of the seventh, after an exhausting day, we hoisted the tower aboard and loaded it into the hold. Operation Deep Water was over.

We now had aboard the *Calypso* several pounds of carefully labeled specimens from the grotto, from the wall of the cliff at various depths, and from the ancient "walk" that marked what we believed was the fossil level. Everything was carefully put away to be examined later by specialists. Such objects are, in our opinion, as valuable and as interesting as rocks from the moon.

Perhaps that seems an exaggeration. But not to me. The study of the living animals of the reef has always fascinated me; but it is dead coral that really fires my imagination as we attempt to piece together the physical life of the atoll and its history. It is possible that our specimens — and the specimens taken from sea bottoms all over the world — will make it possible for scientists to decipher the secrets that coral has preserved for millions of years. Our fondest hope in our work is to be able to contribute to an understanding of the origins of the earth.

On the occasion of this dive, our team found, at the base of the reef, traces of the life forms that built these walls. The massif itself grew as the tiny polyps formed their skeletons from the lime of the water. Countless generations of coral were born and died, piling up one atop the other, according to nature's intricate blueprint. The reef that they began is still living, and it is still growing. On its walls, and in the grotto, one can read the story of the complex relationships that existed between its flora and its fauna when cave men still walked the earth.

I dream of the day when man will be enabled, by new techniques, to dive to even greater depths without having to make use of equipment as delicate and as cumbersome as that which we use today. When that time comes, we will discover secrets that now are beyond our imaginations. We, at least, have the consolation of knowing that we are blazing the trail, that we are showing that the ocean depths can be explored.

It was not quite twenty-five years ago that my friends and I made our first dive to 150 feet and 175 feet. At that time, we did not even know the laws of physiology governing the survival of man in the water. And what a lot we had to learn! But twenty-five years is very little when

(Above) This fish (a Platax) developed an attachment for our divers and would not go away. He followed them throughout their descent and was interested in all they did.

(Facing) Descending along the face of the cliff for about three hundred feet, our divers discovered, and photographed, a wealth of animal life.

it is a question of opening up a world that had been closed to man for millennia. Today, we are much better informed and much better equipped. By the time this book is published, it will no doubt have been discovered that man can dive to a depth of two thousand feet. And, in another twenty-five years, we will have succeeded in going down ten times deeper than that.

ELEVEN

Island of the Absurd
The "demolition area."
Egg-laying rites of the turtles on Europa.
Massacre of the baby turtles
by frigate birds and crows.
A note on conservation of the turtle.
First phase of the Calypso's *expedition completed.*

The exigencies of our deepwater dives and the handling of the Galeazzi tower had exhausted everyone aboard the *Calypso*. We needed relaxation and a period of relative inactivity. Europa, however, is not a place to which one goes for a restful vacation. It is cursed — cursed with a plague of mosquitoes.

During the cyclone, the plague had vanished. Now the mosquitoes assembled again in force. On one occasion, Dr. Millet went ashore with Zoom. We were supposed to pick them up later in the day; but, somehow, no one remembered. The doctor and the dog were left standing on the beach for two hours. Zoom, every few minutes, would run into the shade of the underbrush — and then immediately run out, almost invisible under a coat of mosquitoes. By the time we remembered to send a boat for the unhappy pair, they had both been horribly bitten.

The mosquitoes by themselves might have been made bearable by the single expedient of staying away from the island. But the water around Europa also had a curse of its own, although a less irksome one: jellyfish, tiny Portuguese men-of-war whose sting produced an anaphylactic reaction among our divers. Laban, particularly, was badly stung, and his lips were grotesquely swollen and very painful for several days.

The accident had occurred in the course of a dive that began well, but could have ended in tragedy. Laban and Philippe Sirot had gone down in the open water not far off Europa. The sea was rather rough that day, and the runabout that accompanied them lost track of the two divers: the waves were so high that they obliterated all traces of their air bubbles. Delemotte, who was aboard the runabout, became alarmed and notified the *Calypso* of the situation by radio. Laban and Sirot, unfortunately, were not wearing the new diving suits, which are equipped with underwater telephones, and there was no way to make contact with them.

Meanwhile, the two men had surfaced a good distance away from the *Calypso*. Because of the waves, they could not see Delemotte or his boat, and Delemotte could not see them. To make matters worse, a strong current began dragging them out into the open sea. Laban and Sirot were both too experienced to waste their strength in trying to break

(Facing) Turtles showed not the slightest sign of fear in the presence of our divers. Some of them are huge, weighing well over two hundred pounds and only seldom going up to breathe.

There is no evidence of any aggressiveness on the part of a turtle with respect to man. We were able to touch them, and even to handle them, with no difficulty, but they refused to eat.

We attached kytoons (marker balloons) to the shells of several turtles so that we might follow their movements after they had laid their eggs. Some come back for further egg laying.

free of the current. They simply relaxed and allowed themselves to be carried along. Laban had with him an underwater camera with a flash attachment, for which he had a few flash bulbs remaining. He shot off the bulbs one after the other, and then, holding the camera as high as he could, he began flashing signals by catching the sunlight in the reflector.

As soon as we heard that Delemotte had lost sight of the two divers, everyone about the *Calypso* dropped whatever he was doing and began to scrutinize the surface for a sign of the pair. Even with field glasses, however, two men are hard to find in the open sea, particularly when the water is rough. It was a half hour before they were sighted, by Jean-Paul Bassaget. A boat was dispatched immediately to pick them up — but not before Laban had been stung by several jellyfish. Sirot was stung, too, but not as badly. The flashbulbs, it seemed, had attracted the jellyfish to Laban. Neither man seemed particularly upset, or otherwise moved, by the adventure.

Despite the jellyfish, and despite the occasional roughness of the sea, the water seemed preferable to Europa's mosquitoes, and it was decided that we would spend a few days of relaxation in observing the sea turtles and in diving.

During one of those dives, Chauvellin, Jaubert, Deloire, and Coll were filming the turtles when they discovered an area that they immediately named the "demolition area." It was a relatively large field of dead coral. Even worse, there seemed to be little, if any, fauna of any kind in the area. Not a sea fan; not a fish. As far as they could see from any one spot, it was a field of grayish, dead coral. The reason for death on such a scale remains a mystery. Like Bassas de India, Europa is an old atoll, and it is undergoing a process of decomposition. It is no longer even an atoll in the proper sense. The lagoon is enclosed and filled with brackish water. And the transformation seems to continue at a rate almost perceptible to the human eye. In the water around Europa, it is true, there is still coral; but it is not a coral that gives signs of great vitality. The madreporarians are quite obviously degenerating throughout the vicinity. Perhaps our team's "demolition area" is but a sample of what the future has in store for the entire region.

By now, Europa itself held few surprises for us. We had explored virtually the entire island. And it was not always a particularly enjoyable task. The interior is flat and inhospitable, and over the whole there hangs the fetid odor that we normally associate with swampland. It would require courage to live here permanently. Some have tried it, and failed; and such attempts have often ended in tragedy.

Falco, while he was marooned on Europa during the hurricane, had found several tombs, which were the only remaining signs of one such drama. Many years earlier, several families had come to the island in an attempt at colonization. But, as I have said, there was no fresh water on Europa. As soon as their own supply gave out, therefore, the men of the colony went out in their boat to search for a spring or other source on other islands, leaving their wives with a group of African servants. When they returned, their wives had all been raped and then killed. The men massacred the Africans, and then left Europa forever. Such was the origin of the graves Falco had seen.

A stretch of beautiful weather provided an ideal opportunity for us to film the turtles at Europa. Coll and Goupil were lucky enough to come across a group of about thirty of these enormous animals in the water, in the midst of which swam two equally monstrous stingrays.

A turtle in the act of laying her eggs. The eggs can be seen emerging in the right-hand picture. Each turtle lays more than a hundred of them. The eggs are soft but tough and resilient.

Deloire also saw a very large group of turtles behind a coral massif, lying along the bottom on a strip of sand. As Deloire and his companions approached, the turtles, slowly and with every sign of reluctance, rose from the bottom.

Finally, one of the teams was successful in filming the love-making of several pairs of turtles — a sequence that occupied the couples for a full ten minutes. The male seizes the female turtle from the rear and hooks on to her shell with his front paws and tail. (Males, incidentally, can be distinguished from females by the size of their tails, which are considerably larger.) If the couple is disturbed, the female is the one who flees. The male refuses to be interrupted. He hangs on to the female and is pulled, like a trailer, through the water.

It is difficult to say whether sea turtles are intelligent or stupid; their small heads, it must be admitted, are not the picture of intelligence. Divers have often noticed, however, that turtles have exceptionally keen hearing. When divers approach a group of turtles, some will rise and swim away while the humans are still a good distance off; others remain on the bottom until the divers are upon them. These latter are the sleeping ones. (Turtles seem to spend much of their lives asleep.) Their eyesight, however, does not match their hearing, and it is probable that their small eyes have only dim perception in the water.

Raymond Coll was swimming beneath the surface in shallow water one day when he saw an enormous turtle swimming directly toward him, its mouth open. Raymond — who is able to notice such things about marine life — saw immediately, from the way the turtle was swimming, that it was blind. He waited motionless until it was almost upon him; then he reached out and touched it. Immediately, it shot away in a zigzag pattern of flight, thoroughly frightened. Raymond's guess is that that particular specimen must have been over a hundred years old. Its shell was covered with growths of various kinds — algae, small shellfish, etc. — and its black head was so wrinkled that this turtle must have been the dean of all turtles of Europa.

Hitherto, the turtles I have mentioned were those known as leatherbacks, which take their name from their smooth, leathery skin. We also saw a few hard-shelled turtles — the so-called "true sea turtles." However, they were all of comparatively small size, weighing from thirty to forty pounds.

I must say, in favor of sea turtles, that they almost all are models of patience and gentleness. No matter what we did, it seemed nearly impossible to make them lose their tempers, and not one of our divers was even bitten. It is true that a turtle charged me one day, but she had been badly frightened and obviously was in a panic. A turtle charge, however, is not the most fearsome thing in the world, and I turned my attacker aside merely by giving her a shove.

Although generally unoffended by our presence, the turtles did not respond to our friendly overtures, and refused to accept food from us. Although they are generally herbivorous, we offered them a selection of delicacies: fish, mollusks, and algae. We ended up by holding the food an inch from their beaks — but with no sign of interest on their part. It may be that they do not eat at all during the mating season.

Sea turtles spend their whole lives in the water, except when the female comes ashore to deposit her eggs. On this occasion, the females allowed themselves to be washed up on Europa's beaches by the tide. Then they began dragging their ponderous bodies forward, under the blazing sun, until they reached a point beyond the high-tide line. The passage was made in single file, one turtle behind the other, with the lead turtle seeking out the smoothest path; and the progress of the line, as one may imagine, was incredibly and exasperatingly slow.

By the time the females had reached a point sufficiently high to be safe from the tide, they obviously were exhausted. Nonetheless, they set to work immediately, digging holes with their flippers in the sand. Each hole was large enough to contain the expectant mother's entire body. The turtle then placed herself in the hole and dug, with her hind paws, a smaller but deeper one, a round well, the purpose of which seems to be to protect the eggs from the island's crabs. Into this she dropped her eggs, one by one. There are usually around one hundred eggs, rather soft and resilient, but tough; reptile eggs, in other words. The laying sometimes continued the whole night. And throughout it all — while digging the hole and while laying the eggs — the turtles cried, with real tears rolling down their faces. These tears, however, are not a sign of pain, but a physical necessity; for unless the turtle's eyes are kept constantly moist, it is likely that she would go blind.

The turtles then covered the eggs with sand. At that point, her responsibility ended. The rest was up to nature. The heat of the sun, beating down on the sand over a period of about sixty days, would incubate the eggs.

In the morning, it was necessary for the turtles to return to the sea before the heat of the day began to be felt; otherwise, they would die. They therefore began dragging themselves once more across the sand. A small rock or a protruding root was enough to stop a turtle and to trap her until the sun killed her only a few feet from the life-giving water. The beaches of Europa are littered with the remains of turtles who have experienced this fate. The effort that a full-grown turtle must make to breathe and to lift her enormous bulk, when combined with the heat of the tropical day, is sufficient to kill her. To add to this suffering, the turtles were devoured by Europa's mosquitoes, which covered their heads and paws.

Our men were filled with pity at the sight of the turtles who seemed destined to die only a few steps from the sea, and they tried to save as many of them as they could. It was heavy work. Some of the turtles were so heavy that they simply could not be moved by hand. Others, however, were helped to free themselves by groups of three or four men.

(Facing) Newborn turtles, even if they move quickly, seldom escape the voracious frigate birds. To the right is a bucket containing baby turtles saved by Falco and his friends.

Turtles swimming, with apparent indifference, among a group of fish. Our divers tried to feed them, but the turtles consistently refused to accept anything they were offered.

And, as soon as the turtles realized that they were again able to move forward, they headed straight for the sea. The men are willing to swear that the turtles knew they had been helped.

I wanted to find out what happened to the turtles after the eggs had been laid and the mothers had returned to the sea. Did they remain in the vicinity of Europa for a time, or did they leave immediately? The only way to find the answer was to mark several of them. We did so by boring a small hole, with a drill, at the edge of their shells, and attaching a kytoon, or balloon, similar to those we had used earlier on whales. The

turtles did not seem to mind in the least, for their shells are hard and apparently have no more sensation than, say, a human fingernail.

As it turned out, the marked turtles seemed never to wander very far from Europa; at least not so long as we were in the area.

It would seem that the mother turtles, whether they survived or not, had accomplished their biological task of replenishing the species. But that would be a hasty conclusion. The last act of the drama was still to be played out.

When it came time for the eggs to hatch, Goupil and Deloire hid themselves at the edge of the beach with their cameras ready. All along the beach, the eggs were splitting open, and young turtles, resembling green toads, were emerging from their holes. As soon as they were in the open air, instinct propelled them toward the sea. And at that instant, there appeared thousands of birds — frigate birds and crows, mostly, which were apparently the same ones that, on the night of the cyclone, had attacked our men on the island. They had lost nothing of their ferocity since that time. They immediately fell upon the newborn turtles in such numbers that it seemed not one of the latter would escape. Even the turtles who had already reached the shallows were taken.

Our men were shaken by the violence of the slaughter. They ran down to the beach and attempted to protect some of the young turtles, but the birds were bold enough to grab the turtles away from them. Seeing that this was hopeless, the men then tried to save some of the turtles by picking them up in buckets and carrying them into the sea beyond the shallows. But the turtles had to remain on the surface in order to breathe — young turtles require much more air than mature turtles — and they were immediately seized by the birds. The frigates had apparently understood what the men were doing, and had followed them out over the water. It was difficult not to hate the birds, even though they were fulfilling nature's first law, which is the assurance of self-survival through the search for food. Even so, the frigates, particularly, seemed so unrelenting that it was hard not to accept that theirs was not a conscious cruelty.

There remained but one way to save any of the baby turtles. The men began picking them up as soon as they emerged from their holes and hiding them in a tent that had been erected on the beach.

Falco, Goupil, and some of the others also dug a large hole, filled it with turtles, and covered it with the plexiglass dome that had given

Chauvellin so much trouble during the cyclone. The birds attacked the dome with their beaks but they were not able to break it. Then, after dark, the turtles were put into the sea.

We do not know exactly how many turtles were saved in this way. We estimate about 750 were protected by the plexiglass dome and hidden in the tent, of which perhaps a hundred survived. Several of these were brought aboard the *Calypso,* and later given to friends at Tuléar, or brought back to the *Musée de Monaco,* where they are still alive and well, and considerably larger.

Apparently, none of the other turtles hatched during the daylight hours escaped the birds. Of the approximately two hundred and fifty thousand eggs laid by the mother turtles, the only small turtles to make it to the safety of the sea were some of those that had the good fortune to emerge from their holes on a dark night. The rest, except for those saved, were all eaten by the birds a few minutes after hatching.

It may seem that nature's way is the way of madness. Hundreds of thousands of turtles sacrificed so that a few species of useless and disagreeable birds may survive. Yet, upon reflection, it appears that man's way is little better. For centuries, he has hunted the sea turtle with such ferocity that the species is on the verge of extinction. If they were bred by man — as, say, chickens or cattle are bred — they would provide an abundant source of food in a world in which two thirds of the population exists at the level of starvation. That is not the least of the lessons that the tragic scene on Europa's beach taught us that day.

Obviously, it is possible to breed turtles. In Indochina, it is already done, though for the purpose of obtaining the turtle's shell. These turtles are carnivorous, and therefore easy to feed by means of mollusks and small fishes.

In Japan, the soft-shelled turtle has also been domesticated for use as food. It, too, is carnivorous.

Specialists consider the true sea turtle, or green turtle, to be the most difficult to breed, since it is thought to be herbivorous, and must be either provided with large quantities of algae or else allowed to graze. Even so, on Cosmoledo we saw sea turtles being bred successfully enough — although on a relatively small scale — to be a source of food.

The fact is that the sea turtle adapts very well to a meat diet. Those that we have captured and turned over to the *Musée de Monaco* now feed, with good appetite, on mollusks and small fish.

Many of the forms and colors of colonial animals are an enigma for man. Here is a red zoantharian, which is related to coral but is soft. It may be a Palythoan.

EPILOGUE

*Destruction of the oceans by pollution
and ecological balance is reversible.*

The cruise of the *Calypso* continues; and it will continue, I hope, for years to come. In the present work, I have limited myself to an account of our travels through the coral jungle of the Red Sea and the Indian Ocean. I hope I have succeeded in acquainting the reader with that strange and unearthly world that has hitherto been the preserve of a few privileged men. It is my fondest wish that the world below, hidden in the deeps, may become as well known to future generations as the continents are to us today.

For this to occur, it is necessary above all that that world survive. Man is just beginning to explore the seas and to know them, and already he has discovered that they are dying. The gold-flecked madreporarians, the translucent alcyonaceans, the gorgeous sea fans — all these things, and many more, are threatened by the side effects of our civilization. Let us not forget that we are responsible to posterity for the preservation of the beauties of the sea as well as for those on land. And at the risk of using an old-fashioned term, let me point out that we have a moral obligation toward our descendants. We must not pass on to them a legacy of empty oceans and dead reefs.

The animals of the coral world are not like other animals. They are more vulnerable, their lives more precarious. They are more quickly ruined by man's touch. They cannot flee, as do the sea lions and the sea elephants, and take refuge in some far-off haven that is, as yet, safe from man. The butterfly fish of the reefs are sedentary animals, and they must live or die among the coral. The animals who build the reefs and the atolls — the acropores, the giant clams, the spirographs, and all the others — are "fixed animals," who must also die where they live.

Let no one say that I am unduly pessimistic concerning either the present or the future. I know whereof I speak. For thirty years, my friends and I have explored the seas. We have designed, built, and made use of devices that have allowed man finally to feel somewhat at home in the oceans, from the autonomous diving suit that bears my name and that of Gagnan, through the diving saucers and underwater scooters and the techniques of deep-sea photography, to the *Argyronète*, a revolutionary type of submarine to be used for scientific research.

These are our credentials. They qualify us, I think, to give direct testimony on what is happening in the sea. We have been diving in the Red Sea, for example, for seventeen years. And we are probably the only ones who are able to compare the present condition of the coral in that area with what it was in 1953. We know every wall, every sea fan, and every tuft of black coral around many of the islands, banks, and atolls. And on this voyage we have seen — at Mar Mar in the Farasan Islands, and at Europa — the "demolition areas," the sick and colorless coral, in places that before were throbbing with life and color. If such destruction can take place in only a few years, then the future seems bleak indeed.

This is all the more true in that it is not only the Red Sea and the Indian Ocean that are affected. I am familiar enough with the waters of the world to know that pollution, and therefore disaster, is everywhere — in California, in the Caribbean, as well as in Micronesia.

I have spoken often in this book about the decline of coral. It was appropriate that I do so, because the Red Sea and the Indian Ocean are the sites par excellence of the world of coral, and they are therefore especially sensitive to the pollution of the water. This decline, if it continues, will mark the end of one of the great beauties of creation, and the end of a great hope — that of discovering life forms hitherto unknown on earth. If what I have said earlier proves to be true — if our grandchildren never have the opportunity to see living coral — it will be to the everlasting shame of our age.

Even if coral does not die immediately and finally, it will remain always in danger. The reefs are at the mercy of storms, which destroy their exterior; of heavy rains, which reduce the salinity of the water; of currents, which cover them with river mud . . . These are the traditional threats to coral. But there are new dangers as well. An oil tanker has only to empty its tanks near a reef, or an oil spill from a well has only to spread; and polyps will die over a large area. The solution, theoretically, is simple: there must be a strict enforcement of international regulations.

Above all, however, it is human attitudes, rather than human laws, that we must try to change. We must modify our ideas on the sea. By reason of its immensity, its depth, its seeming invulnerability, and its wealth, it appears to us to be inexhaustible. But we have now discovered that, far from being proof against any and all depredations, the sea is surprisingly limited, and astoundingly fragile.

The reefs, for example, of which we have spoken as teeming with life, are nothing more than closely circumscribed, and precariously maintained, oases. The area in which life exists goes only from the surface to a depth of a hundred or a hundred and twenty-five feet, and it includes only the exterior of the reef. There, there is place only for a limited number of fishes. These fishes are sedentary creatures, and to seek them out and kill them is child's play. Three good divers with weapons can irrevocably ruin a reef such as Abulat or Maf Zuber, for we have no reason to think that the fish killed will be replaced by others of the same species. We must therefore fight, not only against pollution, but also against the senseless massacre of fish. A first step in this direction is to establish marine preserves, as has been done in the United States at Key Largo, and in the Mediterranean, by the French, around the Island of Port-Cros.

It is, however, by example, by word, and by the media of communication above all that we can teach respect for marine life. The ease with which that attitude can be developed is a source of encouragement to everyone who loves the sea. The public reaction to our films, which have been seen everywhere in the United States and in Europe, has revealed — to everyone's astonishment — how many millions of people are fascinated by marine life, and especially by the great, wild, and free inhabitants of the sea. Perhaps it is because we recognize in those creatures the existence of a freedom we ourselves have lost or surrendered. And perhaps it is a reaction to modern man's alienation from his natural environment, and to an innate yearning to return to the sea, from which he came. If so, man today has the means necessary to enter into the sea and live from it. Let us hope that it will not be an empty sea to which he returns.

(Above) Surgeonfish and a group of young Naso swimming about a stylaster fan.

(Below) An Oreaster (starfish), which lives on coral bottoms.

(Facing) The clown anemonefish enjoys an immunity to the tentacles of the sea anemone, poisonous to most other fish. Here it brings food to its anemone.

For two decades now my friends and I, by means of the cruises of the *Calypso,* have been involved in the life of the sea. We have had to solve many problems dealing with animal psychology as well as with diving equipment and cinematographic apparatus. In other words, we have done more than merely go from place to place in the sea. We have had time enough to note a trend, a tendency, the end result of which will be the destruction of the sea. And the destruction of the sea, of course, implies the destruction of the planet Earth. The vegetable life of the ocean provides a large part of the oxygen that we breathe. If the sea is poisoned, marine flora will disappear. And with it will disappear a large part of the oxygen that is necessary to the survival of life on land.

The situation, however, is not hopeless. There is still a chance. Man can still put a stop to pollution and preserve the life of the seas. We must not be content, however, to recognize what is happening and then to do nothing about it. We must mobilize all our resources and energies in a crusade on behalf of all mankind.

Thus far, however, man has been concerned exclusively with the seas as a hunting ground rather than as a breeding ground. Fishermen, with their nets and harpoons, their modern arsenal of radar and electronic fish-finding devices, and their explosives, are exhausting and emptying the seas.

Our friend the turtle shows us how to correct this mistake: the breeding of marine animals must be undertaken, just as our ancestors, twenty thousand years ago, undertook the breeding of land animals. For our future is in the seas, just as that of our predecessors was on land. Man, therefore, must learn to care for and cultivate the waters of the earth, and the creatures that live in them.

A few years ago, it was fashionable to speak of the seas as "the farmland of the future," as a storehouse capable of feeding an overpopulated earth. It was not an impossible dream; but it would have required, first and foremost, an intelligent and planned management of the ocean's capital, that is, of its life. For the present, therefore, it is absurd to pretend that what we seem intent on destroying can possibly act as a means of saving the world from starvation.

This is not the first time — nor, probably, the last — that man has acted so foolishly. Africa, for instance, was at one time regarded as an inexhaustible source of wealth. The truth is that the uninformed exploitation of resources can exhaust a continent as quickly as it can an ocean. The difference is that in the ocean the depredations of man are more systematic and therefore more serious. On land, we try to tame, to cultivate, and to civilize — however clumsily we go about it. In the seas, however, there has been no attempt at cultivation. All our technology is concentrated on one end: to kill, as much and as expeditiously as possible; to kill, at all times and in all places and by whatever means. We attempt to invest fishing with an aura of "sportsmanship" and of respectability because it is an ancient human activity going back to the time of the prehistoric hunters. It is, however, at the present time, an archaic exercise in malevolent absurdity. The application of modern technology to fishing has produced not a sport, but a system of wholesale destruction that must eventually empty the seas of all life.

We must keep in mind that what man may safely take from the ocean without destroying its ecological balance is very little. And as soon as man exceeds that small amount, the results are catastrophic. The wealth and variety of life in the sea can be preserved only if the laws of biology are observed. And we must know them before we can observe them. Every attempt to tamper with life in the sea results in a chain reaction, for the "living sea," though it is indeed a paradise, is a tragically precarious one. There is a place for man in it, just as there is a place for sharks. But it is a small place — and infinitely disproportionate to the devastation that man causes among marine life forms.

It is not impossible, of course, to increase the amount that we may presently (and reasonably) take from the sea. But to do so, we must adopt the proper means. We must begin an intelligent program of breeding and domestication. There is simply no other way. Otherwise, we must give up all hope of feeding the world from the underwater resources of the planet.

Modern man, finally, must emerge from the age of romance so far as the sea is concerned. We must no longer think of the sea as "mysterious." There are no longer "mysteries"; there are only problems to which we must find the answers. We are entering a new era of research and exploration. We must learn how to make use of the biological and mineral resources of the oceans, how to harness and control their energy. But we must also learn how to preserve the integrity and the equilibrium

I am always astonished at the wealth and splendor of life in the sea, on land, and in the sky.

of that world which is so inextricably bound to our own. Soon, perhaps, we will realize that the sea is but an immense extension of our human world, a province of our universe, a patrimony that we must protect if we ourselves are to survive.

Appendixes

APPENDIX I

About diving

The Aqua-Lung, or self-contained underwater breathing apparatus (SCUBA) was invented in 1943 by Jacques-Yves Cousteau and an engineer, Émile Gagnan.

The principal characteristics of the outfit are that it is an "open-circuit" apparatus — that is, the used air is expelled directly into the water — and that the air is provided not in a continuous fashion, but whenever the diver inhales. The air itself is stored in one or more air tanks (or "bottles," or "cylinders") strapped onto the diver's back, and its flow is controlled by a regulator, which delivers air whenever the diver inhales and which assures that the pressure of the air corresponds to that of the water surrounding the diver. When the diver exhales, the used air is fed into the water by

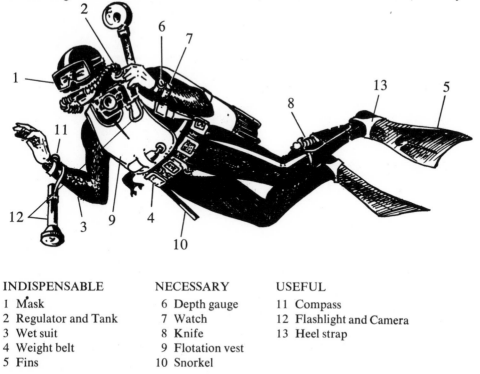

INDISPENSABLE	NECESSARY	USEFUL
1 Mask	6 Depth gauge	11 Compass
2 Regulator and Tank	7 Watch	12 Flashlight and Camera
3 Wet suit	8 Knife	13 Heel strap
4 Weight belt	9 Flotation vest	
5 Fins	10 Snorkel	

Cousteau-Gagnan self-contained underwater breathing apparatus, Mistral type, and diving accessories.

means of an exhaust located under the hood of the regulator. Two flexible tubes run from a mouthpiece to the regulator; one is for inhalation, the other for exhalation.

The invention of the Aqua-Lung was a decisive step forward in man's conquest of the sea, and even in the history of human progress. And yet, it is basically a simple and safe apparatus, entirely automatic and easily mastered, that has, in effect, opened the doors of the sea to man and made it possible for a large segment of the public to take up diving.

The Cousteau-Gagnan independent diving unit was a revolutionary departure from the old "hard hat" heavy diving rig, which most of us recall from the movies. The hard-hat apparatus (so called because of the heavy copper helmet that it included) was complicated to use, uncomfortable, and dangerous. Moreover, it required a long period of training, and it limited the diver to a small area of bottom. If in the

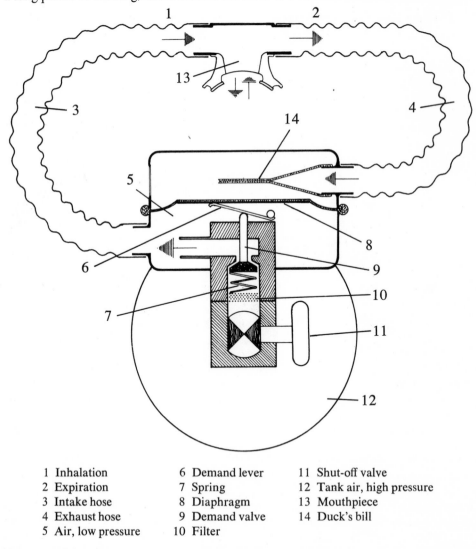

1 Inhalation	6 Demand lever	11 Shut-off valve
2 Expiration	7 Spring	12 Tank air, high pressure
3 Intake hose	8 Diaphragm	13 Mouthpiece
4 Exhaust hose	9 Demand valve	14 Duck's bill
5 Air, low pressure	10 Filter	

Diagram of the Cousteau-Gagnan regulator

past twenty years the sea has truly opened up to man, therefore, it is because of the independent diving gear — and its accessory equipment, such as the "fins" invented by Commandant de Corlieu, the mask, and the weight belt used to regulate buoyancy — which has proved its value as a means of exploration and scientific research even more than as a piece of sporting equipment.

Even though man has now learned to operate independently in the sea, he is still susceptible to two of the dangers with which the hard-hat divers had always to contend: rapture of the depths and decompression accidents.

Rapture of the depths is a form of narcosis, induced by the presence of nitrogen, that seriously impedes a diver's reasoning processes. The depth at which it affects the diver depends upon the individual. Some divers experience its symptoms at, say, 135

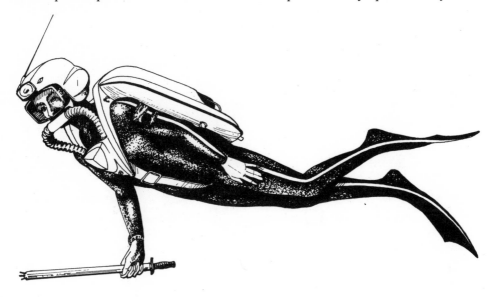

Our new self-contained hydrodynamic diving suit, with helmet and built-in telephone.

feet, while others are affected only at greater depths and after a longer period of time. And some first become aware of the onset of this narcosis when it is too late. The diver's threshold of susceptibility to rapture of the depths can be pushed back by many hundreds of feet, however, by replacing the nitrogen in one's breathing mixture by a lighter gas, such as helium.

Decompression accidents, on the other hand, are due to the fact that, during a dive, gas from the diver's air tends to go into solution in the diver's blood. If the diver rises to the surface too quickly, this gas comes out of solution in the form of bubbles in the blood stream. The result is decompression sickness, which is more or less serious according to the speed of the diver's ascent, the depth from which he began the ascent, and the amount of time spent at that depth. Decompression sickness may be prevented by timing the ascent in such a way that gas may be diffused normally. And for that purpose, tables have been worked out that indicate the number and duration of the pauses that a diver must make during his ascent, according to the depth he has reached and the time spent at that depth. If a dive has been very brief, these stages of ascent are not applicable, since the diver's system has not had time to absorb a dangerous quantity of gas. But as depth and duration increase, so does the time required for decompression.

Drawing illustrating the helium dive at Europa. The Galeazzi tower is hanging from the Calypso's rear, and serves as an underwater decompression chamber. The helium divers are entering the grotto. Other divers, with ordinary equipment, are waiting at the tower to help the helium divers in their ascent at the end of the dive.

The phenomenon of decompression was the reason for our experimenting with the "undersea houses." In the course of that experiment, a diver's body became saturated with gas after a few hours, and it was allowed to remain so, regardless of the amount of time he spent at the depth of the houses. It was necessary for the diver to decompress only once, and that was when he regained the surface at the end of the experiment, which ran for several days, or as in the case of Precontinent III, after a month spent on the bottom. Thus it was possible for a team of divers to remain under water for a prolonged period of time at the price of only one ascent and one decompression. "Pay as you leave," the divers called it.

The use of a decompression chamber makes it possible for a diver, during the ascent, to remain at the same pressure as that of the depth at which he was working. Then, back on the surface, he can be decompressed gradually, and under medical supervision. In this case, the diver may be given oxygen when he attains a pressure equivalent to that which exists at a depth of less than forty feet. Aboard the *Calypso*, the Galeazzi tower does double duty as a submersible decompression chamber and as an observation chamber.

APPENDIX II

The World of Coral

The world of coral is an extraordinary one, even by marine standards. It is a world that is at once very complex, very well defined — and very little understood.

If the tiny animals we call "coral" are to develop and subsist, several environmental conditions must exist simultaneously. The water must be warm, with temperatures never going below 50 °F., and it must be clear, and free of sediment, sand, slime, and mud. Coral, therefore, is found only in tropical and subtropical water; that is, in a belt lying no more than 32° north, and no more than 27° south, of the equator. And, within that area, it is found where the water is not only warm, but in other respects suitable. There is no coral, for example, off the coasts of Brazil, India, or West Africa, because of the mud that is carried into the sea by the great rivers of those regions.

Coral reefs are deposits of which only the chief constituent is coral. These reefs are of three kinds: The *fringing reef* "fringes" the shore, lying a short distance from it, and is separated from it by shallow water. The *barrier reef* lies a greater distance from the shore and is separated from it by a wider and sometimes deeper channel. The third type of reef, the *atoll,* is a ring-shaped reef, which encloses a circular lagoon.

Coral, despite the environmental demands that it makes, exists over a huge area of the earth — about eighty million square miles, or approximately twenty-five times the area of the United States and twenty times that of Europe. The reefs that we find today — which are enormous colonies of living coral — are the result of a process that has endured for hundreds of millions of years. So far as we know, coral first appeared on earth some four hundred million years ago. In certain eras, when the seas were warm, coral stretched as far north as Greenland, and there are traces of its existence in France and England from a time when the sea still covered parts of those countries. When I say, therefore, that coral today can exist only in a narrow "belt" of water, I am obviously speaking in comparative terms.

I have said that coral is the principal constituent of coral reefs. The reefs, in fact, are a composite of many life forms existing together in various relationships — in commensalism, in symbiosis, or simply in promiscuity. There are huge mollusks *(Tridacna),* annelids *Spirographs,* and such hydrozoan coralloids as *Stylaster, millepora,* and calcareous algae — none of which are sufficiently "popular" to be known by any names other than those that scientists have bestowed upon them.

Despite the abundance of life forms in a typical coral reef, I ordinarily use the name "coral" to designate a colony of individual coral animals, each of which is known as a polyp. Each polyp consists of a jelly-like body enclosed in a skeleton (a theca) of calcium carbonate. This body — which tends to group with other bodies into solid masses — is generally a hollow digestive system with an opening at the unattached end of the body. The opening — the "mouth" of the polyp — is surrounded by tentacles, and leads into the gullet. The gullet itself empties into the main digestive cavity.

In the public mind, the word "coral" is a blanket term that covers the precious *Corallium rubrum,* or red coral, of the Mediterranean area. This is the "coral" that we often see used in jewelry. Red coral, however, from a strictly zoological standpoint, is distinct from the corals that build reefs and islands. The former is an octocoralliform; the latter, a hexacoralliform — which means simply that red coral has a radial symmetry of eight, while the reef-building coral has a radial symmetry of six, or multiples of six. Coral is sometimes also called "madrepores" — but that term is no more precise than any other, for in its true sense it designates only a particular group of coral (the "stony coral").

The fixed polyps that I call coral are, to be scientifically precise, members of the phylum Cnidaria, class Anthozoa, order *Scleractinia.* The older zoological textbooks classified corals as coelenterates — a term that included both the cnidaria and the ctenaria. Today, however, scientists recognize the two as separate, though related, branches.

Among the scleractinia there are three groups:

(a) The Aporosa, which include both simple and colonial scleractinia: the *Caryophyllia,* the *Lophophelia,* the *Meandrina,* the *Coenocyanthus.*

(b) The Fungina, which are also solitary or colonial *Scleractinia.* The most typical genus of this tribe is the *Fungia,* which is characterized by its mushroomlike lamella.

(c) The Porina, which are colonial scleractinians. There are two genera: the *Dendrophyllia* and the *Acropora* (which is divided into numerous species).

A massive colony of Porites, *a Madreporarian formation made up of tiny, cuplike, porous beings. Colonies such as this sometimes reach a height of several yards.*

Fungia, *a solitary Madreporarian. The* fungia *is a fixed animal until it becomes an adult; then, it is free-floating. The cavity in the center of the animal, to which lead the radial elements from the fungia's periphery, is the mouth.*

The Cnidaria as a whole are characterized by their poisonous cells, which are called "nematocysts." The nematocyst, essentially, is a minute capsule containing a stinging filament equipped with harpoon-shaped hooks. When the organism is excited or disturbed, the filament is ejected and attaches itself, by means of its hooks, into the flesh of an attacker (or of a diver).

The coral world exists only in comparatively shallow water, There is no trace of it at a depth of more than 130 or 135 feet. The reason is that coral lives in a symbiotic relationship with *Zooxanthellae* — algae they carry in their tissue, which, in addition to acting as a dietetic supplement, serve to rid the coral of certain ammoniac and phosphatic wastes. Beyond that depth, there is not sufficient light for these algae — or for another microscopic plant, called a "green filament," which also lives inside the polyp — to achieve photosynthesis.

All together, there are approximately twenty-five hundred species of coral, and a great diversity of forms. Some are regular, and others are branched. The formations they achieve are often as fragile as they are diverse. The "branches" of certain madreporarian formations, for instance, would crumble if exposed to gravity in the open air. In the sea, however, they are sustained by the water. The variety of color is equal to that of shape — pink, blue, purple, red, yellow, and golden brown. These colors are the result of pigments contained in the tissue of the madreporarians.

The variety in the form of colonial coral is mainly the result of the form of reproduction, through budding that takes place. Reproduction also occurs by the production of eggs and sperm. In the latter instance, the eggs and sperm form in the mesenteries (thin sheets of tissue that are vertical partitions extending inward from the body wall) and are expelled into the water, where fertilization occurs. A microscopic larva emerges from the egg and swims about before attaching itself, becoming a polyp, and secreting its skeleton.

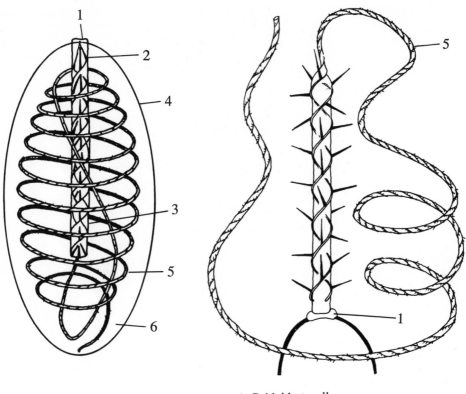

1 Operculum (door)
2 Spines
3 Shaft
4 Cnidoblast wall
5 Filament, or terminal tube
6 Capsule contents

Drawing of a Nematoblast, or Cnidoblast, which is essentially a stinging apparatus. To the left is the stinging filament, rolled up within its capsule. To the right, the filament has been stimulated and is ready for action.

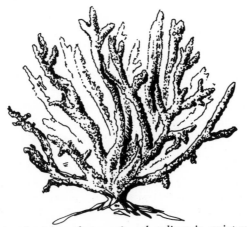

Acropora pharaonis. A colonial madreporarian that lives in quiet water because of the fragility of its branches.

As the colonial forms produce more and more polyps, those lower down die, and new layers of polyps are built up on the dead skeletons. Eventually, the skeletons are broken up by the action of the waves, by other animals, and in other ways, and when the broken skeletons have been piled up in sufficient number, vegetation may become established, and islands and reefs may eventually be formed.

Acropora hebes. *A colonial madreporarian also, but with sturdier branches than those of the preceding species.*

APPENDIX III

Coral Fishes

The coral massifs of the tropic seas are home to numerous species of fish remarkable for their form and color. These fishes are found only among coral formations, where they spend their whole lives, since they are sedentary animals. Consequently, their swimming habits are adapted to the nature of the environment — to the corridors, mazes, and crags of the reefs. They are better called reef fish than coral fish, since some of them in fact live in environments that are similar to those in which coral is found, but in which the temperature of the water is not suitable for the development of coral. Only those fishes who feed on coral — such as parrot fish — are truly bound to a coral environment.

Scientists at present recognize some thirty thousand species of fishes. Of these the species who live among tropical reefs are undoubtedly the most striking. They come in red, yellow, blue, orange; almost every color of the spectrum, and every combination thereof, can be found. Moreover, these vivid colors are often displayed to advantage in patterns formed by stripes, dots, lozenges, and other elements. Even within a single species, there can be a great variety of color and pattern, for the individuals of many species change their appearance with age, sex, or the season, while those of other species do so either when frightened or out of a taste for mimesis, or imitation.

Most coral fish are flat and round, having more or less the configuration of a disc. They are able to swim in almost any position — which allows them an extraordinary mobility when it is necessary for them to flee or to hide in the minute grottoes of a coral formation. Moreover, their comparatively large tails and short fins make it possible for them to spin around quickly and to stop "on a dime."

In the past few years, more and more divers have discovered and been enchanted by coral fishes; and, in their enthusiasm, they have bestowed names on them without reference to scientific principles of classification. Taken from various languages, such names, as descriptive and appropriate as some of them may be, have created considerable confusion among divers and non-divers alike — a situation as unnecessary as it is unfortunate. For these species already have universally accepted and instantly recognizable names; indeed, they have had them since the eighteenth century. These scientific designations, by genus and species, are indispensable for the scientist and the specialist. Nonetheless, man's relationship to the sea — of which language is, after all, only a reflection — has changed considerably in the past twenty years. Today, tens of thousands of men and women have taken up diving as a hobby, and these enthusiasts are constantly observing tropical fishes in their natural habitat. Quite naturally, they feel the need to label what they see. A few scientific names of fish have thus found their way into everyday language — tilapia and albacore, for example, But, for the most part, the layman's mind resists the somewhat ponderous, albeit precise, Latin terminology of science. Consequently, divers everywhere have made up names, based principally on physical characteristics of species, which have become the "popular" designations of those species. The following are a few of those names which, it seems, are commonly accepted, and which I use in describing the expeditions of the *Calypso*:

Parrot fish is generally used to designate the various species that are known to eat coral. Scientifically, parrot fish fall under the categories of Scarus and *Sparisoma.*

Surgeonfish is an apt name for the Acanthuridae, who live in schools and are armed with a sharp, pointed spine on the side of the body immediately in front of the tail.

One can also see the appropriateness of the name trumpet fish for the Aulostomidae, who have slender, stiff bodies and very long heads and snouts. The same holds true for fish of the family Pomadasyidae — which are known as grunts because they actually do make a grunting noise by grinding their teeth, the sound of which is amplified by the gas bladder. And similarly, trunkfish is the common name for members of the family Ostraciontidae because of the bony "box," composed of fused scales, in which they are encased. One can even admit the logic of porcupine fish for designating the Diodontidae — even though the more scientific and accurate name of "diodon" is not particularly difficult to retain. And it would be hard to argue with a diver who insisted on referring to a *Lactophrys bicuspis* as a cowfish — especially since this fish has spines, or "horns," growing from the top of its head.

There are few more-beautiful sights in the tropical sea than the dragonfish — also known as the lion-fish, turkey fish, and zebrafish — with its magnificent stripes and its array of veil-like fins. But, in this instance, the popular designations of the *Pterois* are misleading, for this handsome species is armed with eighteen dorsal spines, which are elaborately striped and spotted — and dangerously venomous.

Many popular names for tropical fish have had their origin in the United States, and these English-language terms have been translated literally and adopted into other languages. Some of these terms are, by their nature, very general; and here is where the trouble begins. "Butterfly fish," for example — which we French have accepted in the form of *poisson* (fish) *papillon* (butterfly) — is used indiscriminately to designate a number of species that actually have nothing in common except that they are lively and colorful. Moreover, some of these species have additional popular designations — which makes the situation almost unbearably complicated. Among the genus *Chaetodon*, for example — which are favorites among the "butterfly fish" — there are spotfins *(Chaetodon ocellatus)*, four-eyes *(Chaetodon capistratus)*, four-spots *(Chaetodon quadrimaculatus)*, and raccoons *(Chaetodon lunula).*

Another problem is that a name that is appropriate in one language will often be meaningless in another. Americans, for example, know the *Abudefduf saxatilis* — a yellow fish with heavy black stripes — as the sergeant major. No doubt, this is a fitting designation to anyone who has served in the American Army. To a Frenchman, however, "sergeant major" conjures up the image of a brand of pen. And therefore the descriptive value of the term is lost. Under such conditions, it becomes almost impossible to develop a popular international vocabulary of marine life. (And, in this case, the difficulty increases when one realizes that the *Abudefduf saxatilis* is also commonly called a butterfly fish and a damselfish!)

The situation is no better when it comes to "angelfish" — a term that crosses the lines of recognized genera to include members of *Pterophyllum, Pomacanthus, Centropyge,* and *Holacanthus*. And to us French, of course, a sea angel is what Americans call a monkfish — which is a cousin of the rays and the guitarfish.

One could multiply examples indefinitely — as divers have — but I think the point has been made. Somewhere, somehow, there must be a system established that will enable an American diver to know what a Frenchman means when he says "sea angel," and a Japanese or German or Indian to understand what species an American means when he says "angelfish."

The entire problem, obviously, is man-made, and extrinsic to the world of coral. It is merely a question of organization and method. There are many other problems, of course, that are not so easily solved, and that have to do with the enigmatic aspects of coral life. One of the most intriguing of these was mentioned by Charles Darwin in 1835, when, aboard the *Beagle*, he visited some of the islands of the Indian Ocean that we explored in the course of this expedition. "I employed myself in examining the very interesting structure of these islands," Darwin wrote in his diary. "In some of the gullies and hollows there were beautiful green and other colored fishes, and the forms and tints of many of the zoophytes were admirable."

The riddle of the colors of reef life forms that Darwin noted has still not been solved. We, and other divers, have gone down with our diving gear, our cameras and diving saucers, and with means of investigation and analysis of which Darwin never dreamed. And still the problem exists: Why do coral fishes have so many colors and patterns and bizarre markings — like the four-eyed butterfly fish *(Chaetodon capistratus)*, which has a large dark spot, rimmed in white, on each side of the tail, resembling an extra set of eyes, as though the fish wished to deceive a predator as to the direction in which he is fleeing? It is possible that such characteristics may be linked to the problem of territory, which we discussed in this book with respect to the grouper.

Konrad Lorenz recently proposed an explanation to which we have already referred. After years spent in observing life on the coral reef, Dr. Lorenz concluded that coral fishes have their colors in order to be able to recognize each other as members of the same species. Every area of the reef is a territory that belongs to a single member of a species; and that individual fish defends his territory with all his strength against any other member of the same species. Only fish with other colors and markings do not constitute a threat to that fish's domination of his territory; and therefore only fish of other species are not attacked and driven out. This manifestation of territorial behavior in the sea is, of course, linked to the reproductivity of the fish.

In the text of this book, I have often mentioned life forms, other than fish, that multiply and live and die in the world of coral. These forms of animal life, which are so different from the life forms of the world above, are of an extraordinary diversity — and fragility.

For aeons, they existed unknown to most men. But today, man's invasion of their world threatens to disturb the environmental equilibrium necessary to their existence — an equilibrium that is the end result of a long and complex biological process in which a large number of marine species have had a part.

For complementary information on such of these life forms as have been mentioned in the text of the book — the sea urchins and the giant clams, the starfish and the mollusks and the sea worms, and many of the other inhabitants of the world of coral who have no equivalent on land — the reader is referred to the Illustrated Glossary, which follows these appendixes.

APPENDIX IV

Turtles

Turtles[1], or chelonians, constitute an order of the class of reptiles. They are characterized by their massive skulls; strong, sharp, toothless jaws; and a body encased in a shell that generally consists of bony plates fused with the ribs and vertebrae and covered with horny plates. The upper half of the shell (known as the carapace) and the lower half (the plastron) are connected at the sides. Most species of sea turtle have less-massive shells than their land cousins, and, instead of feet (like land turtles) or webbed toes (like fresh-water turtles), they have paddle-like limbs. Like all turtles, however, they are oviparous.

There are two suborders of turtle, the Cryptodirea, which conceal their heads by retracting them, telescope style, into their shells; and the Pleurodirea, which lay their heads to the side, horizontally.

Sea turtles are Cryptodirea, the three most important species being:

(1) The true sea turtle *(Chelonia mydas)*, also known as the green turtle, the largest, which we observed on the island of Europa. They ordinarily weigh up to 150 pounds, but there is a record of a specimen that weighed over eight hundred pounds. The green turtle, which is primarily herbivorous, is the source of turtle soup, and it has been hunted long and relentlessly for its meat.

(2) The loggerhead turtle *(Caretta caretta)* is carnivorous (or perhaps omnivorous), and is also edible. It prefers shallow water and is found mostly near coasts and in shallow bays. It is distinguished from the green turtle by its brown color.

(3) The hawksbill turtle *(Eretmochelys imbricata)*, which rarely exceeds a length of three feet and a weight of 150 pounds, is blessed, or cursed, with armored plates of unusual beauty. These plates constitute the world's sole supply of commercial "tortoise shell," for which reason the hawksbill is as prized, and as hunted, as the green turtle. The tortoise-shell plates are removed by immersion of the carapace into boiling water.

All species are found in tropical and subtropical seas.[2]

The turtle's hard shell is protective in nature. Ventilation of the lump is effected by movements of the head and limbs, which, in moving in and out of the shell, act as

---

[1] According to American usage, "turtle" is used to designate any reptile of the order *Chelonia*. Land turtles, however, are sometimes called tortoises, and fresh-water species, when edible, are called terrapins. This appendix, obviously, is concerned only with the sea turtle.

[2] There is a fourth species, the Atlantic ridley *(Lepidochelys kempii)*, which is the smallest of the sea turtles, rarely measuring more than two feet in length. Its Pacific cousin *(Lepidochelys olivacea)*, the Pacific ridley, is slightly larger.

pistons to modify the internal volume of the body. To this is added the action of muscles moving against the soft tissue that serves to seal the orifices of the shell.

Turtles, being reptiles, have a comparatively low metabolic rate, and therefore do not require a great deal of oxygen. (Proportionately to their size, they use three hundred to four hundred times less oxygen than man.) They are therefore able to spend long periods below the surface of the water.

Turtles are a miracle of survival. Two hundred and fifty million years ago, there were twenty-four genera of turtles — of which today eleven remain. For one hundred and fifty million of those years, reptiles — including turtles — were the lords of the earth.

Illustrated Glossary

Acropora

A colonial scleractinian, of the madreporarian group of coral, which is extremely common in tropical and subtropical seas. It is found in green, mauve, or blue, and its formations take the form of branches, or "umbrellas." The latter are of considerable size, sometimes attaining a height of seven or eight feet.

Alcyonians

Alcyonium is a genus of Cnidaria, class Anthozoa, subclass Octocorallia. The true alcyonians are what divers know as "soft coral." They are colonial, and tend to form huge congregations of individual polyps.

Alcyonians, as distinguished from the "stony corals' of the madreporarian group, have less-substantial skeletons, since they do not produce the hard, limy secretion that characterizes the madreporarians. Instead, they have stiff, calcareous spicules.

Soft coral is remarkable for the variety and translucent beauty of its colors — pink, greens, and blues — and for the fact that, at night, the coral swells to large proportions, and then, during the day, resumes its normal size. This transformation is one of the wonders and delights of nighttime diving in tropical waters. One specimen of *Spongodes merletti* was observed to grow, within a period of several hours, from a height of two and one-half inches to about sixteen inches.

Anaphylaxis

Anaphylaxis is the state of an organism whose sensitivity to a certain substance has been heightened by the previous introduction into the organism of a certain quantity of that substance. The organism then may react violently and dangerously to a new dose, however small, of the same substance.

Anaphylaxis was discovered in 1902 by two French physiologists, Charles Richet and Paul Portier. In the course of an experiment, they injected a small amount of an extract from the tentacles of a sea anemone into a dog, with no observable effect. Three weeks later, they repeated the injection, this time using only one twentieth as much extract as in the previous injection. This time, however, the dog became violently ill, and died shortly thereafter.

On the face of it, the results of this experiment seemed to contradict the then commonly accepted theory of immunology. The dog, instead of having been rendered immune by the first injection, had instead been "sensitized" and made exceptionally vulnerable. The explanation — which was unknown to the science of the time — was that the anaphylactic state results from the development of "antibodies" in the organism following the introduction of "antigens."

Angelfish

The angelfish is a disc-shaped fish, round and very flat, which is native to tropical reefs. Individuals sometimes show brilliant hues. The young fish are orange or yellow, while the adults assume more-somber coloration and are striped in black and white.

The maximum length of the angelfish is about two and one half feet, while the height of the body (including the fins) varies according to the species.

The angelfish travels in schools. It is omnivorous, and feeds on small life forms and vegetable waste. Its flesh is edible. (See also Butterfly Fish.)

Argyronète

The *Argyronète* is a submarine conceived and designed by Jacques-Yves Cousteau and built by the Institute of Advanced Marine Studies of Marseilles, for the French Petroleum Institute and the National Committee for Oceanic Exploration. Its purpose is oceanological and petroleum exploration, and it is so designed as to allow a team of ten men — including four divers — to live on the ocean bottom for three days.

The submarine comprises two principal parts, one kept at regular atmospheric pressure and the other able to be pressurized to a degree that corresponds to a given exterior pressure. The two parts — which are connected by a series of air locks — therefore constitute a mobile underwater house.

The *Argyronète* can be used to a depth of about two thousand feet. Its surface range is four hundred nautical miles, and its surface speed is seven knots. Under water, its maximum speed is four knots.

The name *Argyronète* is taken from the Greek words *argyros* (silver) and *nein* (to spin or weave). It is the name of an aquatic spider who lives in the water within a bell-shaped "house" that she spins. The spider's lair is stocked with air she brings from the surface in the hairs of her abdomen. She is therefore able to live confortably and securely below the surface of the water — which is also the purpose of the *Argyronète*.

Ascidians

Ascidians — more generally known as sea squirts or tunicates — are chordates. That is, although they have no backbone, they have, when in the larval stage, a tough, flexible cord (called a "notochord") running through their bodies which serves the same purpose.

The sea squirt is, in effect, a small water bag, yellow or red or violet, which is free-floating as a larva but becomes fixed at the adult stage. There are two openings: one to take in sea water from which it takes oxygen and the tiny organisms on which it feeds, and the other to "squirt" the waste water.

Despite their primitive appearance, ascidians have gills, a stomach, an intestine, and a heart. They are hermaphroditic, having both a testicle and an ovary.

Some ascidians reproduce by budding. Sometimes, the new ascidians are united by stolons (extensions of the body wall) and form tufts. These are the social ascidians.

In other instances, the individual ascidians cluster around a common cloaca. These are called synascidians, or composite ascidians.

Barracuda
(Sphyraenidae)

The barracuda is a well-known flesh eater of the tropical seas. In appearance, it somewhat resembles the pike, with its prominent teeth, well-defined jaw, and its elongated body the color of polished steel.

The largest of the barracudas is the great barracuda *(Sphyraena barracuda)*, which sometimes reaches a length of over six feet. It prefers to travel in groups of three or four when fully grown. Smaller barracuda are often found in schools comprising individuals all of the same size and of the same age or generation.

Barracudas have a bad reputation. In certain areas, they are even more feared than sharks. This reputation is probably due, at least in large part, to their ferocious appearance, razor-sharp teeth, mean-looking eyes, and general behavior. A barracuda will, for example, follow a diver relentlessly, circling about him and never taking its cold eyes off him. Some authorities attribute this deportment to the barracuda's stalking habits. On the whole, however, it has been my experience that the barracuda's behavior is more dramatic than dangerous.

Barracudas are found in the tropical Atlantic and in the Pacific and Indian oceans, often in the form of local species.

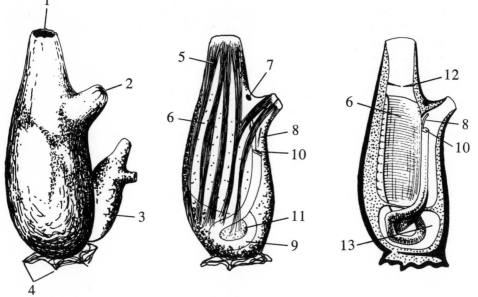

Ascidian

1 Buccal siphon (incurrent: food and oxygen)
2 Cloacal siphon (excurrent: wastes and reproductive products)
3 Young individual or bud
4 Stolons (rootlike extensions)
5 Muscular bands
6 Branchial sac (food filtration and oxygen absorption)
7 Cerebral ganglion
8 Genital canal (male and female openings)
9 Intestine
10 Anus
11 Ovary
12 Tentacle crown
13 Stomach

Black Coral

Black coral is a hexacorallium, of the class Anthozoa, subclass Geriantipatharia, order Antipatharia. It is a colonial animal and its colonies are similar to those of the sea fans, although the individual polyps are different.

The skeleton of black coral is exceedingly hard, a quality that allows it to be worked into the beads and necklaces so highly prized among the Arabs.

Blind Man's Canes

The so-called "blind man's cane" is an octocorallan and a pennatulid. In certain parts of the bottom of the Red Sea, individuals grow to a height of over three feet and constitute a veritable prairie of white canes. In French, we call these canes *virgulaires*.

Brittle Stars and Basket Fishes
(Echinodermata, class Ophiuroidea)

The Ophiuroidea constitute one of the five classes of echinoderms. Their bodies are in the form of a disc, from which grow the arms (usually five in number). These arms are long and thin in relation to the central disc, and very mobile. In the brittle star, for example, the body disc may be only an inch in diameter, while the arms may be well over a foot in length.

There are more than fifteen hundred species of brittle stars (so called because their arms break off so readily), many of which are brightly colored. They are found in all seas and at every depth, among rocks and coral and seaweed.

Brittle stars, like their cousins the sea stars, have amazing regenerative powers. They can lose, or drop, one or several of their arms and grow new ones very quickly, and they are able to regenerate up to half of the central disc.

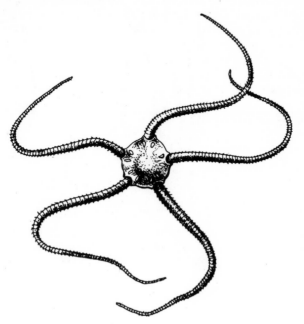

Brittle star

Butterfly Fish
(Chaetodontidae)

The Chaetodontidae, commonly called butterfly fish because of their vivid colors, are disc-shaped coral fish with short, beaklike snouts. Unlike the parrot fish, however, butterfly fish do not eat coral, but live from the minute organisms they find in rubbing their brushlike teeth against calcareous algae.

There are dozens of species called butterfly fish, some of which are not Chaetodontidae at all. Butterfly fish, in the proper sense, are seldom more than six or eight inches long. Like the angelfish, however, to which they are often assimilated (although angelfish are really of the genus *Pomacanthus*), they are remarkable for their astonishing beauty of line and color. (See also Angelfish.)

Cachalot
(See Sperm Whale)

Clown Anemonefish
(Amphiprion percula)
A member of the family of Pomacentridae (or damselfish), which is very common in coral waters. Its popular name is singularly appropriate, for its coloration suggests nothing so much

as the costume of a circus clown: an orange body set off by white bands (around the neck, midsection, and the base of the tail).

Clown anemonefish are best known for the mysterious and intimate relationship in which they live with sea anemones, the poison of which is usually fatal to other fish. This relationship has been defined, or at least qualified, as "symbiotic" and "commensal." One eminent authority (Dr. René Catala) suggests that it be defined as a relationship of "mutualism" — inasmuch as "there is a reciprocity of services. The fish feeds and cleans the anemone and stimulates its tentacles, while the anemone gives shelter to the fish and protects it from external dangers."

Except for brief excursions into the outside world in order to obtain food for the anemone, the clown anemonefish spends its life among the tentacles of the sea anemone. When it mates, both the male and the female take up residence in the same anemone, and the eggs are laid next to the anemone, so that the latter may protect them with its tentacles. (See also Damselfish.)

Conch
(Strombidae)

The name "conch" covers more than eighty species of large, warm-water, gastropod mollusks, some of which attain a length of over ten inches. The shells of many species are prized for their beauty and variety — a tendency that natives of the Pacific islands exploit to the detriment both of these mollusks and of the environmental balance in which they play an important part.

Both the Red Sea and the Indo-Pacific (extending from the East African shores through the East Indies to Polynesia) are notable for the abundance and variety of their shells.

Conshelf
(See Precontinent)

Copra

Copra is the albumin of the coconut, which, once extracted from the shell and dried, is ground up to produce coconut oil.

Damselfish
(Pomacentridae)

Damselfish are small, brilliantly colored coral fish found in all shallow tropical seas. The most commonly encountered species is the *Abudefduf saxatilis*, known as the sergeant major because of its yellow body and black stripes. It is not always easily identifiable, however, for it seems able to change from yellow to silver or black.

Most damselfish are small — not more than six inches long — but they make up in beauty what they lack in size. One of the most striking is the blue reef fish *(Pomacentrus ceruleus)*, or blue chromis, which is an iridescent blue with subtle black shadings. (In the Indo-Pacific and in the Red Sea there are schools of chromis of other colors — notably red.) Another is the yellow-tail *Microspathodon chrysurus)*. Both species are frequently seen in aquariums. (See also Clown Anemonefish.)

Doctorfish
(Acanthurus chirurgus)

More than one hundred species of Acanthuridae are popularly called doctorfish or surgeonfish. All species have a marked characteristic in common, in the form of a sharply pointed, erectile spine on each side of the body immediately forward of the tail. This, of course, is the "scalpel" that gives the doctorfish its name. Some species are armed with a double scalpel on each side of the body. Single or double, however, this spine is capable of inflicting a dangerous but non-venomous wound.

Acanthuridae are common in the Indo-Pacific region, where they feed mainly on algae from coral and rocks. Most species grow to a length of eighteen to twenty inches.

Dolphin
(Delphinus delphis)

The dolphin is a marine mammal and à cetacean, with a long beak containing teeth. It is found in all seas, from the Arctic to Antarctica. There are many species, the individuals of most of which are generally about ten feet long. Dolphins are carnivorous and travel in schools. Their backs are black, and their undersides are white, and some have yellow, gray, or white markings on their sides.

The most common dolphin is, appropriately enough, the common dolphin, or *Delphinus delphis*, which prefers tropical or temperate waters and is often seen in groups of a hundred or more. It is capable of speeds of twenty-five knots and is able to make spectacular leaps out of the water.

The species of dolphin usually seen in American aquariums is the *Tursiops truncatus*, or Atlantic bottle-nosed dolphin, which is an easily tamed, playful, and intelligent creature reaching a length of over twelve feet.

It should be noted that there is another marine life form commonly called a dolphin: the *Coryphaena hippurus*. *Coryphaena* has little in common with *Delphinus* other than its popular name. It is a fish, not a mammal, and it is best known for its color change upon capture: its brilliant golds, greens, and blues fade until, at the point of death, it is a drab olive color. It is the *Coryphaena*, of course, to which poets refer when they speak of a "dying dolphin's changing hues."

Dragonfish
(Pterois)

The dragonfish (Lion-fish, turkey fish, or zebrafish) is a scorpaenid, related to the venomous Mediterranean rockfish, and is found only in tropical waters.

It is a strikingly handsome fish, with large, graceful, diaphanous fins and tail colored in hues of pink and purple. These splendid appurtenances, unfortunately, are tipped with poisonous spines. It is said that this poison is fatal; whether this is true or not, it is certain that it is of sufficient strength to inflict a grave and painful wound on the unwary diver.

The Arabs of the Red Sea know the *Pterois* as "the fish of death"; but the Americans, perhaps less realistically, list it among the popular family of butterfly fish.

The dragonfish reaches a length of about a foot, and feeds on crabs, crustaceans, and other fishes. It is capable of swallowing a victim almost as large as itself.

Echinoderms

The echinoderms constitute one of the primary divisions of the animal kingdom and include the sea stars (or starfish), sea urchins, sea cucumbers, and the crinoids.

Echinoderms are distinguished by the fact that they are radial animals with five sectors (as is obvious from the appearance of a five-armed common starfish).

They possess a nervous system, and a means of propulsion: a complex of tubes that are filled with water and that, by means of hydrostatic pressure, enable the echinoderms to move their ambulatory pods, which are equipped with suction discs.

Though their method of reproduction is primitive (they emit their eggs and sperm into the surrounding water and leave it to chance that the two will eventually combine), they are sufficiently numerous to be common in all the seas of the planet, both warm and cold.

Feather-duster Worm
(Spirographis)

The feather-duster worm of the Indo-Pacific area is an annelid, or segmented, sea worm of the class Polychaeta. It includes a variety of species, all of which resemble feather dusters. It is a sedentary creature whose tube-like body protrudes from the sandy bottom and is crowned with a colorful, featherlike crest. These "feathers" serve as gills, and also trap the minute organisms on which the worm lives. When the animal is disturbed, the feathers are drawn into the tube and down its spiral.

Feather-Duster worm

Feather Stars
(Comatule)

The feather star is a crinoid and an echinoderm. It comprises a central disc from which radiate ten arms grouped in pairs. The sexes are distinct, and the feather star multiplies by means of eggs that are fertilized in the water.

There are numerous species of handsomely colored feather stars — reds, yellows, oranges.

These animals are able to swim by using their arms, but they do not move from place to place. They spend their lives attached to coral or to rocks by means of hooked appendages (called *cirri*), and they feed on small fauna, which they thrust into their mouths by means of the minute tentacles with which their arms are equipped.

Frigate Bird
(Fregata)

The frigate bird (also called the man-of-war bird) comprises two species of long-winged toti-palmate sea birds. They are both noted for their size (a wingspread of up to seven feet is not uncommon), strength, and rapacity. Frigate birds have long, hooked beaks, which they use to advantage in exercising the last quality.

The frigate bird lays only a single egg at a time.

Giant Clam
(Tridacnidae)

The giant clam of the Indo-Pacific is the largest of the bivalve mollusks. The diameter of its shell may exceed three and one half feet.

It is a fixed animal and lives within coral reefs. When its shell is ajar, one can see its blue, fleshy mantle, with a central line of emerald green.

The giant clam snaps its shell closed when it is approached by an alien object. Despite this habit, and despite the force with which the shell is closed, there is no authentic case of a diver being caught, Hollywood style, with an arm or leg in the closed shell. Moreover, there is no species of Tridacnidae that is even remotely man-eating. The closing mechanism of the giant clam is activated by a sort of primitive electric-eye device. The clam's mantle contains a number of transparent cells, which focus light onto the animal's tissue inside the shell. When that light is interrupted by the shadow of an object, the shell snaps shut. These same cells, and the light they transmit, also contribute to the development of minute algae, which live in symbiosis with the clam. The algae dispose of the wastes of the clam and, at the same time, provide oxygen by mean of photosynthesis.

Giant clams occasionally produce enormous pearls, some of them the size of a golf ball, which, however, have virtually no commercial value.

Grampus, Orc, or Killer Whale
(Orcinus Orca)

The killer whale, like the dolphin and the porpoise, is a cetacean and a member of the Delphinidae. It is also the most voracious and spectacular member of the family. Like its cousins, it is usually black above and white below, and marked by a white spot behind the eye. A fully grown male grampus may reach a length of thirty feet or more and weigh over a ton. Its dorsal fin — which projects above the water when the killer whale swims — may be as high as ten feet. All this weight and swimming equipment is backed by the largest number of teeth found in any mammal.

Killer whales prey on seals, walruses, sea birds, and other whales, in addition to the standard whale diet of fish, squid, etc. They travel in schools, and, when attacking large prey such as another whale, they seem capable of executing a complex series of group tactics.

Groupers
(Epinephelus)

Groupers are sedentary fish that live in grottoes and coral indentations. They are found among coral at any depth, although they prefer sandy bottoms. They are adept hunters and throw themselves upon their victims with great speed.

Groupers were formerly very numerous along the coasts of the Mediterranean, where they were hunted to excess because of their value as food. They are still abundant along the African coasts and also off the shores of both North and South America.

There are about twenty species of *Epinephelus* in tropical waters. In addition, the term grouper is applied to many fish who are not groupers in the proper sense — the *Cephalopholis argus,* for instance, or peacock coral — but who belong to the *Stereolepis* and *Promicrops.* Among them is the animal known to Americans as the Pacific jewfish *(Stereolepis gigas),* or giant sea bass. In its true meaning, "grouper" is a general term signifying only members of the family Serranidae.

Some groupers grow to enormous sizes. The Queensland grouper *(Epinephelus lanceolatus)* of the Indo-Pacific, for example, is said to weigh as much as a thousand pounds.

Hydrocoral

Hydrocorallia, or hydrocorals, are of the phylum Cnidaria, class Hydrozoa. They belong to the genus *Millepora,* and they are distinct from the madreporarian corals, which they resemble by reason of their squat or branched forms. Along with the Madreporarians, however, they build coral "massifs" or "banks." But they are not themselves scleractinians.

Among the Hydrocorallia is *Millepora nodosa,* which divers know as "stinging coral" because of its poisonous nematoblasts, and the stylasters, which, on the bottom of the Red Sea, for instance, form huge golden fans of complex design.

Jellyfish, or Medusa

Jellyfish of all species have certain characteristics in common: they are generally umbrella-shaped, transparent, and tentacled. They belong to the classes Scyphozoa and Hydrozoa, of the phylum Cnidaria. They are best known for the fact that the tentacles, which trail below the jellyfish and are numbered in the dozens, are armed with stinging cells. These tentacles enable the jellyfish to capture small animals for food. In some colonial hydrozoans — the Portuguese man-of-war, for example — these stings are powerful enough to paralyze a man, at least temporarily.

A marine invertebrate, the jellyfish is related to the coral polyp and the sea anemone, and most species pass through a medusa and a hydroid (or polyp) stage.

Killer Whale
(See Grampus)

Lithothamnion

A red, crusting alga whose thallus is permeated with limestone, *Lithothamnion* is found on rocks, where it forms a mauve-colored, wavy or lobed, overhang. It absorbs and assimilates calcium carbonate from the water, and in tropical seas, plays a part in bonding madreporarians together. It is found in the Mediterranean as well as in the tropics.

A similar limestone alga is *Lithophyllum.*

Mackerel
(Scombridae)

The mackerel, like its cousin the tuna, is easily recognized by its deeply forked tail, sleek body, and smooth, virtually scaleless and iridescent skin.

Mackerel usually travel in large schools — the reef-dwelling wahoo *Acanthocybium solan-*

deri) is an exception — and migrate widely. They are found everywhere in tropical and temperate seas, both along the coast and far out at sea. And everywhere they are hunted relentlessly by commercial fishing interests.

The Pacific mackerel *(Scomber japonicus)* is distinguished by a number of wavy lines descending just below the lateral line. It is between eighteen and twenty-four inches long and weighs about six pounds. Its relative, the Atlantic mackerel *(Scomber scombrus)*, is a bit more handsome, with dark wavy markings on its back and with a light underside. It is highly prized as food and — since the Atlantic mackerel travels in schools of tens of thousands — it is scooped up by the ton, in nets that are sometimes two or three miles long, by commercial trawlers. The largest members of the family are the Spanish mackerel *(Scomberomorus maculatus)*, whose backs are flecked or spotted with gold. They reach a maximum of three feet and weigh between ten and fifteen pounds.

Manta Ray, or Devilfish
(Manta birostris)

The manta, or devilfish, is sometimes also called the "horned ray" because of the two small fins, one on each side of its head, which resemble horns. It is among the giants of the sea, and may be more than twenty feet in "wingspread" and weigh as much as a ton and a half.

Despite its size, rather formidable appearance, and a reputation based on rather tall "fish stories," it is not an aggressive fish. Its diet consists of crustaceans and small ocean life, and its teeth are small and are found only on the lower jaw.

Unlike other rays, mantas live near the surface rather than at the bottom, and they can sometimes be seen basking only a few inches below the surface. They are capable of prodigous leaps into the air — apparently a form of play — from which they fall back into the water with a resounding clap.

The flesh of the manta is highly regarded by some as food, and it is considered a good game fish because of its speed and strength.

There are some ten varieties of manta in the Indo-Pacific region, but it is probable that they can all be grouped within the same species.

Millepora

Millepora is a genus belonging to the phylum Cnidaria, class Hydrozoa. They are colonial animals, and they live in warm seas, where they, like the madreporarian corals, contribute to the building of reefs.

Milleporines are known to divers as "stinging coral" because of their batteries of nematoblasts, which enable them to discharge poisonous "stings" into an enemy. Fortunately, the polyps of *Millepora* are easily discernible because of their bright yellow color.

The reproduction of *Millepora* occurs when the tiny medusae, both male and female, bud in special compartments of the polyps. These medusae reproduce sexually by means of eggs that develop not into more medusae but into polyps. The polyps then grow into branching colonies.

Moorish Idol
(Zanclus)

The Moorish idol is a circular, disc-like fish of the coral seas with an unusually long, backward-slanting dorsal fin. It has broad yellow and black stripes and smaller markings in shades of red, white, and blue. The shape, the antenna-like dorsal fin (because of which, aboard the *Calypso*, we called it the "radio fish"), and the brilliant coloration make it one of the most spectacular of coral fish. These characteristics also caused the Moorish idol to be confused at one time with the Chaetodontidae, or butterfly fish.

Moray Eel

The moray is a finless fish belonging to the family Muraenidae. It is snakelike in form, swimming with a serpentine motion. There are approximately eighty species of moray, all of which live in temperate or tropical waters, in the crevices of coral reefs, or on rocky bottoms. Generally, they hide during the day and hunt at night for small fish and crustaceans.

The moray eel has formidable teeth and can be dangerous if provoked. Nonetheless, despite its forbidding appearance and reputation, it can be tamed — as Frédéric Dumas has proved.

Mudskipper
(Periophthalmus koelreuteri)

The mudskipper, of African, Asian, and Australian waters, is generally sixteen to twenty inches long and is notable for the amount of time it is able to spend out of water on mud flats, on rocks, or among mangrove roots. Despite this ability, it is a true fish, with gills, but is able to survive on land, even under the torrid sun of the tropics, very likely because of the quantity of water that it stores under its gill covers, and because of special physiological equipment.

Out of water, the mudskipper "walks" by pulling itself along on its large pectoral fins. It is also capable of remarkable, froglike leaps, and of "walking" on the surface of the water. Indeed, it behaves like an ordinary fish only in case of danger, when it dives and swims as well as its cousin, the goby.

The mudskipper. In French, we call it the poisson promeneur, *or walking fish. Its scientific name is* Periophthalmus Koelreuteri.

Octopus

The octopus is a mollusk of the class Cephalopoda whose shell is either entirely absent or exists only in theform of an internal bonelike substance. As its popular name indicates, it has eight arms, or tentacles, which are armed with double rows of suction discs.

The term "octopus" (plural: octopuses) covers many species, all of which are sedentary creatures and are found in all the seas of the planet.

Most species of octopus are not the great, writhing monsters so popular among old-fashioned moviemakers. Their size is usually unimpressive — although the giant Pacific octopus *(Octopus dolfeini)* has been known to have an arm spread of over ten feet and to weigh forty pounds. Also, they are timid creatures, not given to attacking human beings. There are species, however, whose parrotlike beaks secrete a strong poison that is used to paralyze their victims (fishes, crustaceans, and other mollusks); and there are cases in which certain species of octopus, when molested or frightened, have inflicted serious bites on human beings. However, there is no known instance of an octopus killing a man.

Parrot Fish

The parrot fish, of the family Scaridae, takes its name from its jaw teeth, which are fused so that the parrot fish's mouth does indeed resemble the beak of a parrot. It makes use of that rather formidable orifice to bite off bits of coral, in order to feed on the polyps and tiny animals — such as worms — that are fixed on a coral wall. It also feeds on the calcareous algae that constitute a large part of coral massifs.

Parrot fish travel and graze in schools, and their tooth marks are easily identifiable on the coral. Moreover, they make a good deal of noise — which is easily audible in the water — when breaking off pieces of coral. They have no trouble digesting the hard coral, for they have platelike throat teeth, which are used to grind the coral. The waste that they expel takes the form of coral sand, and this sand can, in sufficient volume, change the shape of the bottom in certain areas.

In the Red Sea there is a variety of parrot fish characterized by a prominent lump on its forehead. It is the lumpfish. The lump grows as the fish ages. The lumpfish may be observed during its daily peregrinations, when schools of lumpfishes assemble to feed. At night, however, they separate and hide individually among the coral formations.

The size of parrot fish varies widely according to species. Some are only a few inches long, and some much longer — an adult male *Chlorurus gibbus*, for instance, may be over three feet in length.

Polyzoans

The Polyzoa, or Bryozoa ("moss animals"), are tiny animals that live, for the most part, in fixed colonies comprising large numbers of individuals.

Bryozoans often resemble either little, shrubby trees, or plates. Individuals measure about one twenty-fifth of an inch, and possess "houses" with a hole that allows the animal or zooid to spread beyond it. The individual has the shape of an annelid, or worm, and its head is topped with a growth of tentacles that protrude from the hole of its domicile. These tentacles are used for breathing, and also to capture and convey food to the mouth.

Bryozoans reproduce eggs, which in turn produce larvae. The larvae fix themselves on the bottom and become the first section of a colony. This section buds, and soon other individuals are added. All the zooids of a colony share a common nervous system. When the animal in one house dies, its remains occupy one corner therein until they eventually disappear. Then, a new animal buds, and replaces the dead animal as the new resident.

Pompano and Jack

Pompano and jack belong to the family Carangidae, which is related to the Scombridae (tuna and mackerel). They normally live along the coasts, in tropical and temperate waters, but they are often found far out in the open sea.

This family is a uniformly handsome group, usually having blue or pale green backs and gold or silver sides, which resemble polished metal. There is a well-defined lateral line running to the deeply forked tail.

Among the numerous species of Carangidae, the most characteristic, and the most common in tropical waters, are the common jack *(Caranx hippos)*, with its high body profile and massive head, which is snub-nosed and resembles a battering ram. The common jack (or crevalle) is highly prized by native fishermen for its food value, although it is of relatively small size, rarely exceeding two feet in length and thirty-five pounds in weight. The yellowtail *(Seriola dorsalis)* — also called the California yellowtail — is also well known. It is a popular game fish, and attains a weight of about forty pounds.

The bluefish *(Pomatomus saltatrix)* is commonly thought to be a pompano, although it is in a family by itself. It does resemble the pompano in many respects, having a blue back and silver sides, and it usually weighs ten to twelve pounds.

Porcupine Fish

There are some fifteen species of porcupine fish of the family Diodontidae, all found in temperate and tropical seas. The largest grow to a length of three feet.

The porcupine fish is notable for its ability, when frightened, to swell up to a sphere — like its cousins of the family Tetraodontidae (blowfish, puffers, swellfish). The porcupine fish, however, has the additional protection of a very tough body covering and very sharp spines, which protrude when the body is distended.

Despite these somewhat disagreeable talents, the porcupine fish is highly regarded in Japan as a culinary delicacy — and this notwithstanding its reputation as the cause of many cases of food poisoning.

Precontinent II and Precontinent III
(also Conshelf II and Conshelf III)

Precontinent II was the second Cousteau experiment in underwater living. It was carried out, in 1963, at Shab Rumi in the Red Sea, along the Sudanese coast. On this occasion, a team of two "oceanauts" lived for a week at a minimum depth of ninety-five feet.

In the course of a subsequent experiment (Precontinent III) off the French coast near Cap Ferrat, in 1965, a team of six divers was able to remain at 325 feet for three weeks.

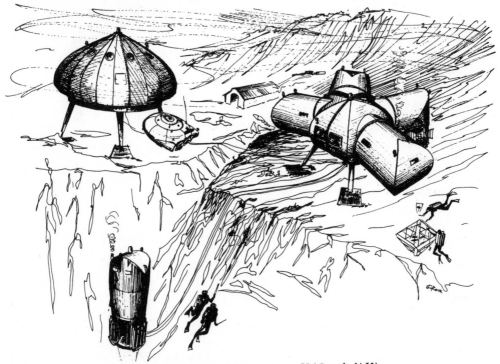

The undersea houses of Precontinent II (Conshelf II)

In the course of a subsequent experiment (Precontinent III) off the French coast near Cap Ferrat, in 1965, a team of six divers was able to remain at 325 feet for three weeks.

Rorqual

The term rorqual refers to any of a family *(Balaenopteridae)* of large whalebone whales characterized by a dorsal fin, a recessive upper jaw, and numerous parallel grooves on the underside.

The largest of the rorquals is the blue whale *(Balaenoptera musculus)*, which can grow up to a hundred feet in length and weigh as much as 136 tons. It is commonly agreed among scientists that the blue whale is the largest and heaviest animal that has ever existed on earth, either in the sea or on land.

The common rorqual *(Balaenoptera physalus)* sometimes reaches a length of eighty feet, although the average is closer to sixty-five feet, with a weight of some sixty tons.

(There is a whaler's rule of thumb to the effect that whales generally weigh one ton per foot of length; this system, however, ignores the fact that whales, like other mammals, are sometimes fat and sometimes thin, and also that body size increases in three dimensions.)

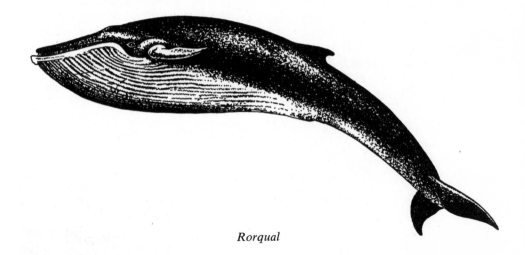

Rorqual

Saprophyte

Any form of vegetable life that feeds on decomposing organic materials.

Scorpion Fish

The scorpion fish, or stonefish, or rockfish, is a cousin of the dragonfish, and, like it, a member of the family Scorpaenidae. It is likewise venomous. There the similarity ends, for the scorpion fish is as repulsive in appearance as the dragonfish is gorgeous.

The scorpion fish is called stonefish and rockfish because it lives on the bottom among rocks, close to land in cold and in warm seas. Its body is lumpy and rocklike in appearance, and poisonous spines grow from its head and back. It has been called, for good reason, the most venomous fish in the world, and there are many authentic instances of human beings dying, in terrible agony, from the sting of the scorpion fish.

Sea Anemones
(Actinia)

Sea anemones are Cnidaria, class Anthozoa, order Actiniaria They are solitary animals, without skeletons, which attach themselves by a basal disc to rocks or, in some species, to shells. Although sedentary, they are able to move over a very small area. They are found in cold and temperate seas as well as in the tropics.

All sea anemones have the same general form: a muscular, cylindrical body, surmounted by hollow tentacles, in the center of which is the anemone's body cavity. The tentacles bear the anemone's stinging cells (the nematoblasts, with which it paralyzes its prey), which serve to capture its food — tiny marine organisms, and even small fishes and crabs — and to stuff it into the cavity.

The sea anemone's reproductive organs are situated within its body cavity, and its offspring, in the form of larvae, are released through its mouth. Some anemones also reproduce asexually by budding.

Sea Cucumber

The sea cucumber is an echinoderm, class Holothuroidea. It received its popular name from Pliny, nineteen hundred years ago, because this animal does, in fact, resemble a cucumber. At the top of its soft, tubular body is the mouth, through which the ten tentacles draw mud, which passes through the body and is expelled through the cloaca at the other end.

The sea cucumber is able to resort to a form of self-evisceration by expelling its internal

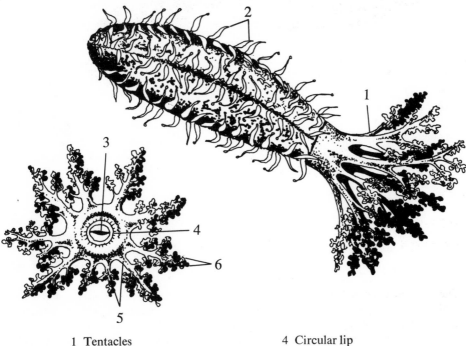

1 Tentacles
2 Ventral ambulacral podia (foot)
3 Mouth cavity

4 Circular lip
5 Large tentacles
6 Small tentacles

Sea Cucumber

organs through the cloaca when frightened. This may be simply an "offering" to appease an attacking predator; or it may be defensive, to the extent that the organs are accompanied by tough, viscous threads that often envelop the predator. These organs are regenerated in four to six weeks.

Some species of sea cucumber secrete a strong poison, called holothurin, which researchers believe may prove valuable as a drug. In any case, the sea cucumber has long been prized by the Chinese (who know it as trepang) for its alleged aphrodisiac qualities.

Sea Fans

Sea fans, which are of the same class (Anthozoa) of the phylum Cnidaria as many jellyfish, are octocorallines. They are actually colonies of animals: a large number of individual polyps spread over a calcareous and flexible skeleton. They exist in brilliant reds, yellows, orange, and purple, and are attached to the bottom or to rocks.

Sea fans are found in all seas. In tropical waters, however, they attain large size, being sometimes four or five feet high. Their grace and beauty must be seen in the sea fan's natural habitat to be truly appreciated, for the "sea fans" sold as souvenirs to tourists are nothing more than dried, horny skeletons. In the Red Sea, for example, there are, at great depths, incredible "forests" of sea fans which are breathtaking.

Sea Urchins

Sea urchins are echinoderms of the class Echinoidea distinguished for the prickly spines — over a foot long, in some species — that cover their bodies. Among the spines are tiny pedicels, which are small pincers, some possessing poison glands.

Sea urchins are abundant in the tropics and subtropics and are also found in colder waters as far north as the Arctic Ocean. The body is generally knob-shaped, and the mouth, with its elaborate masticatory apparatus comprising twenty pieces, is located on the lower surface. Some species walk on rows of tube feet, while others travel on the tips of their spines. They sometimes live in holes they dig to fit their bodies, and their normal diet consists of algae and minute organisms.

The sexes are separate, but the sex organs of the two sexes are indistinguishable one from the other. The only way to tell a male from a female (without a microscope) is by color — yellow in the male of the species *Paracentrotus lividus*, for example, and orange for the female.

Sea urchins are found in a variety of forms — long, heart-shaped, etc.

Shark

The name "shark" is commonly applied to numerous species of cartilaginous fishes — so called because their skeletons are made of cartilage rather than of hard bone. This skeletal peculiarity is usually taken as a sign that the shark is more primitive, from an evolutionary standpoint, than the bony fishes. And yet, the shark has a highly developed nervous system, and a varied, complex, and efficient system of reproduction.

With respect to the first, the head and body of the shark are generously endowed with sensory organs capable of perceiving the slightest variation in its environment. These are the "pit organs" described by Professor Paul Budker in 1938. Research is underway today to establish the precise functions of the various sensory organs of the shark by virtue of which, it seems, he is able, for example, to measure hydrostatic pressure, to register sound even at the ultrasonic level, to sense the chemical composition of the water, and so forth. It seems likely that the shark owes to its olfactory organs its celebrated ability to "smell" blood at a great distance.

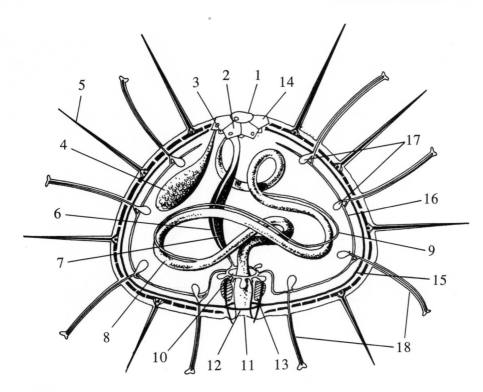

1 Anus
2 Madreporite (water vascular system—WVS)
3 Radial plate
4 Ovary
5 Spine
6 Water vascular canal
7 Axial gland
8 Intestine
9 Intestinal siphon

10 Ring canal (WVS)
11 Mouth
12 Nerve ring
13 Aristotle's lantern
14 Interradial plates
15 Radial nerve
16 Ambulacral radial canal (WVS)
17 Contractile vesicle (WVS)
18 Podium—tube foot (WVS)

Sea Urchin

Regarding mating among sharks, the scientist's chief problem, as Professor Budker has pointed out, is that "observation is neither easy nor frequent." We know, however, that some sharks lay eggs in cases which assume a leatherlike texture in the water, and from which, after several months, young sharks emerge. Most species, however, bear their young alive in numbers that vary greatly according to the species. The sand shark *(Carcharias taurus)*, for instance, regularly bears a litter of two; while the tiger shark *(Galeocèrdo cuvieri)* usually gives birth to six or seven dozen young at a time.

There are more than 250 species of shark, found in both temperate and tropical waters. Of these, only ten or twelve species are known to have attacked human beings. The great white shark *(Carcharodon carcharias)* and the hammerhead shark *(Sphyrna zygaena)* have the distinction of being perhaps the most dedicated, and the best known, of the man-eaters. The white shark is of the family of the so-called mackerel sharks (Isuridae), and it is a monster in every respect, sometimes reaching a length of over thirty-five feet. Size, however, is no indication of the danger that a particular shark represents to a diver. The largest shark is the whale shark

(Rhineodon typus), which reaches a length of sixty-five feet and a weight of twenty-five tons — but which feeds exclusively on small fish, squid, and plankton. One third the size of the whale shark is the other man-eater, the hammerhead, found in all tropical seas, instantly recognizable because its head is, in fact, shaped exactly like an old-fashioned hammer, eyes set at the ends of wide "wings" protruding from the head.

Sharks are caught commercially for the modest value of their skins. Some species are edible, or at least eaten: the *Galeorhinus zyopterus*, or soup-fin shark, contributes its fin to a famous oriental dish, while several species regularly provide the fish for the "fish 'n' chips" on which the British seem to thrive.

Siphonophores

Siphonophores are Cnidaria of the class Hydrozoa. They are exclusively marine animals and are able to float. They are fragile, transparent, and often magnificently hued in iridescent colors.

Siphonophores are hydrozoan colonies that are not fixed, but free-floating. The individuals of the colony therefore develop in such a way as to be capable of performing special and distinct functions. The axis of the colony is a stolon, at the end of which is an air-filled membrane (the pneumatophore) that serves as a floater.

Siphonophores feed on forms of marine life that they capture by means of venomous filaments — a weapon effective enough to be dangerous even to man. They reproduce by eggs, and also by budding in the form of medusae.

Snapper
(Lutianidae)

The many species of snapper of the family Lutianidae are primarily tropical fish, although they are occasionally found in temperate waters, and all are highly thought of as food fish. Most specimens are two to three feet long and weigh five to six pounds, but individual snappers weighing as much as eighteen pounds have been caught.

The best known of the snappers is *Lutianus campechinus*, or the common red snapper, immediately recognizable — in fish markets as well as in Indo-Pacific waters — by its brilliant scarlet color. It often grows to a length of three feet. Another common species is the yellowtail snapper *(Ocyurus chrysurus)*, with its deeply forked tail of yellow, yellow fins, and a yellow stripe along its sides. Although smaller than the red snapper (the average length is about one foot) the yellowtail is reputed to be equally delicious. It is an inhabitant of reefs and inlets.

Spatangus

A spatangus is an ovoid or heart-shaped sea urchin, covered with short spines, that lives on sandy bottoms. It grows to the approximate size of a man's fist. There are numerous species, and they are sometimes called heart urchins or sand dollars. (See also Sea Urchins.)

Sperm Whale
(Physeter macrocephalus)

The sperm whale, or cachalot, unlike most large whales, has teeth rather than horny strips of whalebone. These exist, however, only in the lower jaw (twenty to thirty on either side), and, when the mouth is closed, they are sheathed in scabbardlike cavities in the upper jaw.

Male sperm whales grow up to sixty feet in length, while females are generally from thirty to forty feet long. Usually, the head represents a third of this measurement. Males have been known to weigh over fifty tons.

These mammals are hunted for their blubber and for the spermaceti — which is a waxlike substance, rather than an oil — of extraordinary purity, which it carries in a large closed cavity, or case, in its head.

The sperm whale is one of the best divers of all whales. It is able to remain under water for about ninety minutes — an ability that is perhaps the result of a slow pulse, by virtue of which this whale requires comparatively little oxygen.

The cachalot is found in the warmer parts of all oceans. Like most mammals who are able to live for long periods without breathing, it is characterized by a black, oily skin.

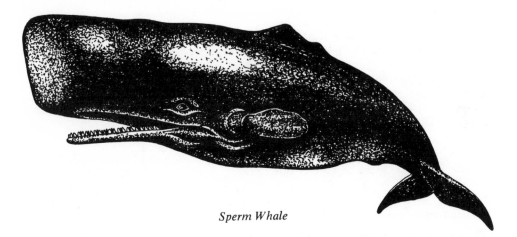

Sperm Whale

Spirographis
(See Feather-Duster Worm)

Sponges
(Porifera, class Demospongiae)

Sponges are the simplest of the multicellular animals, forming the phylum Porifera. Their bodies are covered with holes through which water is drawn. Food and oxygen are then extracted from this water.

Sponges reproduce as primitively and as simply as they live. Fishermen "cultivate" sponges by cutting a piece from a living sponge and allowing it to attach itself to a resting place; soon it turns into a full-grown sponge. Left to itself, the sponge will reproduce by budding, or by shooting out spores that become new sponges.

These animals are found in every sea and at every depth, in a variety of shapes (fans, fingers, spheres, etc.) and colors (blue, yellow, or red) and in sizes from a half inch to six feet tall. There are almost five thousand distinct species. They are sedentary animals. Some (such as the bath sponge) have horny skeletons, and others have harder skeletons made of silica.

Starfish, or Sea Stars

Starfish are echinoderms, of the class Asteroidea, whose bodies are in the shape of a star with five branches or "arms." At the extremity of each arm there is a short tentacle, and at the base of that tentacle is a bright red, light-sensitive, sensory organ. In addition, each arm carries, on its underside, hundreds of tiny podia, or tube feet, equipped with suction discs. A starfish, therefore, is much more mobile than its appearance would suggest.

The starfish's mouth is located in the central disc, and it is a dedicated carnivore which devours mollusks and crustaceans both living and dead. The method of digestion is unusual. Rather than swallowing its victim, the starfish regurgitates its stomach and applies it to its prey, whereupon the victim is dissolved in the starfish's digestive juices.

Starfish can exert considerable pull by means of their remarkably strong arms, which enable them to overcome and consume large quantities of shellfish. A starfish will fold its arms over an oyster and pull until the shell of the oyster begins to give way and a small opening appears. Then the starfish's stomach is inserted into the crack and the oyster is digested.

Starfish are remarkable for their regenerative powers. If they lose one or more arms, or even a part of the central disc that is the body, they can quickly grow new parts.

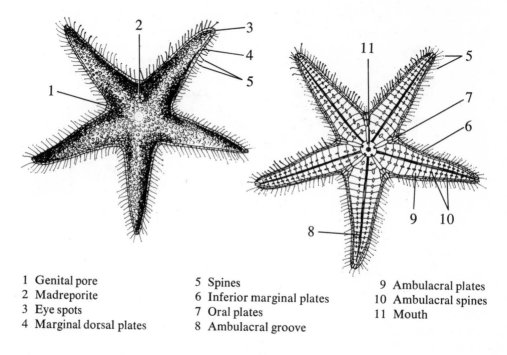

1 Genital pore	5 Spines	9 Ambulacral plates
2 Madreporite	6 Inferior marginal plates	10 Ambulacral spines
3 Eye spots	7 Oral plates	11 Mouth
4 Marginal dorsal plates	8 Ambulacral groove	

Starfish

Stylaster

A bright yellow hydrocoralline of the phylum Cnidaria that branches into formations resembling thickets, which are sometimes of considerable size. Stylaster is a genus closely related to *Millepora* and, like them, is armed with stinging cells.

Triggerfish

The triggerfish, which constitutes the family Balistidae, is notable for two characteristics: One is the beauty of its markings and monochromatic and polychromatic coloration — vivid blues, golds, browns, and whites in a variety of stripes, bars, speckles, and spots — and the other is a defensive spine that can be raised at will and locked into place. This spine is part of the dorsal fin. When the triggerfish is pursued by an enemy, he flees into a coral formation and uses his spine to lock himself into a protected position among the coral.

The triggerfish has a small mouth and leatherlike skin. It is found primarily in tropical and subtropical waters, where it rarely attains a length of more than about fifteen inches.

Troika

A device conceived by France's Centre d'Etudes Marines Avancées, the Troika is a trailer that is towed under water by the *Calypso* to take close-up photographs of the bottom. It carries a camera and a flash attachment, which work from batteries. The Troika is so designed that the camera is activated as soon as the trailer touches bottom. The flash apparatus was designed by Professor Harold Edgerton of MIT.

Tubipora

Tubipora musica — sometimes called organ-pipe coral — is a colonial octocoralline allied to the soft corals. Its skeleton is composed of a complex of red cylindrical tubes arranged side by side, like a pipe organ. These tubes or pipes are not parallel, but lean outward from the base and are interconnected by means of occasional horizontal platforms.

   Tubipora grows vertically rather than horizontally and is a constituent element of the coral massifs in which it is found.

Tubipora

Tuna

The tuna is a member of the Scombridae (mackerel) family. Although the name tuna is used generically for the albacore, bonito, yellowfin tuna, bluefin tuna (sometimes called the horse mackerel), little tuna (or false albacore), and skipjack (or oceanic bonito), there is a great difference in size among the various species. The Pacific species of the bonito *(Sarda sarda)*, for example, grows to a length of about three and one half feet and to a weight of twenty-five pounds, while among the bluefin tuna *(Thunnus thynnus)* a weight of from two hundred to five hundred pounds is common and a weight of one thousand pounds not unknown. Indeed, the bluefin is one of the largest of the bony fishes.

Nonetheless, the Scombridae have many characteristics in common. They migrate in irregular paths and schedules. They all feed on mackerel, herring, sardines, and squid. They are all prized as food. And even the smaller species are famous as game fish.

The natural habitat of these fish is the tropical and temperate seas.

"Walk"

An oceanographic "walk" is a platform situated near the top of a submerged cliff. Its width varies from a few inches to six feet or more. Its origin is often due to chemical erosion, but its development is largely the result of calcareous marine life such as madreporarians and lithothamnion (see entry in this glossary), which is a calcareous alga.

Wrasses

Wrasses are small, bony, shallow-water fishes of the family Labridae found along rocky coasts. There are almost six hundred species, most of which are handsomely colored and patterned. The colors change according to time of life, sex, and age. The males even have a special "wedding suit."

Many species of wrasse are known for the cleaning service they perform for larger fishes. They swim about the body of such animals as groupers and eels and nibble away at parasites.

All wrasses are carnivorous. And some of them, in their turn, are highly regarded as food in the tropics.

Zoantharia

Zoantharia are colonial Coelenterates of the class Anthozoa. They are closely related to coral, but have no skeleton and are sometimes encrusted with sand. The most common kinds are *Zoanthus* and *Polythoa,* and the latter is sometimes so thick as to form a "carpet" on a reef.

Zooxanthella

A flagellate alga that lives in symbiotic relationship to various marine animals, such as scleractinarians, certain alcyonarian corals, and giant clams.

Index